Praise for
Accountability and
White Anti-racist Organizing

What a fantastic and sorely needed resource! In no other volume with which I'm familiar is the issue of white antiracist accountability handled so directly, honestly, and from so many important angles and perspectives. This volume provides insight, inspiration and much needed instruction for those of us seeking to be stronger, more effective allies in the struggle for racial equity.

> **Tim Wise,** antiracist white ally, author, *White Like Me: Reflections on Race from a Privileged Son,* and *Colorblind: The Rise of Post-Racial Politics and the Retreat from Racial Equity*

White people publicly standing up against racism—AWESOME!! *Accountability and White Anti-racist Organizing* lights the path for White anti-racist activists to become effective in their work and build sustainability as a collective. Accountability is the key to building cross racial relationships in the movement to undo racism and create a more just society. This book offers practice guidance, shares the process and pitfalls of organizers across professional disciplines, and gives hope to anyone doing racial equity work who may feel isolated or lost. Despite the book's explicit address to White readers, there is much here that will benefit People of Color as well as organizations who wish to ~ · e of accountability in addressing ins

> **Mary Pender Greene,** LCS\ ist, organizational consultant, a

This is an excellent and much-needed resource for social service workers and all those committed to racial justice. Informative personal stories and practical suggestions make this an accessible, useful, and necessary tool for white activists.

> **Paul Kivel,** white educator, activist, author of *Uprooting Racism*

Kudos to the editors Cushing, Cabbil, Freeman, Hitchcock and Richards for giving us this wonderful ground breaking book, *Accountability and White Anti-racist Organizing*. This book opens up a critical dialogue about accountability as whites in partnership with people of color address systemic racism. *Accountability* provides practical examples of ways that individuals and groups are making real change to create authentic cross racial relationships that address the real issues of the need for systemic change and to address the crux of racism — injustice and the balance of power. *Accountability* is a must-read for any white person who considers themself an activist and is committed to making change.

> **Judith H. Katz,** EdD, white woman, author, *White Awareness: Handbook for Anti-racism Training* (University of Oklahoma Press: 1978; 2003)

I loved this book. These types of stories force a reader to be clear about their own privilege at every turn of the page. In doing antiracist work, it is a necessary step on the journey to self liberation. As a young person, this book proves that there is no one right "next step" on said journey, but rather a myriad of possibilities. If only a copy could be given to every person who identifies as White in the U.S.

> **Maxwell Love,** Afro-American, Mid-East Studies Major at the University of Wisconsin - Madison, member of Promoting Racial Equality and Awareness

The white anti-racist movement is growing, and this powerful and timely collection is for anyone wishing to become a more principled and accountable white anti-racist organizer. With contributors sharing their personal stories, questions, and challenges, *Accountability* reads like a conversation with old friends — the kinds who aren't afraid to challenge you while also holding you close. I must say that once I opened the book I couldn't put it down — it was so wonderful and eerily just what I needed at this time in my life. Thank you for this wonderful resource!

> **Charlie Fredrick,** queer, white and working class ally, Anne Braden Anti-Racist Training Program 2009 alum

Bonnie Cushing and her fellow editors have put together a startling and edifying collection of articles that provide us with a deep insight into the minds of those who have been transformed by their work as whites engaged in anti-racist organizing. It's so easy for people engaged in social change work to get lost in our own self-righteousness and lose a perspective on the limitations of our own impact on those whom we imagine we have come to help. This book should be read by anyone who plans to do any form of organizing work. And organizer or not, if you care to defeat racism in American society, you need to grapple with some of the issues raised in the stories from the actual anti-racist work presented here.

> **Rabbi Michael Lerner,** Jewish American, editor of *Tikkun Magazine* (www.tikkun.org), chair of the Network of Spiritual Progressives (www.spiritualprogressives.org), and author of *The Left Hand of God: Taking Back our Country from the Religious Right*

Congratulations! *Accountability and White Anti-racist Organizing* is an inspirational resource which documents the broad spectrum of white anti-racist organizing perspectives and approaches in America today and courageously names the complexities inherent in putting accountability into practice. I really learned from and enjoyed reading the book!

> ***Beth Applegate,*** MSOD, co-author of *Embracing Cultural Competency: A Roadmap for Nonprofit Capacity Builders*

I was very impressed by this work. Accountability is an important element that facilitates trust between white people and people of color, yet figuring out how best to create processes for accountability has alluded even the most astute among us. Finally there is a well-written book that not only provides ways to better understand accountability but also offers processes for establishing cross-race relationships that encompass accountability. This book will be of great value to those committed to working to transform the ideals of this country into reality.

> **Pamela Smith Chambers**, African American, cofounder and Training Director, Beyond Diversity Resource Center

Excellent book and quite a contribution! This long-awaited book breaks new ground for whites and people of color. Figuring out accountability in the context of white antiracist organizing has been an ongoing challenge, especially with our history of not getting it right. I really appreciated the different voices on what accountability actually looks like. More whites must step up and be willing to risk whatever it takes to co-create with people of color a more racially just and equitable society. This is a must-read book.

> **Maggie Potapchuk,** white woman, MP Associates — building community and organizational capacity for racial justice

This unique book provides a fascinating range of perspectives and examples of accountability and white anti-racist organizing. With candor and insight, the authors offer reflections on their struggles to define and practice. Through their stories, they provide guidance to other white people engaged in dismantling racism. Important food for thought for anyone working for racial justice.

> **Diane J. Goodman,** author, *Promoting Diversity and Social Justice: Educating People from Privileged Groups*

Finally! I'm thrilled that we white anti-racist educators and activists finally have a book to help us understand what it means to be accountable to both ourselves and people of color. As a life-long racial justice educator/organizer/activist, this book means the world to me. The essay by CWS's (Challenging White Supremacy Workshop) Sharon Martinas (with Mickey Ellinger) alone makes this book worth its price. For me, CWS and the People's Institute are the two most important groups that have taught us white people how to live anti-racist lives. Thanks to Bonnie Cushing and her colleagues for creating such a thought provoking collection of essays.

> **Lisa Albrecht,** white antiracist educator, Associate Professor, University of Minnesota, Social Justice Program, long-time feminist writer, and scholar activist

As a local anti-racist educator, I often wonder if white people care. This book heartens me that some do. Our local white women's anti-racist caucus engages a range of women, so the authors' diversity of social location and age is useful. This book offers no easy answers but lots of concrete examples, both what worked and what failed. Let us study and take heed. The chapter "Transformative Alliance Building" shows some of the dysfunctional behavior in white people; it was a relief to read!

> **Rachel Koontz,** woman of European descent, cofounder, Ground to Move, Elkhart, Indiana

I was sure that a book dedicated solely to this topic would be difficult to read, but I read it in one sitting. I was very much surprised by the honesty and vulnerability shown by the authors. Specifically, Christine Schmidt's reflections on working in the New York City school system will help anyone in education. The chapter written by AWARE is so honest on the pitfalls of one-way accountability models. Sharon Martinas' experience is a blueprint for anti-racist work. Persons doing anti-racist work look for "tools" and "models." This is one.

> **David Billings,** white anti-racist organizer and Core Trainer with the People's Institute for Survival and Beyond

These editors have launched a book rich with compelling and inspiring journeys of combating white supremacy and unmasking white privilege. Authors from diverse disciplines and communities offer uncompromising and vivid illustrations of white privilege interrupted. Their paths toward equity are humbling as they reflect on the painful and liberatory trajectories critical to the process of accountability. This book should be a standard reader not only for those interested in doing white activist work but for all students of social sciences and the humanities.

> **Rhea V. Almeida,** MS, PhD, founder of Institute for Family Services, family therapist/activist. Creator of the Cultural Context Model, a community healing paradigm

Have you ever been in conversation with someone and want to say—hey…what does that word really mean? This book does exactly that by exploring the term "accountability" and its relationship to white anti-racist organizing. The result: a better place to work and grow from while gaining access to the tools that are necessary to challenge white supremacy, starting from the inside out.

> **Jardana Peacock**, queer white woman, Highlander Research and Education Center

A timely book. White people struggle to become effective anti-racist organizers and our lack of accountability to people of color is one barrier. *Accountability* outlines strategies to develop formal and informal mechanisms of accountability. In one story Christine Schmidt describes her successful strategies, and her failures — which she attributes to solitary actions borne of "a delusion of grandeur that is part of being white." Her clear and honest narratives provide pathways to achieve accountability and to recover when we don't.

> **Marion Riedel,** PhD, white ally and activist, Associate Professor Columbia University School of Social Work

I loved the book. Finally we have captured the stories of our times from antiracist whites across this nation. As the narratives unfold, we gain a sense of connection and membership with a growing collective working towards a common cause.

> **Sandra Bernabei,** LCSW, antiracist white, cofounder, AntiRacist Alliance

This is a courageous book. Ron Chisom says in his foreward that there has always been a question of honesty between white people and people of color. These authors have made a daring start in their efforts to be honestly accountable. The book is an excellent primer highly recommended for any white person endeavoring to work against racism and to address our white privilege.

> **Monica McGoldrick,** MSW, therapist, teacher, author, woman of white background

Accountability and

White Anti-racist Organizing

Accountability and
White Anti-racist Organizing

✳✳✳✳✳✳✳

STORIES FROM OUR WORK

Foreword by Ronald Chisom

Edited by Bonnie Berman Cushing
with Lila Cabbil, Margery Freeman,
Jeff Hitchcock, and Kimberley Richards

Dear Liz,
Thanks for all your
support & encouragement!
love,
Bonnie

Crandall, Dostie & Douglass Books, Inc.
Roselle, New Jersey

Published by:
Crandall, Dostie & Douglass Books, Inc.
245 West 4th Avenue, Roselle, NJ 07203-1135
(908) 241-5439
www.cddbooks.com

ISBN 978-1-934390-32-0

Library of Congress Cataloging-in-Publication Data

Accountability and white anti-racist organizing : stories from our work / foreword by Ronald Chisom ; edited by Bonnie Berman Cushing ... [et al.].

p. cm.

Includes bibliographical references.

ISBN 978-1-934390-32-0

1. United States–Race relations. 2. African Americans–Civil rights. 3. African
Americans–Social conditions–1975- 4. Social justice–United States. 5. Whites–
United States–Attitudes. 6. Social action–United States. I. Cushing, Bonnie
Berman.

E185.615.A24 2010

305.896'073–dc22

2010032197

Table of Contents

Foreword

Between white people and people of color who are working together there has always been a question of honesty. This book begins an important conversation about accountability that needs to continue and to deepen. In my thirty years of working with whites and people of color and all of those dynamics, the question of accountability is still not clear; not fully understood. We don't need to have one universal way to deal with it, but there has to be some consistency in what we are talking about.

We'll be working in more honest relationships if we start and keep this conversation about accountability going. Whites who want to do anti-racist organizing will find this book a valuable resource. It should intentionally be shared with young organizers so they can start off in a good way, with some understanding of what accountability is. This book will help stress to white organizers that doing social change work without understanding accountability will only add to the oppression they are trying to alleviate.

People of color should also read this book. For folks of color it's a good opportunity to learn how accountability plays out, because I don't think we talk about it or understand it enough. Even in our own communities we're not always effective. Then it gets really messy when we work with white people.

Racism dehumanizes, and to do anti-racist work in an accountable way will bring the humanity back into your work. When I first started doing community work over thirty five years ago in New Orleans, the tenants I was giving technical assistance to told me, "Ron, we know you mean well, but the way you do your work, you need to get yourself some more training." I didn't appreciate them telling me that. But I did go to several training schools, all of them majority white, and they gave me the skills and tools, but they never talked about racism, history and culture. I came to understand that if you give someone skills and tools and they have not dealt with their racism, they can become a skillful racist; they can keep a construct like racism going. You have to be accountable about organizing in an anti-racist way, because that will bring the humanity back into it — and that process can transform those structures and ultimately help eliminate them.

When I first started organizing I thought I could work with white people just like we're all even — but we're not. For me to feel I have some even basis with white people, they have to challenge racism, because when I see whites organizing against racism they have put themselves in a vulnerable situation. Other than that, there's no vulnerability for white people because of the privilege and the access, and they can leave when they want and get confused when they want. Today, everybody's talking about white privilege, but some people may not understand that without the anti-racist organizing to back it up, all that rhetoric becomes like a game.

I personally know the editors and many of the contributors of this book, and I support this effort. The relationships have been ongoing over several years, and in some cases many years. There has been consistency in our working together. What has helped me is that they've been willing to listen and to challenge something when it didn't feel right. That's what these relationships have been for me, and it's been good.

This book arrives at a key time in our nation's history. I've never seen such blatant institutional, linguistic, and cultural racism as I see now because we have a black president. Being an anti-racist organizer is not just about helping people of color; it's about changing this country — it's about making it a more equitable place. White people can play a major role in this change. They can begin to use their white privilege in a real way, by speaking out collectively about what's going on. Now is as good a time as any.

Ronald Chisom
Cofounder and Executive Director
People's Institute for Survival and Beyond

Editors' Preface

Editing a book on accountability is a little unnerving. To whom are the editors accountable? Add in topics like race and racial justice, and then inflect that with a racialized viewpoint — that of white people. It seems daunting.

In the late twentieth century some racial justice activists began to introduce the notion of accountability to strengthen the impact of their work. Foremost among these were core leaders in the People's Institute for Survival and Beyond (PISAB). Both white people and people of color need to understand accountability and apply its precepts. But how to do that is often difficult to discern. This book began as an effort by two white people — Bonnie Berman Cushing (lead editor) and Jeff Hitchcock (publisher and editor) — to bring some clarity to an area that has frequently proven nebulous in practice.

From the start we felt the best approach would be to cull stories from activists and organizers involved in the day-to-day work. Initially we conceived that both white people and people of color might be contributors. Early on, with a concern for our own accountable practice, we expanded the editorial team to include Kimberley Richards and Margery Freeman from PISAB, and Lila Cabbil from the Rosa and Raymond Parks Institute for Self Development. Our editorial team thus comprises five editors: three white and two African-American.

Every book must necessarily develop a focus. The first decision that the editorial team made was that the stories should be entirely those of white practitioners, and the book itself should be a product of, and reflect, white anti-racist leadership. In the larger world there is room for anti-racist people of color to comment on white anti-racist organizing, but that is for another book. A second key decision was to bring out the personal side of the stories our contributors tell. Both these decisions were part and product of the multiracial character of the editorial team.

Our contributors form a varied group. Their writing styles, formats, and political ideologies reflect this diversity. We have tried to honor the unique voice of each story while also applying enough uniformity to preserve a sense of the book as a whole. In other words, the inconsistencies you may find from chapter to chapter are intentional. One obvious example is in the use of the word "anti-racist," or is it "antiracist?" Some prefer a hyphen; others do not. We have allowed each contributor's choice to remain as is on this point. In other instances, such as use of endnote style and section headings, we have applied a consistent approach. This is a book that is somewhat "out of the box," written on a topic and by people who are on the leading edge of social change. Given that, it's hard to apply rigid publishing traditions.

PISAB teaches that for every accomplishment there are a multitude of people, visible and not, that helped make it happen. The creation of this book is no exception. And so it is with gratitude and deep appreciation that we name the people who played an essential role in its creation.

We thank our contributors for their patience on what has been a long process.

Without the feedback, support and foreword from Ron Chisom, executive director of PISAB, this volume might not even exist. His wise counsel and ongoing inspiration — along with that of the institute he cofounded more than thirty years ago — is evident throughout its pages.

We thank the board members at the Center for the Study of White American Culture, Inc., the parent organization to the publisher, Crandall, Dostie & Douglass Books, Inc., for underwriting the project and allowing us to pursue our vision.

Our family and friends graciously shared us with this book over an extended period of time. We want them to know that the sacrifices they made did not go unnoticed.

Finally we give a grateful nod and bow to people of color throughout history and in the present moment who have taken the time and made the effort, often at great cost to them, to educate, guide and support anti-racist white people. It is because of their efforts that we who are white are able to do the work we need to do to create a society that is racially just and, in the act, to recover our own humanity.

Introduction

Bonnie Berman Cushing and Jeff Hitchcock

Most people will find the topic of white anti-racist organizing new or unknown to them, yet there exists today in the United States a small and growing community of activists who take it as their work. How that work may be done in an accountable way is the topic of this book. We believe the book has value for several audiences. Clearly we want to reach white people who have a passion for racial justice, who are working for racial equity, and who are joined in the task of building multiracial structures, institutions, and community. We also hope the book proves valuable to people of color who are working in relationship with white people on matters of racial justice. Activists and organizers working in other areas of social justice may find the book a useful learning tool as well. And the larger public, particularly those who live and work in multiracial settings, or who hope one day to do so, can benefit from lessons this book brings from the forefront of white anti-racist organizing.

Since our topic is relatively unknown to so many people, we need to describe what we mean by white anti-racist organizing, and how the concept of accountability bears upon it. Ultimately the best understanding of accountability and white anti-racist organizing comes from the stories and experiences our contributors reveal in the heart of the book. But a little introduction will help the reader enter into the topic.

First, we do not want to mystify the question of who is white. Much has been written on this question in recent years. We know many people who check "white" on US census forms, but who otherwise claim to be something else — almost anything else it seems. In an increasingly multiracial society, the historic and present baggage of whiteness and white privilege lead many to eschew a white identity. Yet the privilege remains. Certainly there are some people at the margins of whiteness, as there are for any given social category, but if you are confused about who is white in the broader context of US society, then this book may not be for you.

Anti-racism is a term that arose in the twentieth century to name a body of social justice work with much deeper historical roots. Before anti-racism there was anti-slavery, and along the way doubtless other names have been used. The work itself has been continuous. The driving force of anti-racism has always been, and continues to be, led by people of color, but white people have always had a part somewhere.

Today anti-racism, as we understand it, is more than simply countering prejudice and discrimination. Racism is a hierarchical system with historical roots in which access to power and resources is granted to one socially defined group (white people) at the expense of other socially defined groups (people of color). The empowered group does the social defining. Anti-racism must begin with that understanding. Subtle differences may be voiced among proponents, but understanding power and privilege is key. White people may be targets of racial prejudice and discrimination, and in some isolated moments these can produce dire consequences, but we do not as a people in the United States suffer a history of genocide, enslavement, and forced dislocation that has traumatized entire families, communities and, indeed, peoples. It is as if white people in the United States live in a town where their houses have survived a conflagration, and their neighbors, having lost all, are only now beginning to rebuild.

Anti-racism is an active way of being in the world. In the United States we each occupy a position in a system of racism. Understanding one's location in the system (privileged or oppressed) is a first step. Working to undo the privilege and oppression the system imposes is another. Passive understandings of racism are not understandings at all. The realization is in the work.

We understand organizing to be the act of bringing people into collective processes and formations in order to pursue goals and foster social change that benefits those people. Any group of people can organize. Their goals may not be social justice; the goal can be enactment of privilege. Anti-racist organizing is that organizing directed toward anti-racist goals, i.e., to overcome and eliminate racial injustice. Finally, white anti-racist organizing is that done by white people, which furthermore is directed toward other white people, bringing them together to challenge racism.

White anti-racist organizing implies white people performing a role for which white status and identity uniquely prepares us, such as working with our own people. Contrast this with simply performing roles in a multiracial setting in which racial identity is not necessarily important to the task, such as showing up as part of the crowd at a demonstration. White anti-racist organizing also implies an awareness of how one's white identity impacts the situation, and thinking strategically about how that impact can be used.

White anti-racist organizing may imply white caucus work and other activities in which both organizers and other participants are all white. But it does not imply working outside of a multiracial context at the highest level. Rather it necessarily implies working in collaboration with people of color. And this brings us within sight of the concept of accountability.

The dictionary tells us accountability has to do with responsibility, being liable for one's actions, having to explain, and/or being legally bound. One can be held accountable to a boss or to the law. Children are accountable to their guardians. Contracts make two parties accountable to one another. In faith communities, people are accountable to their deities.

In order to be accountable, one must be visible, with a transparent agenda and process. Invisibility defies examination; it is, in fact, employed in order to avoid detection and examination. Accountability demands commitment. It might be defined as "what kicks in when convenience runs out." Accountability requires some sense of urgency and becoming a true stakeholder in the outcome. Accountability can be externally imposed (legal or organizational requirements), or internally applied (moral, relational, faith-based), or recognized as some combination of the two on a continuum from the institutional and organizational level to the individual level. From a relational point of view, accountability is not about always doing it right. Sometimes it's really about what happens after it's done wrong.

What, then, is accountability and white anti-racist organizing, the topic and title of this book? White anti-racist organizers might hold themselves accountable to any number of people, including their fellow organizers, those who they seek to organize, and people who they take as leaders and moral guides. All these apply, and some chapters in this book address these relationships to some degree. But we are concerned first and foremost with the accountability of white anti-racist organizers to people of color in general, and to anti-racist people of color in particular.

Simply put, people with privileged statuses who set out to undo oppressive systems often do not have the faintest notion of what is really needed. The balance of power rests with the privileged but the balance of knowledge rests with the oppressed. This creates an unfortunate dynamic in which the least knowledgeable people hold the most power — simply a recipe for ineffectiveness. It is, as Ron Chisom says, a situation in which white people, because of our privilege, do not have to listen and do not have to make ourselves vulnerable. We can offer our "aid" on our terms alone and walk away if we do not like the manner in which it is accepted.

Accountability asks of white people, "What are you willing to give up? How uncomfortable are you willing to be? What are you willing to risk?" Accountability begs the question, "How messy am I willing to get?" People organize to meet their own goals and if anti-racist white people are organizing, the goal they have in mind is to live, someday, in a racially equitable and just society. We want to get to the promised land. There is little difficulty believing that everyone will be better off in a world without racism, and that people of color will benefit. But we do it to create the world that we, anti-racist white people, want to see come about.

In that world we envision that white people and people of color will live in authentic relationship and community with one another, and the differences of racial power and privilege that exist in today's world will no longer exist. But exist they do, and we have only today to do our work, however glorious the future may be. Accountability in the traditional sense implies an underlying power that can administer sanctions, but if there are no sanctions, if one is in the power position, why be accountable, and who can hold you to it? So accountability as we view it in regard to white anti-racist organizing is about a willingness to share power. Indeed, accountability is the balance to power that brings our vision of the future into the present moment.

Since its founding more than thirty years ago, the People's Institute for Survival and Beyond has voiced the need for accountable organizing and, in particular, emphasized the need for white activists to work in accountable relationships with anti-racist people of color. We are a product of the People's Institute training, as are all the editors and most of the contributors to this book. Although the book itself is not a work of the Institute, we are compelled to recognize its leading work, carried across so many years, that now is bearing fruit in hundreds of locations across the United States. In gratitude to its work, its long-term contribution, and its immediate contribution to the ideas in this book, the publisher has agreed to share a portion of the proceeds with the Institute.

What is clear in principle, however, is sometimes more vague in application. Accountability in white anti-racist organizing is one of those instances. There is no rule book, and no set of guidelines, no steps 1-2-3 to teach us how in each instance we might put our concern for accountability into practice. There are only the hard won lessons of experience by dedicated organizers who have remained faithful to their ideals and purpose. And what better way is there to learn? People working for racial justice and equity are, at the heart of it, engaged in a very human undertaking. Rules are good for robots, and for creating orderly societies, but to create social change through building authentic relationships, that calls for a deeper understanding of what we must do.

Accountability is not the be-all and end-all of anti-racist organizing. The People's Institute teaches several principles, including leadership development, networking, and understanding our history. These principles interweave with one another so that any one taken alone is only part of the story. But we can achieve a deeper understanding of what accountability means, knowing that without it we are not likely to succeed. And so we offer these stories.

The contributors represent much of the broad spectrum of white anti-racists living and organizing in the United States today. They span a wide range of ages, do their anti-racist work in a variety of disparate settings and are guided by different perspectives and approaches.

The eleven narratives which follow are singular in many ways, yet what they all hold in common is the contributors' understanding that they answer to something larger than themselves for their actions and inactions. What that 'something' is, and how to develop an authentic relationship with it, rests at the heart of each story.

Chapters may be read independently. Reading them in order, however, will allow you to travel the country from context to context, hearing first from activists working in coalitions and institutions and, later, to the voices of anti-racist collectives. Think of the book as you would a family; you can meet the siblings as individuals, but to get a true sense of the family, you need to attend the reunion.

In the first chapter Jacqui Hermer takes us to post-Katrina New Orleans and the struggle in distinguishing between charity and solidarity work. As a college-sponsored student from the Northwest volunteering in the Ninth Ward, Jacqui reflects on how her privilege can blind and benefit her, even as she engages in work intended for the empowerment of others.

In Chapter Two, Jeb Middlebrook brings us into the world of white hip-hop and the role that popular culture and a for-profit strategy can and cannot play in anti-racist organizing. As one half of the performing duo AR-15 (which stands for the fifteen anti-racist principles he outlines in his chapter), Jeb recalls lessons learned from campus initiatives, trainings, media opportunities, and more.

Christine Schmidt's work as an advocate for youth within a public education system is a study in how professional gatekeeping involves managing multiple, competing layers of accountability. In Chapter Three, Christine shares her frequently harrowing navigation of a complex, interdisciplinary setting in her attempts to bring justice to bear in a resistant environment.

Larry Yates' story of a successful tenant rights campaign in a multiracial effort of national scope illustrates the power of applying anti-racist principles to traditional organizing strategies. In Chapter Four, this long-time activist reflects on how legal policies can be changed with broad-based collective effort and a clear, unswerving commitment to action.

In Chapter Five "Burning Deep Inside," Gillian Burlingham stresses the power of personal relationships and spiritual practices to guide and sustain a racial justice activist. With clear definitions for accountability and a commitment to transparent process to guide her, Gillian ultimately consults her heart to find strategies for making change in her Quaker community and beyond.

Through Ben Kohl and Lisa Blitz in Chapter Six, we gain access to the inner world of a large social service agency in the process of transformation. Ben and Lisa's story, seen through their clinical lens, illustrates the tensions that can arise between professional and moral duty, the challenges that the intersection of other oppressions can play in 'dis-organizing' a caucusing effort, and manifestations of how intellectualization and other characteristics of white organizational culture can stall or derail the transformation process.

Matt Meyers' work with his grassroots organization, Resistance in Brooklyn, is based in radical political ideology and fueled by the commitment, as members of the privileged group, to take risks for the cause of justice. Chapter Seven emphasizes the need for understanding the historical and international context current activism is founded upon, and the imperative to balance knowledge with action.

The need to pass on the political tradition of anti-racist, anti-imperialist solidarity politics to a younger generation is what drives the thirteen year "herstory" of the Challenging White Supremacy Workshop (CWS). Cofounder Sharon Martinas' saga in Chapter Eight is a fearlessly honest telling of the trials and challenges of leadership development among young white activists in the anti-racist movement. Sharon, with the help of CWS cofounder Mickey Ellinger, describes the creation and evolution of an accountable anti-racist pedagogy and in the telling provides critical questions for any accountable practice.

In Chapter Nine, the New Jersey-based Alliance for Racial and Social Justice (ARSJ) addresses the essential role of amends in the reclamation of our humanity as white people and reminds us that the personal is, indeed, political at its core. Based on the work of Pablo Friere, Rhea Almeida, and other liberation theorists, and founded in their shared history of domestic violence, ARSJ tells the story of its formation and internal functioning as a white affinity group's answer to the call for accountability.

The necessity of authentic cross-racial relationships to effective, sustainable anti-racist practice is the central theme of AWARE's (the Alliance of White Anti-Racists Everywhere) Chapter Ten. They thoughtfully critique the prevalent and long-standing unidirectional model for accountable cross-racial relationships, and propose a new model based on reciprocity within a formal advisory structure and white identity development frame.

In the final chapter we return to New Orleans with an offering from European Dissent, a group of white anti-racist activists formed in 1986 in response to a direct challenge from the leaders of color of the People's Institute for Survival and Beyond. In their chapter, they share their Statement of Accountability — an internal document that defines the term and outlines in some detail what a living practice of accountability should look like.

In our Afterword we come back to the place we began — located within the context of a larger movement for racial justice, a broader body of guiding principles, and a longer story; one that includes those who came before us and those who are sure to follow.

Chapter One

Pulling Back the Veil: Lessons from Post-Levee-Break New Orleans

Jacqui "Adhi" Hermer

On January 1, 2006, more than fifty volunteers from across the country drove past military blockades into the mostly vacant and absolutely devastated Lower Ninth Ward of New Orleans. This historically rich and vibrant community was at the bottom of the list for support from the city government and at the top for bulldozing, forced land seizures, and development into "green space" or casino land. At the request of a homeowner, volunteers began a project to gut, renovate, and transform a house into a headquarters for returning residents seeking to rebuild their neighborhood. Volunteers from everywhere, including New Orleans, have played a major role cleaning out and reopening schools, churches, and thousands of homes and businesses. I had the blessing to be one of them.

On August 29, 2005, Hurricane Katrina's 140-mph winds ripped the roof off the living legacy of US slavery and released thirty feet of water over government-designed, constructed, and funded levee walls. More than eighty percent of the city was flooded. Today, that same legacy of slavery — the notion that black and brown lives are disposable — has created the largest gentrification project in US history. From the federal response to the flood to planning for the city's renewal, the government at all levels has continued to systematically push poor black and brown residents out of the city.

Fueled by outrage, disgust, and guilt, I, like thousands of other well-meaning volunteers, came to lend a hand with the rebuilding efforts under way throughout the Gulf Coast. We represented a massive influx of predominantly white, college-educated, and class-privileged folks. We shared living space with other strangers for a few days to many months, showered and ate when possible, and spent our days clearing mold-infested homes. In many ways our free labor was necessary. However, in many other ways, the attitudes, assumptions, and behaviors that we brought with us represented yet another burden for residents and local organizers of color as they rebuilt their homes.

Post-levee-break New Orleans is a window into the long history of racial and class oppression in this country. For weeks after the storm, major media featured images of floating homes and bodies; white shirts clinched in the fists of mostly black, hungry, sweaty, and tired outstretched arms trying to signal a hovering helicopter; and desperate crowds everywhere — waiting — on sidewalks, in attics, on roofs, on the freeway, inside the Superdome. The media's portrayal of the flood's "poor victims" quickly shifted to the "violent savage"; headlines no longer focused on families waiting for help, but on black men taking advantage of the vacant city to loot stores and rape women. They grossly exaggerated or gave blatantly false stories that soon became the justification for a militarized response rather than a humanitarian one. They also set the stage for thousands of "brave" and "courageous" volunteers to paternalistically head into this "dangerous" city with the self-appointed goal of trying to "save" New Orleans.

In this chapter, I hope to offer a critical reflection on the pervasive nature of white supremacy in white activist communities, specifically focused on the primarily leftist organization I worked with in post-levee-break New Orleans. By sharing stories of success and failure, I also intend to spotlight how my own privilege and internalized sense of superiority participated in my response to this tragedy, in the hope that these lessons may be transferable to other white activists as we continue to struggle and understand what it means to work in true solidarity.

Some Personal Context and History

I grew up in Seattle and New York as a white Ashkenazi Jewish South African, privileged both in class and education.[1] When Katrina hit, I was at Burning Man, a weeklong festival dedicated to self-indulgence.[2] Driving home from the week of debauchery while listening to the news of the storm, I was left feeling empty and couldn't help but think that I had spent my entire life basically lost in a desert somewhere in Nevada. A couple of months later, I attended my first "Undoing Racism™ and Community Organizing Workshop," facilitated by the People's Institute for Survival and Beyond (PISAB).

That day, we had the honor to hear PISAB's cofounder and New Orleans native, Ron Chisom, graciously share stories of his experience and tragedy during the storm. I attribute the moment I became radicalized to this workshop, which marked a major turning point in my life. At this time, I was struggling to understand and contextualize my experience as a white African and US-born citizen. I had recently had the opportunity to live and study in Kenya, and returned home in a state of distress and guilt. I really did not know much about New Orleans, other than what I had learned from major news sources and a friend who had been down there for a couple of months. By volunteering, I guess I hoped to do something productive in the south with my privilege that I had felt incapable of accomplishing in Kenya. I asked for a plane ticket as a birthday gift and traveled to New Orleans for two weeks in December 2005. While there, I compiled and distributed a pamphlet on free and accessible medical and social services available in the city.

Common Ground Relief

My host was Common Ground (CG), an activist organization that came together shortly after the levees broke to strategically mobilize volunteers in order to mitigate the inadequate responses of the city, state, and federal authorities. Under the leadership of Malik Rahim, a former Black Panther, CG's most prominent work was and is providing free house-gutting services in the Ninth Ward and free medical services across the city.[3] The accomplishments of the organization are vast and impressive. CG was one of the very first relief organizations in the city, and in spite of all its struggles it has helped thousands of white college-age folks like me to expand our political consciousness.

CG attracted mostly younger lefty activists from across the country. Those who were able to stick around for longer than a few weeks were disproportionately white and middle class. Subsequently, many of CG's volunteers had little knowledge of the history and culture of the people who called New Orleans home. Volunteers stayed in daycare centers, churches, or elementary schools in the middle of a predominantly black neighborhood where few residents had yet been able to return. Most of us had no previous relationship to the city or its people. Therefore, a sense of long-term responsibility or commitment was rare. The only thing consistent within the organization was turnover among its volunteers.

CG prided itself on the slogan "Solidarity not Charity." However, many of its decisions and the work it undertook were influenced by a sense of crisis that did not lend itself to reflection or community outreach. Its quick, crisis-driven decision-making often did not include the voices of the local people most affected by those decisions. Although long-time black organizers held the primary positions of leadership, white folks from out of town were overwhelmingly in the majority. This not only resulted in a serious disconnect with the direct needs of residents, it also permitted the development of many new projects with little chance of long-term sustainability. Moreover, as Common Ground grew and began reaching tens of thousands of volunteers, the resources that poured in came to benefit the organization and not the people it was supposed to be in "solidarity" with.

Following her first visit to the city, Molly McClure, an organizer with the Catalyst Project, an anti-racist collective in San Francisco, commented in an insightful essay on the culture of CG. As she put it, "Racism fosters in white people an easy, unconscious arrogance, an inability to see past ourselves, the capacity to be 'blinded by the white.'"[4] What she and many local organizers saw permeating within CG were paternalistic and egotistic attitudes that confirmed rather than challenged the prevailing culture of white supremacy. Even with good intentions, we were blinded by a veil of whiteness that ensured an organizational culture indicative of the very oppressive forces we were trying to fight against.

Initial Reflections and Intentions

After returning home to Seattle, I committed to expanding my understanding of racism and began my first social justice organizing work with a student organization dedicated to working with white folks to challenge white supremacy on campus. When I returned to the south in April 2006, I hoped that a longer time commitment to the city's renewal, on my part, would enable me to practice true solidarity and support other white volunteers to do the same. Through the work I did and with the patience and intentional support of many inspiring organizers, I gained invaluable insight into the ethics and strategies involved in work aimed at solidarity and inclusion.

At this point, even though the barriers to returning to their homes and communities continued to be extremely problematic for people of color, the disaster response "rush" was over. Unfiltered racism no longer filled the front page of newspapers. Yet, in the time I had been away from New Orleans, the AntiRacist Work Group (ARWG) had been formed within CG through support from Ingrid Chapman of the Catalyst Project[5]; Catherine Jones, a long-time organizer from New Orleans; and several longer-term CG volunteers. European Dissent (ED) — a New Orleans-based, white antiracist collective with strong ties to PISAB — and two movement-building, political-education collectives based in San Francisco — the Catalyst Project and the Challenging White Supremacy Workshop — were all integral in supporting the growth of ARWG, mainly through personal relationship building.

Members of European Dissent and the People's Institute came to the AntiRacist Work Group meetings, offered political education, and mentored different ARWG members during its development. With goals of supporting white volunteers by deepening their analysis of white supremacy and offering tools to ensure accountability to communities of color, the ARWG was and is instrumental in growing a larger antiracist community focused on advocating for the right of return for all displaced peoples.

I immediately began working with the ARWG and a youth- and education-focused project called "Kids and Community" (KNC). Typically, volunteers new to CG are placed in work crews and assigned a house to gut on their first day. I was able to bypass house gutting and move into a position of leadership due to a sense of entitlement I gained from my previous experience. For example, I felt familiar enough with the culture and expectations of CG to move freely though the chain of command and I had a close friendship with a CG organizer who knew of an open leadership position.

As a result, I felt highly qualified to assume this responsibility. I also believed the work that I was planning to do — reframe minds within the organization to be agents of antiracist change — was the most important work to be done, and that house gutting was work for those who lacked my analytical skills. After just a few days of being back, I gladly stepped into a coordinator position with KNC.

Kids and Community: Strategy and Struggles

KNC arose out of outrage about a historically under-funded school system that was undergoing massive privatiza-tion.[6] Many schools across New Orleans were still not open and those that were became highly selective and expensive. Child-care and accessible extracurricular activities for low-income youth of color were still unavailable; this lack was a major reason why families dislocated by Katrina chose not to return to the city. KNC was receiving incredible support and praise from the leadership of CG and major resources were committed to its growth.

Asked to organize a summer camp in New Orleans, I was anxious to tap into CG's resources and strategically use the sup-port that KNC was receiving from the organization's leadership. Two folks from San Francisco showed up with lots of energy, strong antiracist sentiments, and a commitment of two months. We were all thrilled to take the spring to plan a solid summer pro-gram. Knowing how important this project was, I sought support for our work from members of the ARWG. Elders and antiracist peers encouraged me to seek out local voices and listen to their advice about the most effective use of our leverage within CG. I was given a few phone numbers of folks who were familiar with the history of education in the city as well as stakeholders who would be directly affected by how schools and daycare programs were going to be rebuilt.

Through meetings, I began to learn more about the negative ramifications of CG's activities in New Orleans. I heard that many local organizers were tired of having to compete with CG for funding and media attention. I learned that CG was reluctant to publicly support any organization that wasn't already tied to the name "Common Ground." The humbling and honest feedback from local organizers sparked a lot of discussion among those of us who were new to the city and responsible for planning the summer program. It was apparent that the critique about CG applied to the after-school program KNC was currently planning, as well as to the summer camp I envisioned.

Based on the feedback received, we decided to significantly shift our focus for the summer and use CG's access to volunteers to launch a project that would be created at the discretion of, and with support from, local organizers and groups involved in ongoing work with youth in New Orleans. We planned to develop a volunteer program that would screen and train long-term volunteers with previous experience working with youth and then refer them to local summer programs and schools needing volunteers to get up and running again. We specifically hoped to support organizations with radical leftist politics and schools that had external monitoring systems in place.

As it took shape, the core goal of the KNC summer volunteer program was to maintain internal and external accountability to everyone we would be working with. Internally, we intended to do this through open communication, transparency, and building an infrastructure for the fall program. Externally, we planned to share CG's access to resources, support local education programs with leftist politics, provide a safe and uplifting space for children, and ensure that every decision we made and action we took would be at the discretion and in the interests of folks who were most affected by Katrina and historical oppression.

A lot of dissension emerged when we proposed to the larger KNC organizing body that it adopt goals similar to those of our summer program. A small group of us were very vocal about wanting to change the direction of KNC so that it supported local organizations. Another group about the same size was deeply committed to the expansion of CG. Members of this group had experienced joy watching their students grow through the after-school program and were excited about the prospects of designing new programs which they hoped would offer the same benefits to families throughout the city. This conflict between outreach to local residents and institutional goals, which continued throughout the spring and summer, highlighted the strong emotions that are often deeply rooted in community organizing. It also shed light on the historical baggage that white folks bring to our work and our struggles to give up leadership and recognition.

Arguably, one of the most damaging aspects of white organizational culture is the value placed on individual achievement over community or relationship building. In our summer project organizing group, we understood that we needed to model what it looked like to challenge white culture in our own internal organizing approach first. We were a small, predominantly white group of folks, only one of whom was from New Orleans. Transitioning from an environment in which one white man had been making most of the decisions that affected KNC, we intended to make all subsequent decisions based on consensus and develop an organizational structure that demonstrated a spokesperson model. We also spent time together away from meetings getting to know one another.

As a group, we made a commitment to deepen our collective and personal understanding of racism. We attended ED and ARWG meetings, and three of us traveled to St. Louis for the seventh annual White Privilege Conference. We were determined to seek out resources so we could build a comprehensive training program that would not only ground the new volunteers in antiracist analysis, but would also contextualize the history of education in the city and create a support network for the volunteers whose role it was to help young people deal with trauma.

We expected each volunteer to commit two months. We reached out to people of color and working-class folks by sending letters to ethnic student centers on campuses and publicizing our project on many different web sites. However, we knew that being free to devote two months of unpaid work necessitated some sort of economic privilege on the part of volunteers. Therefore, we required volunteers to attend a six-day orientation designed to address the power differential between themselves and the youth they'd be working with. Some of the goals of the orientation were to dispel myths about the city; build group unity; introduce volunteers to long-time, local education-justice organizers; and support the volunteers to accept leadership from the program directors and teachers they would be working with. To model these goals, local organizers facilitated most workshops. The program included a shortened People's Institute "Undoing Racism™ Workshop"; signs and symptoms of post-traumatic stress; abuse prevention; conflict management; nonviolent communication; history of the educational system in New Orleans; and a CPR/first aid course. On the last day, the twenty volunteers, four of whom were local residents, were assigned to one of five schools, two art camps, or a day camp (based upon their skills and requests) and met with their respective project directors to learn more about their specific expectations and responsibilities.

As a pilot project, the summer volunteer program was successful. As expected, a large majority of the volunteers able to commit to it for the entire summer were white. We spent much time during the orientation discussing why each volunteer had chosen to come, how their lives and situations made this possible, and how they each could hold themselves accountable to provide access to and transparency in their work in New Orleans and after they returned home. Despite our passion, aspects of white organizational culture pervaded the summer program. Most arguably, this was seen via the competitive, results-based approach that we, as organizers took.

What Is Our Legacy Going to Be?

With the summer program concluded and the future of KNC uncertain, the decision-making body of KNC met several times to discuss the future goals and direction of the project. Our summer program planning group focused on being clear and honest about what we hoped the legacy of our work would be and what we could commit to move forward. I intended to leave, and worried that KNC might lose the community relationships we had built.

With the support of several mentors, I wrote a letter to the KNC Spokes Council, modeled after Catherine Jones' "love letter" to the CG Health Clinic a year earlier.[7] My letter included a list of questions about the possible negative effects we could have on New Orleans.

This led to a day-long strategic planning session facilitated by a local educational justice organizer of color. The meeting was a great opportunity to identify the mission and future goals of the project. As a result, the KNC leadership body committed to a number of actions: maintaining a model of accountability based upon input from elders and leaders in the community; specifying who would provide resources in order to maintain accountability; adopting a majority-based decision-making structure; and building institutional memory for sustainability. Members of the core summer group and I left the meeting feeling hopeful.

I left New Orleans not long after this last meeting. For a while, I maintained close contact with a few of the organizers within KNC. Two months later, I heard that CG had cut funding for KNC and that the fall project could not get off the ground. The Spokes Council turned its energy to supporting the work of local organizers, such as the woman who facilitated our meeting.

What is "Solidarity"?

Effective solidarity work can restructure resource distribution and power differentials. Participating in solidarity work implies that I am not from the community in which I am working, that I have skills or privilege to offer, and that I am constantly and consciously working towards developing others' leadership and access to resources. This process includes political advocacy, building valuable relationships, reallocating resources, being transparent in my actions, and being strategic and sustainable with my energy. The key word — accountability — means recognizing that this work is about supporting folks and their projects in a way that is not about me and my involvement, but is about the people directly affected and the way they wish to express their needs and greatest potential. In the previously mentioned love letter by Catherine Jones, she ends with a really powerful statement:

> [Ultimately] this work is not about you, or me, or any one of us. It's about building a world where all of the structures that keep people down don't exist anymore, and where any human being among us has the power to decide, for real, how they will live their own life. Right? And for that to even begin to happen in a legitimate way, we need to own up to our role in that whole process. How we help it along, and how we stand in its way.[8]

My biggest personal challenges in New Orleans were overcoming my ego and Eurocentric cultural traditions. I made a grave number of mistakes and learned a thousand more invaluable lessons. My biggest mistake was losing sight of the importance of building valuable relationships. From day one, I prioritized work over friendship and ultimately limited the long-lasting impact and relationships that I might still have today if I had acted differently. The greatest lesson I learned was passed on to me through mentors. It is one that prioritizes leadership development and ensures that this work continues to new generations.

The many mentors who supported me while in New Orleans and long after I returned home continue to humble me. Thank you especially to members of the People's Institute for Survival and Beyond, European Dissent, AntiRacist Work Group, Catalyst Project, and the Challenging White Supremacy Workshop for showing me with love, patience, and courage what it looks like build a movement that works to challenge white organizational culture. Thank you to the folks in KNC before and during that summer for sharing and struggling with me. Thank you to those within CG who have continued to gut, clean, cook and fight for the right to return for all displaced New Orleanians.

And, in no particular order, thank you also to Catherine Jones of ED, ARWG, and LHOP; Ingrid Chapman of ARWG and Catalyst Project; Sharon Martinas of Challenging White Supremacy; Molly McClure of ARWG and Catalyst Project; Sherry Frohich, Bridget Sumser, Todd Cooley, Tyler Norman, Emu Sandall, Kiyoko McCrae and Jeffrey Boston of KNC; Amy Lafont, NOLA school board candidate; Ms. Estella Johnson of Mt. Carmel Baptist Church; Kimberly Richards and Ron Chisom of the People's Institute for Survival and Beyond; Rebecca Mintz, Bay Love, and Steve Peace of ARWG; Bridget Lehane, Laura Manning, Doug Henderson and Rachel Luft of ED and PISAB; Toph West and Dix deLaneuville of ED; Greta Gladney of the Renaissance Project; and so many more.

I cite all these names to remind me of all of the folks who are doing this work, continue to do it, and have been doing it for centuries. They helped me ask the right questions and learn the importance of planning for meetings. They pushed me to be strategic about building allies, to come from love, to avoid being subversive or divisive, and always to assume good intentions. They reminded me to check in, and they cared first and foremost about our friendship. They showed me by example that this work is not just about me or them, but about all of us and our role in creating radical social change and reclaiming our humanity.

Applying Hard Lessons at Home

I brought home with me an urgency to carry the same degree of energy into struggles for liberation in my home community that I put forth while in New Orleans. I brought home a passion to build sustainable and radical community with folks that I share a common history and struggles with. I brought home a desire to stay grounded in my work by focusing on building strong and honest relationships first.

One of the key strategies in white antiracist organizing that I will continue to pursue is what I have come to call the "Three Pillar Approach." The three "pillars" are simply a tactic for doing this work accountably. They are: maintaining a strong connection with a white antiracist affinity group; working in solidarity with a multiracial, people of color-led radical leftist project; and building up the leadership and antiracist analysis of other white activists new to activism.

Today, I practice the three-pillar strategy through my work with Jewish Voice for Peace-Seattle (JVP). Not long after I graduated, I moved back to Seattle to be near my family and a larger population of Jews. Through JVP, I have had an incredible opportunity to grow on many fronts by building community with other radical Jews challenging racism within the mainstream Jewish community and larger US society; supporting others as we speak out against the occupation of Palestine; and braiding our traditions into our political work and relationships.

Through coalition organizing and national campaigns, I have worked alongside local Palestinian communities to commemorate the 60th anniversary of al Nakba — Arabic for "catastrophe" — the date that, for them, marks the beginning of the occupation. In terms of my role in building others' leadership, I recently organized and co-facilitated a three-part workshop for young Jews at a campus Hillel center on challenging what we've been taught about Israel and Palestine and our role in working for peace between Jewish and Palestinian communities.

There is no doubt in my mind that my experience in post-levee break New Orleans has benefited my life significantly. To name a few of the results: I received college credit, have been sought out to speak about the situation on the ground in New Orleans, have enriched my resume experience, and received (undeserved) praise for just going down there. These career-enhancing benefits speak to the ways that even the stories of Katrina passed onto future generations will be filtered through a racialized and classist lens. These benefits also speak to the ease with which solidarity work can be co-opted by self-serving charity.

As a white person working towards building a world that is based on equity, justice and self-determination, I have a responsibility to struggle to pull off my veil and challenge white supremacy in my own behavior and in the well-intentioned organizations I am a part of. In order to build a movement aimed at collective liberation, I must support others to do the same. As Aboriginal activist Lilla Watson is often quoted as saying, "If you have come to help me, you are wasting your time. But if you have come because your liberation is bound up with mine, then let us work together." This quote speaks truth to the power of solidarity organizing. It also offers a tremendously energizing strategy for rebuilding our communities, manifesting radical change, and reclaiming our humanity.

Author's Note

The author would like to thank Bonnie Cushing and all of the editing staff. Thanks especially to Molly McClure, Ingrid Chapman, Antasia Parker, Becky Renfrow, Ian Morgan, and Carol Hermer for guidance, support, and really good and hard questions while putting this piece together.

Notes

1. I share this history to contextualize my complicated history of Diaspora and racialization. All of my great-grandparents sought refuge in South Africa in the late 1800s from the anti-Jewish pogroms of Eastern Europe. Both my parents grew up during the height of apartheid. The passing of this tragic and violent legislation marked the first time my family was classified as "white" and received all the privileges attached to that title. My parents tried to raise us "colorblind," and an early childhood memory is of my mother's pride in my oldest brother when he was explaining a fight on the basketball court and never used the other boy's race as a descriptive word.

2. "Burning Man" is a week-long festival that has been going on for decades and is held each year in what is known as "Black Rock City," a city that is constructed in the middle of a dried-up lake bed in the middle of the Black Rock Desert of Nevada.

3. For more information about Common Ground Relief, see its website, http://www.commongroundrelief.org. To read more about the Common Ground Health Clinic, check out http://www.cghc.org.

4. Molly McClure, "Solidarity Not Charity: Racism in Katrina Relief Work," A Katrina Reader: Readings by and for Anti-Racist Educators and Organizers, http://www.cwsworkshop.org/katrinareader/node/461.

5. See Ingrid Chapman, "Hearts on Fire: The Struggle for Justice in New Orleans," A Katrina Reader: Readings by and for Anti-Racist Educators and Organizers, http://www.cwsworkshop.org/katrinareader/node/425.

6. Immediately after the storm, the state seized each school and began selling them selectively to large international and U.S. corporate bidders. For more information about this process and the current state of New Orleans schools, visit http://www.nola.com.

7. Catherine Jones, "Love Letter to Common Ground Clinic," A Katrina Reader: Readings by and for Anti-Racist Educators and Organizers, http://www.cwsworkshop.org/katrinareader/node/459.

8. The Common Ground Health Clinic was one of the first projects started by Common Ground. For more information about the clinic's inception and development, see its website, http://www.cghc.org. For further information, read Challenging White Supremacy Workshop's A Katrina Reader, especially Catherine Jones' letter referred to in the above note.

Chapter Two

Rhyme and Reason:
The Making of a White Antiracist Rap Group

Jeb Aram Middlebrook

Mic Check

> *I choose to be an ally / we cruise the sidelines / recruiting white guys / school 'em to fight lies.*
>
> Jus Rhyme, "Million Allies"

> *Real recognize revolution.*
>
> Raw Potential

I was not always committed to antiracist principles, and I definitely was not always touring the United States as a white antiracist scholar, organizer, and rapper. I came to be who I am through a political process, through "study and struggle," as my friends at the Catalyst Project would say. This is a story about the process which made me, and also which made a rap group called AntiRacist 15 (AR-15).

AR-15 was a collection of fifteen antiracist principles that guided me and my rap partner, Trevor Wysling aka Raw Potential, in our work as rappers and activists. Some called it a rap group, others called it an organization. We called it a way of life. These principles were largely inspired by the work we did with the Challenging White Supremacy Workshop and the Center for Third World Organizing at the time of the rap group's inception. My story is organized around these principles, as was the work of AR-15.

The seeds of the group were planted in the fall of 2000 at Macalester College in Saint Paul, Minnesota through my attempts to politically organize friends on campus. **Principle 1: Practice Non-violence** was also formulated during this time. Non-violent social change, I understood, could come about through community organizing, and I intended to do just that.

Asking questions about social change at Macalester led me to friends who asked similar questions. They were student organizers on campus fighting for justice on issues ranging from sweatshop-free college apparel to gay visibility to representation by and for students of color. They were women, people of color, GLBT people, and international students. I wondered what my cause was as a straight white guy of economic privilege. Out of my desire to know, I called a formal meeting of my organizer friends in November 2000.

Thinking back to this now, I wonder about this search outside of myself for answers about race, gender, sexuality, and class. I lived race (whiteness), gender (maleness), class (upper-middle), and sexuality (straight), but these identities were invisible to me, normalized by racist, sexist, homophobic, and classist institutions in the United States. **Principle 2: Learn Antiracist History** led me to learn the history of the United States with regard to race, oppression, and privilege, and my role in it. I carried the answer to what my cause was and how I could contribute to social change, but I did not know that then.

During that first meeting at Macalester, I sat looking at my friends, some of the most committed activists and organizers on campus. They represented working-class and elite class backgrounds, gay and straight sexualities, and a multitude of different races and nationalities. I wanted to know their histories — their ways of resisting, organizing, and surviving systems of oppression that were not designed for their well-being. Without knowing it, I had begun to practice what would become **Principle 3: Study Legacies of Resistance.**

Looking around the room, I realized that I was the only white guy.

"What are we here for?" my friend Melissa asked.

"We're here to talk about what we do on campus," I said. "To figure out how we can support one another's causes."

Overwhelmed with school work, part-time jobs, student organizing, and life itself, my friends stared back at me bleary-eyed. Silence. I tried to kick off the discussion. Silence. The meeting ended. The following week, I called another meeting. This time, fewer people showed up: "I'm busy," "I have too much homework," "I can't miss sports practice," the people I invited told me. This meeting played out the same way as the first one. Melissa: "What are we here for?" Me: "To support each other's causes." Blank stares.

I called another meeting for the next week, but couldn't make it due to my own busy schedule. Another white friend of mine, Scott, who had similar interests to mine in finding his cause attended in my place. I don't know what happened at the meeting, but from what my friends told me, Scott said some inappropriate things that were borderline racist, sexist, and homophobic. I confronted Scott one evening in the dorms and told him he wasn't allowed to come anymore—he'd messed up.

"Where's Scott?" Melissa asked me at the next meeting.

"I told him not to come anymore. He messed up," I said.

My friends looked at me, stunned. "You should've talked to us about it," they said.

"I handled it," I said.

But by the look of growing distrust in their eyes, I clearly hadn't "handled it." I'd messed up myself, in more ways than one. My friends stopped coming to the meetings. I couldn't figure out what had happened and mulled this over with Scott into winter break.

Deciding to formalize our thinking, Scott and I put together a proposal for an independent study project. Our research questions focused on two themes: "What didn't work in our attempt to organize students across race, class, gender, and sexual lines on campus?" and "What can two white guys do to challenge oppression?"

We called our study "Synthysys," an intentional—and we thought cooler spelling—than *synthesis,* a term gleaned from our reading of the philosophy of Karl Marx. We understood synthesis, as Marx used it, to mean what happens when two opposite ideas (*thesis* and *anti-thesis*) come together to make something new. We meant to write a paper. We ended up building an organization.

After weeks of debate and writing we came to the realization that it wasn't the job of two white guys to organize women, people of color, GLBT folks, and international students to support each other's causes. These students were already doing what they could when they could. Also, in many ways, we hadn't challenged our *own* racism, sexism, classism, and homophobia, so perhaps we weren't even ready to come to the table and strategize with our friends. Indeed, it was a table *we* had set up, and to which *we* had invited *ourselves.*

We learned the next two principles back to back, **Principle 4: Research Your Family History** and **Principle 5: Respect Leadership of Color.** Scott and I did not know our family histories. We did not know what it had meant or did mean to be white in America. As a result, we played out personally destructive dynamics with our friends of color. We learned **Principle 5: Respect Leadership of Color** the hard way. We did not respect our friends' experiences with racism in the United States. We did not honor their direct experience and expertise in dealing with their own oppression. And we certainly were not showing leadership in the white community in challenging our own racism.

What we demonstrated was not solidarity, it was two white guys running the show. What else was new? We realized that if we wanted to support women, people of color, GLBT folks, and international students on campus, then we should educate ourselves

— and other white people — to be the best allies we could be. We would do what became AR-15's next principle — **Principle 6: Stand in Solidarity.** We decided that we could best stand in solidarity with people of color by taking responsibility for our own and other white people's racism, men's sexism, straight people's homophobia, and wealthy people's classism. In this way, we imagined ourselves to be in alliance with both antiracist organizers across racial lines and with people of color who experienced systemic racism most directly.

Scott and I felt our job was to fulfill what became **Principle 7: Challenge Oppression** by acting within our spheres of influence, to make changes where we could. We began reaching out to other white guys on campus to talk about race. What we found when we broached the topic with other white friends was the same bleary-eyed look we'd seen in the eyes of students of color when we tried organizing them. Whatever their race, people were already too busy, too tired, too stressed out. So we asked ourselves, "What are white guys already doing on issues of race that we could connect with them on?"

The answer? Watching movies! So we organized movie nights, complete with suitable college drinks, and screened Spike Lee's classics. Our plan: to watch movies in which race was an undeniable theme and then use the movies as jumping-off points to get white guys on campus to talk about race. We attempted what we later learned was a tried-and-true organizing strategy: **Principle 8: Listen Actively.** We hoped to meet other white guys where they were at in terms of their thinking, talking, and acting with regard to race. In this way, we hoped to move them toward antiracist consciousness and action. We screened, *Do the Right Thing* and *Malcolm X.* But before we could screen *Bamboozled,* I dropped out of college.

I was becoming bleary-eyed myself. I needed some time to think. My world had been turned upside down by the question Scott and I had asked: "What can two white guys do?" The prospect of the amount of work that white people, including me, would have to take on to fix our own racist behavior and institutions overwhelmed me. I needed a break.

Only later did I recognize that the fact that I could take time out to *think about* oppression, rather than *survive it,* was in itself a privilege — made possible by the complexities of race and class advantage. I couldn't go to class at Macalester, let alone eat in the cafeteria, without the constant realization that my white skin got me things in this world that some people of color would never have. In this, I recognized the need for a revolution in the United States and realized that I — and white people in general — stood in the way of it happening. But in order to face racism, I first had to face myself.

People Before Profit

> *I drop the topic properly / rich folks got O.P.P. /*
> *other people's property.*
>
> Jus Rhyme, "People Tell Me"

I had read in a book in college that the true test of any nation is how it treats its lowest resident. Given what I'd learned about race, class, gender, and sexuality, I figured that person in the United States would be homeless, black, a lesbian, and a recent immigrant. I wanted to test my theory through personal experience, but I wasn't black, nor was I a lesbian or a recent immigrant. Well-read but undereducated, I thought, "I could be homeless." I hopped the first plane I could find to San Diego (a city I knew because I'd lived there after high school in AmeriCorps, plus it was warm) with one change of clothes and a toothbrush, looking forward to all the great insights I'd gain from being homeless in the United States.

Instead of learning about oppression, I learned about privilege. I had *decided* to be homeless — an act seeped in ignorance. Instead of listening to what poor people and people of color said, I wanted to *be* them, to take their place, to speak for them. Plus, my ranking system for determining who was most oppressed in the United States ignored the complexity of how oppression actually works. In reality, I realized later, oppression operates through a complicated web of systems of inclusion and exclusion that privileges and oppresses all of us in different ways. I had a lot to learn.

Despite my best intentions to be homeless, I had a place to stay the night I landed in San Diego. I had a shared room within a week, and a library card and job within a week-and-a-half. I quickly realized that I couldn't escape privilege. The United States wouldn't let me, a white guy from money, slip through the cracks. So I returned to Minnesota, stayed with friends until I could get my own place, and dedicated myself to *using* my privilege to end oppression.

I spent the next three months, however, staring at the ceiling of my bedroom trying to figure out how use privilege to end oppression. I worked odd jobs to pay my rent and buy groceries, but basically, I thought. *Use privilege.* Not knowing what to do, I applied for college, again, this time at the University of Minnesota (U of M). I was accepted and would start in the fall of 2001. *Use privilege.* I kept thinking. Sometime around June 2001, I discovered what would later become **Principle 9: Create Antiracist Culture.** I had the desire to create a community around my developing principles. I called Scott and a friend from AmeriCorps, Trevor, and pitched them the idea. The organization, to be called Synthysys, would merge art, education, and activism. Its main purpose would be to make space for discussions, realizations, and mobilizations around issues of race and privilege. Hip-hop would be the vehicle; it was the first thing I'd seen unite people of different backgrounds in a real way. I found out about community organizing later.

I made it official by building a website for Synthysys and incorporating it as a non-profit. I made flyers. But Synthysys never did anything. It existed as an idea, a space in my mind where people of all backgrounds would come together to make revolution. I talked about Synthsys with everyone I met. People were inspired: "Sounds cool." "Where do I sign up?" "How do I get involved?"

I had an org, but no organization. *I* was Synthysys—the site of opposing ideas (oppression and privilege) coming together and working themselves out to become something new. Instead, I was becoming something new.

My life became a microcosm of what I imagined the revolution would look like: rallies, protests, concerts, conferences, house parties—all multiracial, intergenerational, multi-class, diverse in gender and sexuality. I knew, perhaps, what revolution looked like at a house party, but on a societal level I had no clue. And what was my contribution?

"What does Synthysys do?" people asked. I didn't know.

I scrapped Synthysys. **Principle 9: Create Antiracist Culture,** echoed in my mind, however. It was time to get organized. I looked at what I already had: a website, a non-profit, and three recipe-card boxes full of contacts—artists, educators, and activists. I flipped through my contacts and stopped at Donald aka Rhyme Chyld. We'd freestyled together for several months at Macalester and later, while I was at the University of Minnesota. He'd heard me work out my thinking and my identity through hip-hop, as I evolved from Jeb Middlebrook to Lonely Poet to Privilege (eventually I'd become Jus Rhyme). I thought he'd get what I was trying to do.

We decided to meet at a pizza place on the West Bank of the U of M. He told me he had a good friend, Denario, who he thought would like my idea, so he brought him along. I gave them my pitch: "The Hip-Hop Co-op: Get Free. Make Change." "Get Free" was a call to all hip-hop artists who wanted free stage time and promotion for their work in the community. It was also a call to community organizations that wanted free performances to draw people to their meetings and protests. "Make Change" was a call to the same groups. Hip-hoppers could sell their merchandise in a cooperative fashion through the organization and donate a portion of their profits to our work. Community organizations could receive money from concert fundraisers that the co-op would put on and split the profits among themselves to support their work. Donald, Denario, and I started the organization.

In the fall of 2002, within three months of its inception, the Hip-Hop Co-op boasted over 500 email addresses, thirty regular volunteers, and a small office in the commercial district around the University of Minnesota. We had relationships with most hip-hop promoters in the city and a mobile entourage of six to eight volunteers. We began to purchase cooperatively owned equipment and began to throw our own shows.

We supported a variety of community causes. We wrote a hip-hop play for an organization supporting women in prison. We recruited hip-hop emcees to freestyle call-and-responses as part of a march against police brutality and detentions after 9/11. We set up hip-hop performances and fundraisers for anti-war organizations after the United States invaded Iraq. We performed at the Saint Paul capitol side by side with women of color from the Welfare Rights Coalition, and raised our voices to senators and congressman to support poor people in Minnesota. The Hip-Hop Co-op mattered. We were making change.

Then a phone call came. It was a reporter writing a piece about us for a community newsletter. She asked me, "So don't you think it's weird that a white guy runs a hip-hop organization?" I informed her that I was co-director of the organization and that my partners Donald and Denario were African-American and Latino/African-American and that she should talk to them, too. She did later.

But that call left me wondering if it *was* weird. Was I repeating the same mistake I'd made at Macalester? Was I, once again, the white guy running the show? I realized I needed to stand up and be counted as a white guy against racism. I needed to do what the next principle instructed: **Principle 10: Act on Your Principles.** But I was not sure how. I decided to call Trevor, my friend from Ameri-Corps. He was also a white guy into hip-hop. I had learned to freestyle side by side with him and a Filipino guy, Roy, while doing community service projects around the southwestern and western United States. Maybe Trevor would have an answer.

It was now December 2002, four years after another friend of mine in AmeriCorps, Lakiesha, told me that the United States "is made for white people." After four years of conversations with Trevor and Scott about the meaning of race, whiteness, and white privilege, I was still trying to understand what Lakiesha meant. I was now on the phone with Trevor. "The Hip-Hop Co-op needs to do a training for white guys in hip-hop," I told him. "Whites in Hip-Hop: Roles & Responsibilities." Trev laughed. He already had a reader put together; he just didn't have a title. Perfect. We set the date for the training and began to take responsibility.

The training was a mild success. Only one of the five white hip-hoppers the Co-op invited showed up. But all of the people of color we invited appeared. We came together in a powerful afternoon of multiracial conversation, in which each participant presented their perspective on hip-hop and race based on their own background. There was an African-American male emcee, an East-Asian American female hip-hop activist, an Indian-American female singer, and two white guys in hip-hop who now had an idea of what they could do. When it was our turn to present, Trevor handed out the collection of readings he'd compiled. The room smiled.

Flip the System

> *We organize by day, our nights are political/*
> *AntiRacist 15, our lives are our principles.*
>
> Jus Rhyme, "AR-15 Anthem"

I had incorporated the Hip-Hop Co-op as a non-profit because I figured that this was the kind of organization you set up if you want to create change on a community level. A cooperative made sense to me because racism, sexism, homophobia, and capitalism were hierarchical enough, and the least I could do was create an organizational structure that everyone could benefit from. What you put in, you'd get out. The contribution could be something as simple as donating time.

But money got the best of the organization. Isn't that usually the case? Wanting to show people that what we were doing was working. Wanting to be symbols of hope by showing people what a cooperative, multiracial space looked like, we overspent on office space and sound equipment, and found ourselves in debt. I burned out as well. Tired of managing thirty people a month and a 500+ person newsletter for free for a year, I longed for a break — for someone to mentor *me,* to show *me* what a cooperative, multiracial space looked like. I retired from the Co-op. Donald and Denario didn't want to keep it going without me, so we closed the doors in May 2003. It was a good run, but in the end it wasn't sustainable.

I graduated from the University of Minnesota in August 2003. Trevor had recently moved to Oakland and I had nowhere to be — so Oakland became my destination. I drove west in my dad's car the week after I graduated. Once I arrived, my goal was to learn from organizers who were creating multiracial spaces. After a couple of phone calls, I reached the co-founder of the Challenging White Supremacy Workshop (CWS), Sharon Martinas, who would later become my mentor and friend. I signed up for CWS's fifteen-week training for antiracist organizers, and there learned what antiracist organizing meant. I realized I had already been doing some of this work with the "Whites in Hip-Hop: Roles & Responsibility" workshop I'd put together a year earlier. A couple of weeks later, I met the program director of the Center for Third World Organizing (CTWO), a racial justice organization led by people of color, and landed my first job in the Bay Area, doing database entry for this long-standing multiracial organization.

The three biggest realizations from my time with CWS and CTWO were 1) privilege could be used to fight oppression; 2) this work was most effective when done from within white-led antiracist organizations in solidarity with organizations led by radical activists of color, and 3) I should surround myself with people and organizations who would keep me politically accountable. With this grounding, I set my sights on gaining all the privilege I could in order to further the antiracist movement and effectively "flip the system."

Attempting to walk my talk, I applied for PhD programs in Ethnic Studies around the United States, and Trevor and I started a political rap group. We met with antiracist organizers at CWS and CTWO to discuss what kind of rap group we might be.

"You're mobilizers, not organizers," said Sharon of CWS. "As performers, you guys have the power to get a lot of people in one room at one time. Use that space to do antiracist education and raise money for local, racial justice organizing led by people of color. Twenty-five percent of your income would be a good start for a donation." Sharon had virtually written a mission statement for our rap group. Now, we needed a name.

After a couple days of brainstorming, we had it: AntiRacist 15. AR-15, for short. It was the term used to describe the police issue version of the M-16, the weapon of choice for the US military and one of many guns popularized by gangsta rap. But antiracism would be our weapon. *Our* AR-15 would be fifteen antiracist principles. These principles came from the organizing work of CWS and CTWO — principles passed down through generations of antiracist organizers from the 1960s and decades before. Now it was our time. Our turn. We reserved the last five principles, 11–15, for future generations. I became Jus Rhyme. Trevor became Raw Potential. Together we became AR-15.

It's Bigger than Hip-Hop

> *I'm the product of the each one, teach one/*
> *A soldier leaned over and banged on my ear drum.*
>
> Raw Potential, "Soldiers Anthem"

Increasingly conscious about our identity as white antiracists and our role as hip-hop performers, Raw and I looked for white role models that merged the worlds of hip-hop and antiracism. But

we couldn't find any contemporary white artists who were publicly against racism. It seemed that white hip-hop artists and their
fans chose to make race an unmentionable, since focusing on it
might draw attention to their already precarious individual and collective position in relation to a black-and-brown-run art form. White
hip-hoppers would rather attempt to blend in, citing the utopian
promise of hip-hop as a space where "color doesn't matter" and
"belonging is based on skills," an ironic inversion of the dream of
Dr. Martin Luther King, Jr.

Raw and I soon realized that the growing white fan base of
hip-hop could effectively create majority white hip-hop scenes,
from promoters to performers to fans. So where was the accountability structure for white people in hip-hop? Accountability not
only to hip-hop culture—which was birthed and nurtured by predominantly Black and Latino artists—but also to the broader society of people of color and white people who were affected and
influenced by popular culture. Despite the utopian promise of hip-
hop as a space "beyond race" that filled the minds of many hip-hoppers, the fact remained that after a hip-hop show people returned
to their respective communities where race still operated, where
white privilege and racial oppression still worked to keep neighborhoods of color more segregated, more policed, and more poorly
funded than white neighborhoods. As the rap group dead prez
said, "It's bigger than hip-hop."

Raw and I felt a need for consciously antiracist whites to
pick up the mic. We wanted to hear the stories and rhymes of
how white people negotiated the issue of race in hip-hop. We
wanted to hear their understanding of and engagement with
larger issues of white privilege, white supremacy, and racism in
the United States. Instead of criticizing white hip-hop artists who
ignored issues of whiteness, white privilege, and white supremacy,
we decided to be the example. Following the lead of hip-hop
artists such as Public Enemy, KRS-One, dead prez, Toni Blackmon,
Immortal Technique, and Invincible, we wanted to walk our talk
as community activists. We would tell our story as white antiracist

hip-hoppers in our rap songs. We would demonstrate antiracism with intentional and organized strategies, plans, and practices. We would make the music we wanted to hear.

Two main ideas governed AR-15: "people before profit" and "flip the system." For us, "people before profit" meant that we gave higher priority to our relationships with each other and people in local communities than we gave to making money. Having learned from my experience with the Hip-Hop Co-op, I knew that financial independence was crucial to ensuring that a social change project would last, but that money did not solve everything. I also recognized that the federal government often tied the hands of non-profits, trading tax exempt status for the promise that funds would not be used to lobby or elect policymakers.

For these reasons, we intentionally made AR-15 a for-profit organization, with socially conscious goals and guidelines. We performed shows and sold merchandise as a grassroots fundraising strategy. In this way, we functioned as a radical community organization. To us, "people before profit" represented a different kind of money-making strategy. In the words of rapper Talib Kweli, we considered ourselves "revolutionary entrepreneurs." We used capitalism to fund social change efforts. In our case, this meant funding work against racism. Our business moves were simultaneously political moves. We strategized on how to raise money as we raised consciousness. We also strategized on how we could share our resources — money, space, visibility — with antiracist and racial justice organizations. In this way, we hoped to "flip the system" by using privilege to end privilege.

We donated twenty-five percent of our profits to racial justice organizations led by people of color and shared the stage with these organizers as part of a community panel after our performances. In this way we challenged the white privilege and male privilege that benefited us in business and entertainment. We contributed to community organizations led by the people most affected by racism, and we demonstrated solidarity between white antiracists and organizers of color at our public appearances.

Our political business strategy revolved around touring college campuses and communities with a live hip-hop show and panel featuring local, racial justice organizers of color. With this strategy we created a financially sustainable and politically accountable way for us to challenge white supremacy. Our selling points for AR-15 were also our political commitments. "What does it sound like when two white guys raised on rap speak truth to power? It sounds like AR-15," read our one-sheet. Colleges that booked us could expect "a live hip-hop show with danceable beats and conscious rhymes" and "a Q&A panel with local, racial justice and antiracist organizers."

When a gig was booked, we did research on racial justice campaigns in the community surrounding the area where we would be performing. We contacted the organizers directly and explained our mission and political commitments, and offered to share the space in any way that would be useful to the organization, from fundraising to political education to membership recruitment. In this way AR-15 worked as a bridge between college campuses and local community organizations. Through concerts and panels, we helped build relationships between local academic and activist communities, and acted as a catalyst for antiracist student organizing on campuses nationwide.

We also learned to embrace the contradictions inherent in our work, especially as business owners and entertainers. We were comfortable using our privilege to generate more gigs and visibility for our work, knowing that we were simultaneously generating money and visibility for racial justice organizing. We were fortunate to receive advice from organizers of color and white antiracist organizers since the beginning of our work, but also gave ourselves credit for taking the time to listen. "People before profit" meant, in part, that we regularly checked in with our advisors on our political business strategies, and also made sure that our practices were transparent to the general public.

Embracing contradiction led AR-15 to make inroads into popular media and culture on a broad scale. We pursued media coverage for every performance and successfully received full-page coverage in local newspapers around the United States, opening discussions about antiracism, white privilege, racial justice organizing led by people of color, and white people's investment in antiracist work. We also intentionally engaged in book, film, and television projects in order to widely disseminate our ideas.

AR-15's introduction to film was among friends. Dr. Shakti Butler, filmmaker, workshopper, and friend of AR-15, produced the film *Mirrors of Privilege: Making Whiteness Visible,* which profiled white people who were taking on questions of whiteness, white privilege, racism, and antiracism. Dr. Butler approached Raw and me about filming one of our performances for the documentary. Knowing Dr. Butler's intentions and other people involved in her project made it easy for us to do our thing while the cameras rolled. We were the youngest voices, and the only hip-hop artists featured, and served as an important intergenerational and artistic link in the film.

In 2006, Raw spotted a call for applications for a new show on MTV Network's channel Vh1 called *ego trip's The (White) Rapper Show.* We understood that the concept of *The (White) Rapper Show,* which featured white emcees, was problematic. It carved out a space for white rappers to "make it" in a black-dominated art form, to "make it" in a nation already steeped in material and psychological advantages for white people. But thousands, if not millions, of white kids, hip-hoppers and otherwise, would be watching. The show ended up with three million viewers weekly for eight weeks during its run in early 2007. We hoped to use our appearance on the show to reach and potentially politicize other white hip-hoppers.

Three weeks after I submitted my video application and posted it on the Internet to advertise AR-15, I received a call from one of the executive producers of the show, Sacha Jenkins. He'd seen the video while randomly searching the Internet days before the final casting call in New York.

"We received thousands of applications from white rappers around the nation," Jenkins told me, "and we want you because of your politics. We don't have anyone else like you." I knew Sacha and his crew, *ego trip's,* work. They were a creative collective of hip-hop writers, editors, and artists — a multiracial group of men of color, including a mix of artists of African-American, Asian-American, Latino, and Jewish descent. They'd written *The Big Book of Racism* and *The Big Book of Rap Lists* and had published a respected underground magazine called *ego trip* in New York in the '90s on hip-hop and politics. They had a three-part series on Vh1 called *Race-O-Rama* which dealt with race and hip-hop. It seemed like a perfect fit for AR-15 and I trusted them, if anybody, to represent our brand of antiracist politics.

Vh1 offered to fly me to New York for the final audition call. I would spend two months in a house with nine other white emcees and be tested on my hip-hop skills and knowledge of race, class, and hip-hop culture for the chance to win $100,000 and the title of the "next great white emcee." I wasn't interested in the title or the fame. One hundred thousand dollars would mean a $25,000 donation to local racial justice organizing, as well as capital to sustain the work of AR-15.

After thousands of auditions and applications for *The (White) Rapper Show,* the casting directors could not come up with a white rapper who wanted to engage issues of race and antiracism the way that I and AR-15 did. I knew that it was not a choice but a responsibility for me to be on the show. I knew my job would be 1) to win the show and 2) to represent antiracism as best I could while on camera. I tried out and I got on.

I didn't win the show, but I was able to use my air time to bring some attention to antiracist issues and principles. The response that AR-15 received was incredible. Over six thousand people added us as their "friend" on MySpace. Over two hundred people wrote to volunteer to help AR-15 in any way they could. We got hundreds of emails from white people and people of color internationally of all ages, sexualities, classes, and genders who identified with what we were talking about and encouraged us in our work.

AntiRacist 15 released our debut album, *Stand in Solidarity,* through iTunes in December 2008. We hired a top-level publicist who had worked some of the biggest names in underground and conscious hip-hop. We also began to build the AR-15 team. We hired our first employee, a booking agent, to help grow the AR-15 fan base through touring one venue, one city at a time. We will see what the future holds.

I share this information and this story to show the power of merging popular culture, socially conscious business practices, and antiracism in an accountable and sustainable way, and to testify from firsthand experience about the power of this combination to move people politically. I also share my story and the story of AR-15 to show that the risks involved in putting antiracist ideas and strategies out there, individually and collectively, are worth it.

Let me end by quoting my rap partner, Raw Potential, when I say, "The end of white supremacy is not the end of me / it's the beginning of we / so come on, let's get free."

Resources

Alliance of White Anti-Racists Everywhere – Los Angeles. http://www.awarela.org.

AntiRacist 15 (AR-15). http://www.thisisAR15.org.

Catalyst Project. http://www.collectiveliberation.org.

Center for Third World Organizing. http://www.ctwo.org/.

Challenging White Supremacy workshop. http://www.cwsworkshop.org.

Jus Rhyme. http://www.jusrhyme.com.

Lee, Spike. *Do the Right Thing.* 40 Acres & a Mule Filmworks, 1989.

_____. *Malcolm X.* 40 Acres & a Mule Filmworks, 1992.

_____. *Bamboozled.* 40 Acres & a Mule Filmworks, 2000.

Marx, Karl. *Capital: A Critique of Political Economy* [1867]. New York: Penguin Classics, 1992.

Malcolm X, with Alex Haley. *The Autobiography of Malcolm X.* Ballatine Books, 1987.

Chapter Three

From Within: Practicing White Antiracism in Public Schools

Christine Schmidt

Public education in the United States began as a social movement in the mid-nineteenth century. Inextricably linked to ideals of democracy and equality, public schools are responsible for preparing children to become productive and contributing citizens. This charge is profound. It is also fraught with contradictions between the ideals of democracy and the reality of racial discrimination and inequality. Social work is a profession committed to promoting and ensuring human well-being. School social work emerged one hundred years ago as a specialization dedicated to removing obstacles that prevent children from participating fully in school. Racism — an anathema to the ideals of public education and to social work — is deeply woven into the fabric of our educational institutions. True equality and real democracy cannot be achieved until this injustice is rooted out and dismantled.

I am a white antiracist bureaucrat. Professionally trained as a social worker, I have been employed by the New York City public school system for twenty-six years — twenty in district-level special education and six in alternative school programs. I was drawn to school social work because I believe that education has the power to transform lives and that social work is charged with dismantling historical injustice.

My school social work practice has been informed by multiple commitments — my convictions as an antiracist, my core values as a social worker and my professional allegiance to the New York City Department of Education. These three commitments don't reside easily with each other, and I struggle to maintain integrity — moral, professional, and institutional — in my daily work.

Complicating these delicately interwoven commitments is that insidious monster known as "internalized racial superiority." As a white person, I have benefited from economic privileges, excellent education, and access to countless opportunities. When I am remiss and fail to recognize that my actions are influenced by my privileged experiences, unconscious blind spots lead me to make assumptions about what is right, fuel my impulse to forge blindly ahead towards my goals, and entitle me to act on behalf of others instead of empowering them to act on their own behalf.

American public schools are institutions of education that are rarely accountable to the students and families they serve — rather, they pursue institutional visions of success that generally reinforce white privilege and maintain the institutional status quo. I strive to be vigilant about the racist character of the schools I work within and attempt to be accountable to multiple constituencies whose objectives are often affected by race — students and families, co-workers, and supervising administrators.

In this chapter I will offer examples in which I struggled to balance my institutional responsibilities, professional integrity, and moral convictions as a white antiracist. I will describe my process of "checking in" with persons of color and my efforts to find white allies to pursue institutional responsibilities in an antiracist way. I will also examine moments when I lost sight of my white privilege. I will illustrate the challenges, dilemmas, mistakes, and resolutions I've made in my efforts to maintain moral, professional, and institutional integrity in serving students, families, co-workers and supervisors.

The following demographic information serves as a backdrop to my narrative: There are 1,013,472 students in the NYC public schools: 86 percent are students of color — 35 percent African-American, 37 percent Latino, and 14 percent Asian. Only 14 percent of the public school population is white.[1] More than 14 percent of NYC public school students are mandated to receive special education services.[2] However, a disproportionate percentage of special education students are students of color. (For example, 1.59 percent of all African American students are classified as Mentally Retarded, whereas only .57 percent of all white students are classified as such.[3]) Disproportionality is most pronounced in the subsystems of special education and incarcerated education. Nearly all of the 2,000 students incarcerated each day in New York City are students of color.[4] This correlates with statewide figures that indicate more than 80 percent of youth in residential placement (criminal justice systems and treatment facilities) are youth of color.[5] In programs for incarcerated students, 36 percent are mandated to receive special education services.[6] This is nearly three times the prevalence for all NYC public school students and nearly four times the national average.[7] At the largest school for incarcerated students, 58 percent of those mandated for special education services are classified as Emotionally Disturbed.[8] This data illustrates the gross over-representation of students of color in programs for the disabled and incarcerated and suggests the historical pattern of racial steering of students of color into special education programs for "emotionally disturbed" youth and eventually into jail. Institutional racism in our public school system is responsible for creating what the Children's Defense Fund has aptly termed the "Cradle-to-Prison Pipeline."[9]

Students and Families

As a supervisor for district special education programs, I represented the school district at administrative proceedings conducted with parents who refused to allow their children to be placed in special education programs. More often than not, I was mandated to represent white administrators against students and families of color. My supervisors reviewed the Impartial Hearing Office decisions of cases I presented. I was accountable to them for the strength of my defense of the school's positions and I held myself accountable to the students and families I faced across the hearing table. I will offer two illustrations in which I was charged to act on behalf of students and families of color while complying with my mandate to represent the interests of the school system. It was a challenge to simultaneously to maintain my commitment to antiracist principles, professional integrity, and institutional responsibilities.

Situation A

A middle school principal requested an impartial hearing against Kathy Baines,[10] an African American mother, because she refused to consent to place her son Larry[11] in a class for students classified as Emotionally Disturbed. The school submitted reams of anecdotal notes substantiating their position. Although not required, I prepared for the hearing by consulting with Kathy in an effort to understand her position. Disparity was already firmly imbedded in these administrative procedures by not requiring the representative school to seek understanding and documentation of the parent's position. Kathy was reluctant to speak with me and, although she eventually did, maintained an air of wariness and hostility. Long after this event I realized that I addressed her by her first name, as the school principal referred to her. She did not give me permission to address her by her first name, so my failure to acknowledge her adulthood and title was a sign of disrespect.

I encountered her as an angry parent who believed that the school system was out to get her son by attempting to push him into special education. Larry's mother declared that he was very bright, read at grade level, and didn't need special education. When I asked her to respond to the school allegation that he had behavior problems, she stated that the previous and current schools failed to provide daily physical activities for boys. She also stated that his teachers were racists and didn't like Larry because his complexion was dark. She described attempts to meet with school administrators about these matters, but her requests were denied. I consulted with school administrators about Kathy's report. They described her as an irrational and angry woman and described Larry as "the apple that doesn't fall far from the tree." The principal described an incident when Kathy jumped onto the counter in the main office and shouted that she would not place her son in special education. The principal interpreted her action as a personal threat and called the police. Consequently, he decided to pursue a special education placement for Larry in a program for emotionally disturbed students, which his school didn't offer. This "solution" would remove Larry and his family from the school community. I realized that the school administration had not only deemed Larry a problem but had deemed Larry's family undesirable. As a school social worker, my responsibility was to advocate for Larry. As the district representative in an administrative proceeding I was responsible for presenting the school's position that Larry should be in a special education setting. As a white antiracist, I wanted to support Kathy's contention that Larry was being unfairly treated because he was African American. I wanted to expose the institutional injustice in the special education evaluation and placement process, and I wanted to help Kathy use the administrative proceeding as a forum to be heard for the first time. Acknowledging her wariness of me, I invited an African American male social work colleague to join me at the hearing. I hoped that he would be able to gain her confidence and offer support. The proceedings took two days instead of the usual half-day because Kathy had much to say. My colleague engaged her in discussions about Larry's strengths and interests and she used the opportunity to offer a perspective about Larry that hadn't been considered by school personnel. The outcome of the hearing was an interim agreement to maintain Larry in his regular education class for the remainder of the year because my social work colleague offered to meet with and mentor Larry each morning. He viewed the outcome as "saving another African American boy from special education." For me, this was an instance in which I was able to use my position of institutional authority to allow an African-American mother's voice to be heard. The result was that one less African-American boy was steamrolled into the pipeline of educational failure. My strategic decision to seek support from an African-American colleague was critical to the successful outcome. He was able to establish a trusting relationship with Kathy and Larry, whereas alone, I couldn't. I was a representative of the repressive institution.

Situation B

The white principal of a Brooklyn elementary school threatened to take Ms. Clark, Raheem's mother, to an impartial hearing because Ms. Clark wouldn't consent to classify Raheem as Emotionally Disturbed.[12] Ms. Clark pre-empted the principal by filing a request for a hearing, charging that the school had failed to educate Raheem and was therefore responsible for paying the tuition at a private school where he could receive an appropriate education. This is known as the Buckley Amendment to New York State education law. Savvy white parents who hire attorneys to force the school system to pay private school tuition for their mildly disabled children have often used this legal technicality. I have reviewed hundreds of detailed evaluations directed by attorneys and written by highly paid, private educational consultants. The consultants were contracted by parents to substantiate their cases for private school placement at public expense. The evaluation reports documented disparities between the child's cognitive potential and current achievement level and concluded that educational remediation could only be offered in a small private school setting with teachers who had specialized training in specific — and sometimes esoteric — methodologies. Ms. Clark, an African-American single parent who lived in public housing, didn't fit the typical profile for this high stakes litigation.

I was assigned to represent the principal and the school district in the impartial hearing. In preparation, I contacted Ms. Clark and the principal to collect pertinent information. Ms. Clark informed me that Raheem had been attending a private academy in central Brooklyn for the past two weeks. The school was known for its Afro-centric curriculum. It attracted middle- and working-class African-American families. I asked if she would give me permission to visit the school and interview staff about Raheem's experience there. She reluctantly consented, with the condition that she accompany me on the visit. During our day together at the academy I observed a proud mother determined to do right by her child. She interviewed teachers about Raheem's behavior and progress while I assumed the role of listener. The reports about Raheem contained numerous descriptions that he tested authority and that he responded positively to their firm structure. For the hearing, I was expected to present a case to show that Raheem's school behavior met the criteria for "emotional disturbance" and I was expected to defend a public school program for emotionally disturbed students as the appropriate place to meet his learning needs. On the other hand, Ms. Clark had persuaded me that the private academy was a viable alternative to special education.

The hearing was held. I did not present a case to show that Raheem was emotionally disturbed. On the record, I described a child whose public school had been unable to address his outbursts of frustration and that his current school was successfully helping him to learn to read and to relate appropriately to other students and staff. The hearing officer ruled that the board of education was required to pay Raheem's tuition at the academy. I thought I was satisfied with the outcome.

When my special education administrator read my testimony and the hearing decision, I was reprimanded. He accused me of failing to develop a case that supported the school's contention that Raheem was emotionally disturbed. Determined to advocate for Raheem, I had misjudged the way to influence the outcome within the boundaries of my responsibility to the school district administration. I realized that, in the future, if I chose to challenge the school system I needed to form an alliance with the parent, seek allies within the administration and develop relationships with staff who would provide appropriate testimony at these proceedings. The outcome of this case nearly resulted in my removal from impartial hearing responsibilities. I was stunned by the reprimand and, on reflection, came to terms with an aspect of my own internalized racial superiority — my desire to be effective was so intense that I acted without the support of others. Hubris and arrogance fueled my solitary activity. I thought I had the power to change the system from within — and alone, as an individual. It's a delusion of grandeur that is part of being white.

Co-workers

Most of my tenure in the school system has been as a supervisor or administrator. Within this rigidly hierarchical system, I have strived to maintain antiracist principles in my relationships with other professionals, including supervisors, social workers, and student interns — of color and white. It has been through these deep and caring interpersonal relationships with colleagues that I have become more aware of my own racial identity. Through their nurturance and gentle, constructive criticism, I have been able to learn about myself and to continue growing as a human being. In the following anecdotes, I will critically examine the impact of my emerging white identity in incidents when I attempted to engage in antiracist practices.

Example 1

For fifteen years, my closest supervisory colleague was an African-American woman. We developed an ongoing, open, and honest conversation about the impact of institutionalized racism on our professional work and relationships. Because we had achieved a degree of comfort in conversation, we relied on each other to 'perception check' in settings where one or the other of us experienced the affront of racism. On one such occasion, we were participating in a large clinical meeting convened by staff from the central office. As usual, we sat together. My colleague was the only person of color in the group of fifteen. At the beginning of the meeting we introduced ourselves to facilitators. During a discussion, one of the facilitators misaddressed my colleague by using the name of an African-American clerical worker in our office. We immediately used our 'perception-check code' to acknowledge the racism inherent in her being stripped of her name, stripped of her professional identity and attributed a name of another African-American woman in the unit. We both felt angry. When the meeting ended, I approached the facilitator to introduce my colleague by name and title. The facilitator apologized to my colleague, but my colleague was furious with me. There I was, feeling good about myself for stepping up to interrupt a moment of overt racism, without realizing that I'd robbed her of her voice. My white privilege enabled me to speak freely and easily, as I have often done in speaking out against injustice. It hadn't occurred to me to check in with my colleague to see if she wished me to intercede on her behalf.

Example 2

The conversation my colleague and I kept on the table about institutional racism led us to develop workshops to examine how racism impeded our working relationships. She was not available to facilitate the third workshop, so I asked an African-American social worker familiar with our work to collaborate with me. The process of developing the workshop was difficult. It required us to speak about our experiences with racism in a deep and personal way, yet the social worker and I hadn't built the trust that comes from working together and being friends. As we talked and planned, her intense anger frightened me. My fear made it hard to talk and our planning suffered. The workshop was offered and we managed to support each other throughout the six-hour event. At the end, we both seemed satisfied but emotionally exhausted. I thanked her for co-facilitating with me. She acknowledged my gratitude and asked me to put it in writing. I was offended and told her that I preferred to consider her as an equal and not a subordinate, which would be suggested if I issued a written commendation. She declared that I was another white person robbing her of her due recognition. I felt hurt. My tears angered her more. She seethed that she was tired of African American women taking care of white women. Try as I might, I couldn't understand why my refusal to write a thank you note was so offensive and why my effort to explore the issue was so infuriating. I so desperately wanted to imagine us as equals that I determined a thank-you note would be an expression of my superior position. It took me several years before I understood that we were locked into a system that treated us as unequal, and that no desire or gesture on my part could change that. I was deluded by my white privilege into thinking I could change the playing field — rather than simply appreciating her professional skills and talent, and using my access and credibility to let those in power know about her skills and talent as well.

Example 3

Working as an education administrator in jail schools on Rikers Island was the most difficult assignment I accepted. While my assignment was manifestly to "offer support and specialized training" to social work staff, I grew professionally from my relationship with an African-American social worker in the women's detention facility. Dedicated to her students, she took risks and spoke critically about conditions that young women, whom she referred to as "her girls," confronted. In her words:

> Most of the young women detained at Rikers are there for non-violent charges. It is horrific to see how African and Latino adolescence is criminalized. Teens of color do not have the same liberties in exploring risks that is said to be characteristic of normal adolescent development. In this jail school I stand with young people in the crossfire of multiple systems. Each of these systems has their own special brand of racism, classism, and sexism. I've had to find a way to negotiate and navigate those systems while holding the hands of young women. They don't let every adult touch them you know. I've had to earn that right. As a result, my own growth and development have been reignited. I owe that to the young women who have so willingly taught me some valuable lessons. I've gained knowledge on how to create environments where young people can have a voice and realize and actualize their power and their activism. All this being done in the context of school social work.

She indicted the school and jail institutions for failing to meet their needs and took risks to share her opinions with me, fully knowing that I reported to the district superintendent. I viewed myself as accountable to her, a person of color working on the front lines, as well as to the white superintendent and the white principal.

We had a difficult and painful conversation one morning in which she expressed anger about the school administration's directive for her to review high school transcripts with students in order to engage them in educational planning. She repeatedly pointed out that she was being asked to do work assigned to another professional. Each time I failed to understand the meaning of her anger, she became exasperated with me. I realized that I was missing something important that she was communicating. Thoroughly frustrated, I could not hear her message, even though she told me that she felt dismissed, devalued, and discounted. She continued to tell me that the administration's transcript directive was a racist refusal to acknowledge the emotional trauma experienced by every incarcerated student, and that her school social work practice addressed this critical condition as a prerequisite to educational planning. By disregarding her students' needs, they were also disregarding the core of her work. I kept returning to my own agenda — how to develop individual learning plans for each student. Our long meeting didn't improve my empathy or my understanding. The following week, we met and began our talk by affirming the importance of our relationship with each other. I heard, in a new way, her expression of appreciation to me. Through that lens of appreciation, I began to understand her anger the previous week about being devalued rather than appreciated. I began to hear how she felt diminished by a veil of invisibility and disrespect and by being asked to perform tasks that disregarded the core of her professional social work with her girls. While I lacked the experience of feeling invisible, I was able to hear her pain and anger as righteous under these circumstances. I also began to understand that when she demonstrated her deep passion for her girls and for her work, it was often heard as anger. Later she wrote to me:

> White people are so intimidated by angry Black women. Historically, we Black women have experienced retaliation for being angry. Anger in a person of color is viewed as passion in a white person.... If someone were to write about my experiences in doing social work as an African-American woman, it would read like an epic novel. There have been hits and misses, highs and lows, and a real struggle to survive. My work has not been solely altruistic in that I've continuously had to fight to earn respect. The successes as well as the failures are etched in my heart. Even the training to become a "professional" is designed to keep one in the head and disconnected from the heart. They call it "being objective." Being credentialed and experienced in social work has not gained me the same status as my white counterparts. Our profession claims to use a psychosocial methodology, but in actuality we are heavy on the psych and almost oblivious to the social. In my quest to maintain ethical integrity in my practice, I've had to develop a method that some would say has passive

aggressive features. As an African American social worker
I don't have the same options as white social workers. But
with the options available to me, I do what I can to nurture the promise and the purpose inside the young people
entrusted to my care.

Her determination to help me see that institutionalized and
personalized racism fueled her passionate anger taught me this: As
a white social worker, I need to listen to and learn from social workers of color and to incorporate their understanding of the world
into my own world view and practice. I am also accountable to
white social workers that may not be enlightened and able to see
through the lens of racism. Adhering to antiracist principles means
committing to look and listen for the truth, listening hard, and finally hearing it, making appropriate personal changes so that others can hear it too. The moment I neglect to listen and forge ahead
with my own well-intentioned agenda, I cease to be an effective
agent of change.

My colleague reshaped our school social work agenda. We
committed to creating opportunities for the muted to be heard and
the invisible to be acknowledged, to strengthening our relationships through appreciating each other and consciously including
staff that have been historically disregarded. These efforts are essential elements in an antiracist agenda.

Example 4

During my first year on Rikers Island I re-established my relationship with Hunter College School of Social Work and created
several internship placements. My reconnection to Hunter was ignited
by an Undoing Racism™ Workshop offered by the People's Institute
for Survival and Beyond in which I participated with students who
were passionate, articulate, and committed to dismantling structural racism — beginning with the social work profession. Because
Rikers Island is a high security setting, I interviewed candidates for
the internships and carefully matched them with school social

workers who served as their field placement instructors. Most of the students were white and most of the field placement instructors were white. As the coordinator of the field placement program, I convened regular meetings with the students. Since the mission of social work is to intervene at the "breakdown points" where people interact with their environment, our meetings frequently examined the lives of our incarcerated students within the context of structural racism. We talked about our experiences as white professionals and we talked about how to talk about race and racism with incarcerated students, their families and our colleagues — both white and of color. The social work interns were committed to keeping the conversation about racism "on the table." It was refreshing and somewhat daunting. I'd never encountered a group of white people in the schools who wanted to talk about racism and who felt it was our responsibility to do something about it. As the year progressed, we extended our conversations about racism and incarcerated students to meetings with the social work staff and to citywide meetings of social work field placement instructors. I learned from the interns how important it is to develop white allies amongst peers, colleagues, and supervisors.

Administrators

Promoting change from within the system is a bumpy process of forming alliances, forging ahead, encountering institutional pushback, and then dusting off and continuing on. As a mid-level educational administrator, I continuously sought openings to converse, analyze, and challenge racism. I encountered confusion: an African American colleague confronted me with, *"Why are you concerning yourself with racism? You're a white woman."* I encountered denial: A white administrator declared, *"There's no racism in jail; it's all equal opportunity. Look at all of the African-American captains in the Department of Corrections!"* I encountered distrust: An African-American administrator challenged me, *"We have to keep our focus on students, not tan-gential issues."* I encountered dismissal: A white colleague declared, *"I'm not interested in talking about racism. I know all about it; I've studied it and would prefer to spend my time on issues that directly affect our students."* I encountered relief: African-American colleagues who at first privately stated and then publicly de-clared, *"Finally, we're talking about the heart of the issue that impacts our students' lives."*

Shortly after I began working on Rikers, Dr. Joy DeGruy made a presentation to students and staff. She spoke about historical trauma that African Americans have suffered as a result of enslave-ment of their African ancestors. The students were transfixed but the staff was visibly divided. One white administrator rudely walked out in the middle of her talk. That evening I sent the prin-cipal a note applauding him for keeping this difficult but crucial conversation about racism on the school agenda. I urged him to convey the importance of continuing this conversation. In the weeks that followed, I visited each school site to speak with staff about Dr. DeGruy's talk and how it related to us as educators of incarcerated students. I encountered a divided staff that was visibly uncomfortable with my efforts to talk about racism in racially mixed groups. I realized that I needed to develop this conversation through academic practices in order to be credible.

I began to build credibility as an educational resource through my affiliation with the Cornell University Cooperative Extension's Advancing Youth Development Program. I talked with school staff about youth development and I brought many Rikers teachers and administrators to the Cornell workshops. It was not insignificant that all of the Cornell Extension associates were peo-ple of color. In the youth development workshops we examined racial identity development and talked about internalized racism amongst staff and students at Rikers.

Building upon these positive experiences of learning together, I began to speak with Rikers school staff about the Undoing Racism™ Workshop. Encouraged by their interest, I approached the principal and requested funding to send a group of teachers and social workers to the training. He agreed and I enthusiastically began recruiting participants. Several committed and suggested that I invite a certain white assistant principal. I contacted him and described the program. As we spoke, he became louder and angrier and declared that there was no racism in the school, the jail, or in society. He declared, *"Poor people are African-American because they drop out of school and have babies out of wedlock."* I was so taken aback by his overt racism that I immediately terminated the conversation. Ten minutes later I received an email from the principal rescinding his commitment to pay the training fees. This episode of institutional pushback caught me off guard because staff — both African-American and white — had been so positive. I realized that I'd lost sight of the repressive school culture in a jail school and the threat that an open conversation about racism posed to the administration. I also didn't heed the recent school history in which the same white assistant principal had been formally charged for racially threatening behavior against staff. My white privilege caused me to act without taking this history into account. Once again, my internalized racial superiority blinded me to the deep realities of structural racism. My colleagues of color weren't surprised at what happened because they'd attempted to expose racist practices of the school system in the past, and had lost.

My efforts were not a complete failure: I'd found colleagues — African-American and white, teachers, administrators, and paraprofessionals — who were interested in continuing the conversation about the impact of structural racism on our professional work. I initiated several book groups, each providing an informal forum to read and discuss the impact of racism on identity, education, and community. We read a book about traumatic loss and discussed historical trauma and violence. We read about racial identity development and discussed the stages of racial identity evolution amongst staff. We read about the political and economic inequalities experienced by Native- and African-Americans and discussed unequal justice and the stories of incarcerated youth at Rikers. We read about entrenched segregation in urban schools and discussed how expectations of student performance are determined by the racial identities of students and staff. The book groups kept the conversation on the table. I had to be careful not to lead and dominate these discussions in my enthusiasm to see people evolve in their antiracist consciousness. Finally, we were talking about racism — the heart of the issue that impacts our students' lives.

Keeping true to my antiracist convictions while working in the New York City public schools has been an ongoing challenge. Through trusting relationships with students, families, and colleagues I have learned to see through an antiracist lens — even though it isn't a comfortable experience for me as a white person. It has been a necessary experience, however, and has strengthened my sense of responsibility to dismantle this injustice. I've seen how racism steers children of color into special education programs and into jail. I have also learned how blindsiding white privilege can be. It is the side of racism that dehumanizes white people. I've learned the importance of finding allies because it's strategically wise, and arrogantly foolish to act alone.

As a result of bureaucratic reorganization and my determination to find co-workers who share my antiracist vision, I was recently assigned a position in a district committed to create quality education for disenfranchised, over age, incarcerated and poor New York City youth. Some of my colleagues and supervisors are fearless advocates for students and families. I have found many opportunities to bring the conversation about racism into planning meetings. I am heartened to find others in the educational bureaucracy whose moral, professional, and institutional commitments are similar to mine. Together we may be able to bring our public schools a step closer toward the mission of true equality and real democracy.

NOTES

1. National Center for Education Statistics, Characteristics of Largest School Districts, 2008.

2. National Center for Education Statistics, 2006 data, compiled June 2008.

3. The Schott 50 State Report African American Male Data Portal, 2005.

4. ATS reports on Island, Horizon and Passages Academies, 11/14/2008.

5. Children's Defense Fund, *Cradle to Prison Pipeline,* 2007.

6. ATS report on Island Academy, 11/14/08.

7. National Center for Education Statistics, Status and Trends in Education of Racial and Ethnic Minorities, September, 2007.

8. ATS report on Island Academy, 11/14/08.

9. Children's Defense Fund, *Cradle to Prison Pipeline,* 2007.

10. Name changed to protect identity.

11. Name changed to protect identity.

12. Names changed to protect identities.

Chapter Four

A Case Study:
Professional Advocates Can Be
Accountable to People of Color

Larry Yates

*The simplest answer to the question of accountability is, if you
are a white person, talk with people of color and hear what
they say. There is no substitute for actual human contact.*
Naomi Jaffe, http://www.upstatefilms.org/weather/jaffe.html

Note: This is a story of events in which I participated actively and
about which I have strong feelings. As much as possible, I have based
this account on documentary evidence. While I believe it is a fair account, I cannot claim that it is completely objective.

I am a white male from an academic family, raised partly in
colonial-style comfort in Southeast Asia and partly in the suburbs of
Washington, DC. At the time of these events, I was in my late thir-
ties and early forties. I dropped out of college at the end of my
freshman year in 1968 to get involved in the antiwar movement.
Before I was hired for the work described here, I had worked in
blue-collar jobs and as a jail librarian, coalition director, community

organizer, and housing planner. Since then I have held jobs with nonprofits that have allowed me to support grassroots organizing and, in my personal life, I have become more explicitly active in anti-racist efforts than at the time of these events.

Like most national advocacy nonprofits, the organization described here was foundation-funded and deeply engaged in Washington power relationships. It was — and is — respected by a wide range of national "players." Its staff members were mainly white, and they participated in meetings with the staffs of other national nonprofits, lobbyists for related business interests, Congressional staffs, and federal policymakers. In each case, the majority membership of these groups was white. Each nonprofit was directly involved in national policymaking on its issue and had credibility with America's white-dominated power structure. Each group also operated effectively in all the typical nonprofit advocacy activities, including testifying before Congress, serving as a credible source for mainstream media, and consulting with similar organizations working on related issues.

While the organization described here was solidly rooted in a liberal/labor/civil rights tradition, its major mission was not to explicitly oppose racism. Nevertheless, through its work on a specific issue it succeeded in pursuing effective anti-racist measures based on accountability to people of color. While this organization's story is not typical, it need not be a unique one.

The Organization: The National Low Income Housing Coalition

Since the early 1970s, the National Low Income Housing Coalition has been the most widely respected national organization advocating specifically for the housing needs of lower income people. During the period discussed here (1988 – 1995), the Coalition consisted of two organizations; both shared the same office and most staff members divided their time between the two groups. One was the Coalition itself, which lobbied for low- income housing; the other was the Low Income Housing Information Service (LIHIS). LIHIS was founded in 1975 "to provide information on housing affordability problems and federal housing programs and to offer technical assistance and support to state and local advocacy efforts."[1] LIHIS did not lobby Congress directly, but was closely associated with the Coalition's work. Each organization had its own board of directors, though all members of the LIHIS Board were also members of the much larger Coalition Board. In 1996, LIHIS was merged into the Coalition.

For the purposes of this chapter, I will use "the Coalition" to refer to the overall organization and its shared office and staff. I will refer to LIHIS only when the distinction between the two groups made a real difference.

The Issue: Federally-assisted Housing at Risk of Conversion to More Profitable Uses

By 1988, gentrification, deinstitutionalization, and increasing poverty had created homelessness on a scale unequaled since the Depression. Despite this problem, massive cuts in housing-production programs endangered the future of affordable housing. As this issue surfaced, a few housing professionals also became aware of a housing "time bomb" threatening low-income people. The "bomb" was an inherent flaw in President Johnson's Great Society housing programs. "Housing … programs," as Piven and Cloward wrote, "were designed in the face of pressures from special interests that stood to lose or gain."[2]

Certain Great Society programs gave incentives to private developers — mostly white and mostly politically connected to the Democratic Party — to provide affordable rental housing to lower income people. The original arrangements allowed the owners, usually after twenty years had passed, to convert the projects to more profitable uses. In the 1990s, as the result of a real estate boom in inner cities where much of this housing stood, this conversion option became a real threat to lower income tenants — and an opportunity to turn a profitable program into a bonanza.

Speaking about this situation, Representative Nancy Pelosi said in 1989, "I believe it was intended fifteen, twenty years ago.... that there would be some creative thinking on housing in the generation that ensued. Little did we know that not only would there not be more housing development, but that the federal housing policy would be dismantled in a decade..."[3] In other words, the needs of low-income tenants in assisted housing were put on the back burner, with no one watching the pot.

The Damage Begins

As of 1988, when I began actively working on this issue in Washington, the problem was still understood by a relatively small number of people. The first conversions — prepayments of HUD multifamily mortgages — had already happened. The impact was devastating. They occurred quickly and with almost no notice to tenants, who had no idea such conversions were even possible. Hundreds of tenants lost their homes. After years of living in affordable and regulated housing, many lower-income people were thrown back into a housing market in which they could not compete. While no one had the tools to track them, some undoubtedly became homeless.

Housing advocates began to understand that this could be a serious problem. Though the risk existed in most states to some degree, the most vulnerable housing was concentrated in certain areas, including Texas, California, Massachusetts, Chicago, and New York City. In Dallas and Chicago, where the first nationally visible prepayments occurred, organizing of tenants in threatened buildings began. The Texas Tenants Union took on the issue in Dallas; in Chicago several of the city's many community organizations were involved.

There should be no illusion that tenants in this type of assisted housing enjoyed idyllic lives prior to this crisis. In Boston and Newark, tenants were already organizing around issues such as deteriorating building conditions and unfair treatment by landlords. The US Department of Housing and Urban Development (HUD) — by law the regulator of this type of housing — had rarely been the tenants' champion. For example, tenants did not receive basic information on their Congressionally-mandated right to organize until 2002 — and only after several years of pressure from the nationwide initiative described below.[4]

Still, for the vast majority of tenants, assisted housing was affordable and livable. It was also a resource for future generations, since many residents built up savings and moved on, leaving this housing for others who also could benefit from it. Given this cycle, conversions not only displaced current tenants, they also reduced the affordable housing supply for future tenants.

The Organization's Action Strategy

In the spring of 1988 I was hired as the sole staffer of the Anti-Displacement Project to work primarily on this issue with the Low Income Housing Information Service (LIHIS). The year before, Congress had approved a temporary moratorium on mortgage prepayments, the main form of conversions at this time. Now the struggle was under way to find a permanent solution. At stake were "more than 2 million units of federally assisted housing,"[5] each providing affordable housing to a household of one or more lower income people.

Having worked in 'the boondocks' in Richmond, Virginia for fifteen years, I was geographically not far away, but lacked Washington contacts. While putting together statewide and citywide networks to address the housing crisis and other problems, I learned how to engage people in issues that directly affected both them and their communities. As I came to understand the conversion issue, I focused on the fact that hundreds of thousands of people were facing the possible loss of their homes without even knowing that decisions about their futures were being made. Thanks to my participation in the civil rights and antiwar movements, and community-organizing, I had some experience with empowerment. I knew "that the capability of 'ordinary' people to organize and speak for themselves, to run their own institutions and manage all of their own affairs, can be astonishing."[6]

Over the next few years, I facilitated the creation of a political coalition of tenant leaders and organizers from around the nation. This network eventually became an independent tenant-controlled organization — the National Alliance of HUD Tenants (NAHT) — which has had substantial impact on both legislation and HUD policy. It was — and still is — one of the few national policy organizations controlled by low-and-moderate income people of color. Closely tied to an upsurge of local organizing, NAHT's growth reflected the fact that "tenants were not going to sit back and watch their homes taken away from them."[7]

What Were the Anti-racist Results of These Actions?

In 1987, when Congress visited the issue of conversion of HUD-assisted housing for the first time, the conversation apparently included only one person of color — Representative Henry Gonzales, Chair of the House Committee on Banking, Finance, and Urban Affairs. Yet this issue directly and personally threatened thousands — and eventually millions — of low-income people. About 900,000 of those affected were people of color.[8]

By 1995, when I left the Coalition, dozens of tenant leaders — the majority of them people of color — in more than fifteen US cities, had met with HUD officials, members of Congress, or even the relevant federal Cabinet Secretary. Many more tenants had helped determine the input given to decision-makers. In addition, tenants had established the National Alliance of HUD Tenants, their own voice with HUD and with Congress. Here again, a majority of people of color held leadership positions. By this time most, if not all, major policy discussions on this housing issue included people of color representing their own interests.

The Coalition had substantially aided lower-income tenants, mainly people of color, in entering the national debate about the fate of their homes. Once these tenants took this opportunity, they made more of it than anyone expected. As noted on the National Alliance of HUD Tenants' website, "tenants formed NAHT because we realized that if we wanted to speak for ourselves on a national level, we needed our own national organization."[9] While this went beyond the 'comfort level' of Coalition staff — including me — we remained committed to self-determination and democracy.

I am proud of my part in this process, but I know that struggles for change lead to amazing feats on a daily basis — and this is only one of many. However, relatively few of these amazing feats happen within the "inside the Beltway" circle of national advocacy organizations. Why and how did this one national advocacy organization create an opening for marginalized people of color to speak for themselves — a rare outcome in Washington policy circles?

Organizational Factors Supporting These Outcomes

I believe that the organizational and personal characteristics of the Coalition, its Board, and its staff that led to these outcomes included:

- The impact of the Catholic Campaign for Human Development (CCHD), a LIHIS funder

- The structure and membership of the LIHIS Board

- Staff focus on the population affected

- Staff and board support of self-determination as a principle

- Focus on support of local organizing as a national issue strategy

- Non-partisanship

The Impact of the Catholic Campaign for Human Development, a LIHIS Funder

> Its mission is to address the root causes of poverty in America through promotion and support of community-controlled, self-help organizations and through transformative education.
>
> Founded in 1969, CCHD's pastoral strategy is empowerment of the poor through a methodology of participation and education for justice...[10]

These powerful words describe the mission of the Catholic Campaign for Human Development. This organization is generally not well known to non-Catholics, with the exception of the community organizers who receive a lot of support from it.

The LIHIS Board of Directors was specifically structured and selected to meet the criteria for funding of the Catholic Campaign for Human Development,[11] which reflects the spirit of the time in which it was established. The urban rebellions of the 1960s had led to an ecumenical effort in which Catholics played a key role — called the Interreligious Foundation for Community Organization. This group organized the National Black Economic Development Conference in April, 1969, and that Conference, in turn, supported the Black Manifesto, written by African-American revolutionary and SNCC leader James Forman. The Manifesto called for white congregations to provide $500 million dollars for black economic development. Forman then took the Manifesto to the wealthy Riverside Church in Manhattan, dramatically interrupting a service to do so.

Forman's tactics were widely denounced by churches, white liberals and others. But, as Amy Kedron notes in an article, while the [National Black Economic Development Conference] received a mere $300,000, churches actually donated millions of dollars in so-called reparations monies. The National Catholic Reporter estimated contributions amounting to $127 million. Riverside Church, for example, gave a three-year grant in the amount of $450,000 for what they called, "work among the poor." Many other groups followed suit, allocating monies to programs with ambiguous aims such as "poverty work," "minority group work," and "self development of people..."[12]

It is in this context that we must understand the emergence of the CCHD and its hard-edged focus on accountable organizing. This, in turn, became a factor in how LIHIS was governed, in the work of the Coalition, and in my work on the housing issue. The Campaign was born, in some measure, in response to the most serious kind of call for accountability to oppressed people — a call for reparations — and that call, in turn, had an impact on LIHIS two decades later.

Structure and Membership of LIHIS Board

The LIHIS Board, which initially received substantial funding from the Campaign, was set up to meet the following criteria:

People living in poverty must have the dominant voice in the organization. At least 50 percent of those who plan, implement and make policy, hire and fire staff (e.g., the Board of Directors, etc.) should be persons who are involuntarily poor...[13]

While these criteria do not speak to race or ethnicity, the LIHIS Board had a majority of people of color at all times. It included current and former residents of public housing and other assisted housing. These funder requirements gave the LIHIS Board a clear framework of accountability. Coalition founder Cushing Dolbeare was also well known for "her admonition to focus on those most in need," (in the words of John Henneberger of the Texas Low Income Housing Information Service, a former LIHIS board member.[14])

As a result, when I was hired by LIHIS, my project was under the ultimate direction of a board with a majority of people of color who had experienced housing problems. At a formal level, this provided a genuine process for accountability to the needs of low-income people and people of color. It ensured that a majority white staff had to respond to checks and balances reflecting the experiences of people of color with poverty incomes. I provided the LIHIS Board of Directors with quarterly reports of the Anti-Displacement Project's activities and reported in person to the board at least once a year. My supervisor, the executive director of LIHIS, was in touch with me far more frequently. In practice, he was more accountable to the LIHIS Board than to the separate Coalition Board, which was a much larger and more diffuse body.

Such oversight, in some form, has been widely recognized by activists of color as a necessity for national advocacy organizations. For example, lack of national organization accountability to people of color was a major driving force in the creation of the environmental justice movement. One of the principles of that movement is that "environmental justice demands the right to participate as equal partners at every level of decision-making, including needs assessment, planning, implementation, enforcement and evaluation."[15] This call is very much in the spirit of the Black Manifesto.

In the majority-white peace movement, Pax Christi USA has recognized this principle by establishing "Brothers and Sisters All ... a 20-year initiative to transform Pax Christi USA into an anti-racist, multicultural Catholic peace and justice movement" with a commitment "to transforming its organizational structures, policies, practices, and forms of decision-making to include participation of, and accountability to, people of color."[16]

A major reason for the lack of accountability to people of color in national advocacy organizations is that their staffs tend not to be people of color or from low-income backgrounds. As noted earlier, this was true of the Coalition.[17] Similarly, in the environmental movement, "the staffs of the major national organizations are disproportionately white and middle class."[18] It has been true for some time that "it has become possible for a larger number of professionals to earn a respectable income committing themselves full-time to activities related to social movements."[19] In his argument for funding organizing, *The First Charity*, Robert Johnson notes that in modern public interest organizations, "staffing and governance ....are predominantly middle class... [and] so are most of the active constituents, even when it seems logical that they should include poor people."[20]

The LIHIS Board set an organizational tone that validated the experience and perceptions of low-income people of color in a proactive and effective way.

Staff Focus on the Population Affected

Christian anti-racist Jim Wallis has written "to place the reality of the poor at the center of our attention will require a fundamental change in priorities and direction."[21]

Cushing Dolbeare, the original staffer and founding executive director of LIHIS, substantially succeeded in making this "fundamental change." In the mid-1980s, I observed this at a board meeting of the LIHC during a discussion of public housing issues that included representatives of a national organization of public housing tenants — the National Tenants Organization. Dolbeare, herself white and from an upper middle-class background, visibly worked hard to ensure that the tenants and their points of view were heard and taken seriously by the white advocates in the room. Those white advocates were not only in the majority, but also had the advantage of operating in an organizational atmosphere that valued their style of speech and decision-making. Dolbeare leveraged her high prestige with the group to persuade the white professionals present to take the tenants' points of view seriously.

The Coalition has been known as the organization in the housing field that always spoke up for the housing needs of low-income people. For example, in June of 2006, George Moses, chair of the Coalition (while testifying before a Congressional committee), described the Coalition as follows:

> While our members include the wide spectrum of housing interests, we do not represent any segment of the housing industry. Rather, we focus exclusively on what is in the best interests of people who receive and those who are in need of federal housing assistance. These are people with low incomes.[22]

Moses, incidentally, is a longtime organizer in the Pittsburgh African-American community and was a resident of assisted housing for fifteen years. For thirty years, then, the Coalition and, while it was a separate entity, the LIHIS held as an internal cultural value that the housing needs of the poorest people in this nation were its priority. While the majority of low-income people in the United States are not people of color, because of the economic impact of both past and ongoing racism, this segment of the population is disproportionately represented among the poor. A focus on the needs of the poor can mean charity, not accountability, unless the question of power is faced honestly and openly.

The Coalition explicitly supported an empowerment approach well before 1988. The 1984 National Low-income Housing Conference, held at Howard University in Washington DC, set the direction for the Coalition for years to come. The conference proposed that housing programs should "provide resident control of housing through a strong role for tenant organizations, limited-equity cooperatives, community-based housing groups, and home-ownership."[23]

In addition, the Conference put forward the idea of a funding stream devoted solely to supporting community-controlled housing development organizations. This proposal became reality in the 1990 HOME program — the first federal funding source for housing after President Reagan. Both of these proposals promoted the empowerment of low-income people as a value independent of the provision of safe and affordable housing to them.

The democratic rights of low-income people living in assisted housing were consciously included in the Coalition's agenda. This value was critical to the anti-racist direction that the work against conversion of assisted housing took, because it validated an approach based on empowerment, not charity.

Support of Self-determination of Low-income People as a Principle

From the beginning, the Coalition's approach to self-determination proved to be controversial within white professional advocacy circles. In September 1988, I organized the first national meeting around the conversion issue that included affected tenants. Having been engaged in community organizing for several years, this approach seemed self-evident; I could not imagine finding a solution to an issue affecting many thousands of tenants that did not involve them.

Following this step, the Coalition heard from people I referred to at the time as "techies" — experts in the law and in housing development — that "a tenant-focused meeting would not be worth their while."[24] However, I was supported by the Coalition in my position that "we were committed to involving tenants in an issue that affected them the most." This was not an easy position to take, since some of these techies were friends and close colleagues of LIHIS staff. Some of these techies stayed away from the meetings.

However, as more meetings were held and more outreach took place, an atmosphere of respect for a growing tenant constituency emerged. That constituency included tenant groups in Chicago, Dallas, St. Louis, Syracuse, San Francisco, Los Angeles, Sacramento, New York City, Springfield (MA), Pittsburgh, Burlington (VT), Minneapolis, Newark, Seattle, Hampton (VA), and other communities.

Each local group was organized differently. For some, tenant representation was their sole mission; for others, it was one of several goals. The racial composition also varied quite a bit from group to group. The Northgate tenants in Vermont, for example, were almost all white and native born. In contrast, the tenants in uptown Chicago reflected every major US ethnic group, as well as immigrants from dozens of nations. In the words of a 1996 report on organizing there, "the names by the doorbells are not McGuire, Ianello, or Schmidt; they are Thu, Asoegwu, and Lopez."[25]

In every locale, however, the groups drew their leadership from lower income tenants and in the majority of cases, these were people of color. At the same time, a few white professionals, such as Jim Grow of the NHLP and Victor Bach of the Community Service Society, provided vital and unstinting technical support. In effect, the network that the NHLP created became a kind of multicultural coalition, typical of "arenas in which we can explore new relationships of greater equity and mutuality between groups and individuals."[26]

By early 1989, it was clear that tenant input was going to change the focus we had initially set for the Anti-Displacement Project, which was set up solely to tackle the risks posed by the conversion of assisted buildings. Other related issues quickly surfaced that were more immediate to tenants and tenant leaders, especially those related to current management, the right to organize, and HUD's failure to effectively oversee these properties. Our commitment to self-determination for tenants on one issue all but forced us to make more holistic connections to related issues because this approach was logical and even necessary for the tenants.

This commitment also led us to provide "scholarships to [our] conferences" and workshops at our conferences run by tenants, "staff assistance in planning and organizing and .... logistics of a meeting with high-level HUD staff," and "an insistence that every significant forum for preservation ... be open to tenants."

In 1991, a different kind of challenge emerged when, as noted above, the tenant leaders brought together by the Coalition decided to form their own organization, the National Alliance of HUD Tenants. They made this decision against my advice and that of other LIHIS staff members. I was very conscious of the great difficulty of sustaining a national organization and also wanted to keep the tenants "inside" the Coalition because I saw them as a force for internal reform. Nevertheless, once the tenants made their essentially unanimous decision, we did our best to support it.

The relationship between the National Alliance and LIHIS continues to this day, though it has gone through many changes and tough times. George Moses, the Coalition's chair, has also served in leadership positions in the National Alliance of HUD Tenants. Tim Moran, recently a Coalition board member, is a member of Northgate Residents Association in Burlington, VT, a resident-owned complex that received help in its development from NAHT and from LIHIS.

I know of no other national advocacy organization that assisted in the development of an independent organization of low-income people of color and then provided it with material support. While this is probably not unique, it is unusual. It could not have happened without support from the executive director of the Coalition on down — and this attitude clearly reflected an ethical commitment on the part of all LIHIS staff members.

Support of Local Organizing as a National Issue Strategy

The connection between LIHIS's continued support of an independent National Alliance and anti-racist outcomes may seem to be a stretch, but I think it is critical. The LIHIS initiative that I directed, the Anti-Displacement Project, sought to inform the public about, and have an impact on, policy and legislation. Like other Washington-based programs, it could have focused on contacting policymakers and networking with other national organizations. Most of my days could have been spent in meetings with other white professionals in the rarefied atmosphere of Washington. The Project's communications to the "field" — those concerned about the issue, but outside the Washington process — could have been limited to crisis-driven exhortations, aimed primarily at donors, to support national legislation directly.

This pattern is typical of national nonprofit advocacy groups according to a summer 2006 study, which found that in these organizations, "membership tended to be educated professionals who make financial contributions to their organizations, while their constituents — or those whose interests or concerns they said they represented — tended to be members of under-represented groups such as poor or low-income people, people of color, children, etc."[27]

The Coalition broke this pattern by creating a real and reciprocal relationship with its constituents, who were, after all, organizing themselves to save their homes, not writing checks to support a "cause." The Project both responded to and helped to build a network of tenant organizing groups around the country. As noted earlier, these groups were diverse demographically, but they all shared a commitment to grassroots democracy and organizing. In at least one case, I identified a grassroots group in California with organizing competence and persuaded it to take on the work of mobilizing tenants to protect themselves from conversion of their buildings. This ultimately resulted in increased participation by people of color in this group, as well as the expansion of its skills.

Our emphasis was on providing groups like these with the information they needed to accomplish local goals. This included information on which buildings were at risk of conversion, which state or local solutions were working, and which organizing and legislative strategies other groups were using locally. However, these groups not only consumed information, they also provided and evaluated it. We learned from them what worked locally and what they needed most. We also learned how legislation and policy actually played out. This created a sense of ownership within these groups, as well as a sense of solidarity with each other and with our staff.

The Project's network of tenant groups was also one of the first to use e-mail as an organizing tool. As early as 1990, with support from the Center for Community Change[28] and from HandsNet,[29] we provided most of our constituent groups with computers and began using e-mail along with conference calls, national meetings, and site visits to strengthen our relationships.

This made for an especially effective force in winning policy fights. We had a substantial impact on HUD and influenced Congress as well, based on both our local advocacy results with federal decision-makers and our ability to intensify our presence in Washington as needed. In one case, we mobilized significant groups of local low-income tenants to meet face to face — in their home district — with a key conservative member of a critical Congressional committee. The positive results of this face-to-face meeting with a few dozen personally concerned people could never have been achieved solely through inside-the-Beltway lobbying.

In August 1989, the House Subcommittee on Housing and Community Development held a hearing on developing new housing legislation. Due to the Project's efforts, a Congressional committee heard testimony for the first time from a tenant of at-risk housing — James Fields, a member of ACORN and a tenant in assisted housing in Chicago. He shared personal details such as "eighty percent of the tenants are sixty-five years [old]. We have had one tenant, a lady who is celebrating her 100th birthday September 9…." He also observed that Chicago had a lot of luxury construction, but "low-and-moderate income construction is also needed, as there are far more of us than the very wealthy."[30] The powerful impact of his testimony was clear to everyone present.

I testified at the same hearing and shared recommendations developed via national consultation with local groups in meetings I attended in Chicago, Boston, and Berkeley. Recommendations for a right of first refusal for tenant groups seeking to purchase their buildings and for a requirement of notice to tenants before conversion emerged from this process and eventually became law. Since these were provisions that tenants had themselves developed, they naturally were very helpful in local struggles to save assisted properties.

This process may seem like mere common sense, but the 2006 study quoted earlier found that "80 percent of [national nonprofit advocacy organizations] do not survey their members (or constituents) to find out who these individuals are or what their thoughts are about the activities or agendas the organizations should be undertaking."[31] One of the oddest discoveries I made while working for national organizations in Washington was how little information actually gets from the grass roots to Washington, and vice versa.

Major legislation often moves forward based on one or two anecdotes known to a Congressional aide. And equally often, supporters who are asked to contact Congress have little more than a short letter or e-mail to base their actions on. Because we had a position of trust with people who were actively organizing in some of the communities directly affected by policy decisions, we could not only mobilize support, we could also mobilize information, both to use in Washington and to share with and among local communities.

A commitment to two-way communication was key to our work to empower tenants. The staff on our project was consciously dedicated to service and we worked with a constituency that was ready to hold us responsible for our actions. In this process, we empowered people of color and gave them a means to hold us accountable for reaching goals that they had helped to shape.

Non-partisanship

This may seem like an unlikely value for an anti-racist group. Let's face it, in an era in which one political party has chosen pandering to militarism and a white flight and anti-"welfare" mentality as its central domestic focus, many nonprofit organizations are heavily oriented toward the other, apparently more benign, political party — the Democrats. I suggest that this is, to some extent, a position of privilege — and that the more appropriate position for those genuinely concerned with opposing racism or making any social change is "no permanent friends, no permanent enemies."

While the Democratic Party may be a comfortable home for white professionals with nonprofit careers, it is not as comfortable a home for many people of color. As Sheila Collins notes in her analysis of the Jesse Jackson campaign, the Democratic Party historically "has conceded to black and other minority demands only reluctantly and usually under the threat of massive black electoral defection or militant disruption." [32]

Ernesto Cortes, one of the most widely respected organizers in the United States today, describes what he does as "a process of arguing, bargaining, trading and negotiating" leading to "some form of public trust" and argues that "you don't vanquish or obliterate your foes."[33] Some communities cannot afford to rule out any options. Today's foes may be tomorrow's allies, or at least be neutral. This was also the approach of LIHIS founder Dolbeare — "she freely crossed party lines, forming unlikely alliances of conservatives and liberals, according to one obituary."[34]

In the case of the Anti-Displacement Project, we made this attitude work by building a successful relationship — one with genuine practical value for low-income tenants of color — with the staff of HUD Secretary Jack Kemp, a Republican. Kemp is in some ways a maverick, especially on race, and this has led to his marginalization within his own party. But he is definitely a conservative Republican, with a focus on homeownership that many low-income tenants found wildly impractical for them.

Nevertheless, his race politics and the partisan history of the ownership of assisted housing combined to make him a real ally for tenants in that type of that housing, especially on issues of procedural fairness. Credit here must go to Michael Kane, who later became the tireless executive director of the NAHT, for suggesting in early 1989 that we approach Kemp and his staff.

The fruits of this strategy included a personal meeting by tenant leaders with Secretary Kemp. At a 1991 meeting between residents and high-level HUD officials, tenant leaders "were the first to hear about new pro-resident mortgage servicing guidelines developed by HUD, and...they also witnessed a high-level HUD official calling regional HUD staffers (by speaker telephone) on the carpet in response to [tenant] complaints."[35]

Nor were tenants passive recipients of Kemp's largesse. When Kemp staffers reneged on a commitment to meet with Chicago tenant leaders, tenants coordinated their activities across state lines to correct this behavior. A few days after the planned Chicago meeting, the same Kemp staffers met with tenants in Boston. The meeting included the delivery of a singing telegram to the HUD officials. The song was "Jack the Giant Windbag" to the tune of "Puff the Magic Dragon."[36]

By putting the interests of tenants above our own knee-jerk political responses, we assisted the tenants in building a relationship with HUD characterized by respect on both sides. This relationship went beyond partisanship and continued into the Clinton and George W. Bush years.

Conclusion

I do not mean to idealize the process described here. For example, there were substantial difficulties in the relationship between NAHT and LIHIS — and I am sure that race and class played some part in the disputes that occurred, which were often about resource issues related to meetings. Nor was the problem we were working on solved. Many tenants lost their homes and some of the buildings that were saved are in less than ideal condition. Some of what was gained legislatively or from HUD has since been lost. Nevertheless, I think that housing consultant Emily Achtenberg summarizes the results well:

> ...the history of these federal [housing] programs shows how organized grassroots constituencies can sometimes fundamentally alter political processes and program outcomes to create meaningful opportunities for social housing ownership and finance, facilitating long-term

preservation even under the most adverse of circumstances...[37]

I think there are positive lessons to be learned here, especially for the staffs and boards of national or even statewide advocacy organizations. The critical lesson, I would suggest, is that there is no contradiction between successful advocacy and an anti-racist approach based on accountability to people of color. On the contrary, being accountable to people of color directly affected by an organization's issues can strengthen its impact. As far as the issue of risks to HUD-assisted housing went, "Organized tenants and community members [were] an asset in pressuring both elected and appointed government officials, and in bringing about specific legislative changes."[38]

When LIHIS first took on the issue of conversion of HUD-assisted privately-owned housing, powerful real estate interests were arguing that "owners should not be forced to stay in the program in violation of rights clearly spelled out in the mortgage and the note that the owners sign." The tenants, on the other hand, had "needs" and "interests," but no clear legal rights they were bound to respect, from the owners' point of view.[39]

The echo here of the language of the Dred Scott decision is not accidental, and the legal situation seemed to be as one-sided. As so often happens, the legal situation changed because of political action. In later federal legislation, tenants gained a right to notice, a right of first refusal, and a more sharply defined right to organize, while the owners' rights were limited to some extent. The involvement of thousands of organized tenants in national, state, and local actions, especially through the NAHT, clearly made a major difference.

Yet if LIHIS had had a different structure and different values — and had made different choices — it is possible that most of those tenants would not have heard about this issue until it literally arrived at their front doors. While many tenant organizations would surely have formed and fought effective, and sometimes victorious, fights to save their homes, it is unlikely that they would have been able to build a national organization in time to really help them.

I hope that this will encourage other advocacy organizations, no matter what issues they work on, to reconsider their thinking about their constituencies, how decisions are made, and how campaigns are run. Supporting people who are directly affected by an issue to act on their own behalf is not only morally right, it can also unleash a powerful political force with unequalled authenticity. None of us should forget that when an organized mass of working-class African Americans took on Jim Crow, this apartheid system — which had been deplored for a century — fell in a decade.

Grassroots community-based organizations and networks are not adequately funded and supported in our society, compared to "professional advocacy organizations that rely on a professional paid staff to speak for constituencies but largely mobilize resources from institutions, direct mail contributors, and the general public and thus lack a direct membership base."[40]

Since I am currently working for a grassroots organizing network, I am certainly sympathetic to the case that such groups should be much better supported than they are. However, the Coalition was a professional advocacy organization — and so were 40 percent of foundation-funded advocacy organizations in 1980 and 58 percent in 1990. So it hardly makes sense to ignore these organizations as we develop an anti-racist agenda, especially since most of them have at least a paper commitment to anti-racism.

For a variety of reasons, the Coalition went beyond the usual limitations of such organizations and took an effective anti-racist position. There is no intrinsic reason why the dozens of other such organizations cannot do the same. I personally would find it difficult to support any national advocacy group that failed to take such an approach.

As an individual, I consider my work on the Anti-Displacement Project to be among the most important that I have ever done. There were personal costs — "competencies questioned [and] privileges lost"[41] — but I also learned, as did hundreds of tenant leaders in their own arena, that "often we attribute to ourselves greater risk and less personal power than really exists..."As a white male, my housing advocacy gave me an invaluable opportunity to "adopt new roles and values" and "develop new support relationships" as part of a critical struggle, not just to change bad policies, but also to empower people to protect themselves from those policies.

NOTES

1. National Low Income Housing Coalition, http://www.knowledgeplex.org/partner-details.html?id=15&p=1

2. Frances Fox Piven and Richard A. Cloward, *The New Class War: Reagan's Attack on the Welfare State and Its Consequences* (New York: Pantheon, 1982), 5.

3. U. S. House. Committee on Banking, Finance, and Urban Affairs. Subcommittee on Housing and Community Development. *Housing and Community Development Act of 1989: Hearings before the Subcommittee on Housing and Community Development of the Committee on Banking, Finance, and Urban Affairs, House of Representatives, One Hundred First Congress, first session, May 18, June 29, September 6, 7, 12, and 13, 1989.* (Washington, DC: Government Printing Office, 1990), 119. Testimony of Rep. Nancy Pelosi of California.

4. National Alliance of HUD Tenants, "Access and Reform at HUD," http://www.saveourhomes.org/history.php

5. U.S. House, *Housing and Community Development Act,* 155. Testimony of Marvin Siflinger, Executive Director, Massachusetts Housing Finance Agency.

6. George Katsiaficas, "Organization and Movement: The Case of the Black Panther Party and the Revolutionary People's Constitutional Convention of 1970," in *Liberation, Imagination, and the Black Panther Party: A New Look at the Panthers and Their Legacy,* ed. Kathleen Cleaver and George Katsiaficas (New York: Routledge, 2001), 141–155.

7. Philip Nyden and others, *Saving Our Homes: The Lessons of Community Struggles to Preserve Affordable Housing in Chicago's Uptown: A Report Completed by Researchers at Loyola University of Chicago in collaboration with Organization of the NorthEast* (Chicago, 1996), 37, http://www.luc.edu/curl/pdfs/Saving_our_Homes.pdf.

8. Author's calculations based on data from the U.S. Department of Housing and Urban Development at http://www.huduser.org/datasets/assthsg.html.

9. National Alliance of HUD Tenants, "History of NAHT," http://www.saveourhomes.org/history.php.

10. Catholic Campaign for Human Development, "Mission," on the Website of the U.S. Conference of Catholic Bishops, http://www.usccb.org/cchd/mission.shtml.

11. Renamed in 1999 the Catholic Campaign for Human Development.

12. Amy Kedron, "Freedom, Reparations and the Black Manifesto," Caucasians United for Reparations and Emancipation, http://www.reparationsthecure.org/Articles/Kedron/BlackManifesto.

13. Catholic Campaign for Human Development, "CCHD Community Organizing Grants. Criteria and Guidelines," U. S. Conference of Catholic Bishops, http://www.usccb.org/cchd/grants/criteria.shtml#criteria.

14. National Low Income Housing Coalition, "Memo to Members: March 3, 2006," National Low Income Housing Coalition, http://www.nlihc.org/pubs/entire_issue.cfm?id=58.

15. Environmental Justice Resource Center, "Principles of Environmental Justice," (17 principles adopted at the First People of Color Environmental Leadership Summit, Washington, DC, October 27, 1991), http://www.ejrc.cau.edu/princej.html.

16. Pax Christi USA, "Brothers and Sisters All: The Pax Christi USA Anti-Racism Initiative," Pax Christi USA: The national Catholic peace movement, http://www.paxchristiusa.org/pc_brothers_sisters.asp.

17. Personal observation of author.

18. John H. Adams, "The Mainstream Environmental Movement: Predominantly White Memberships Are Not Defensible", *EPA Journal* 18, no. 1 (1992): 25–27.

19. John D. McCarthy and Mayer N. Zald, "The Trend of Social Movements in America: Professionalization and Resource Mobilization," in *Social Movements in an Organizational Society,* ed. Mayer N. Zald and John D. McCarthy (New Brunswick, NJ: Transaction Publishers, 1987), 337–392.

20. Robert Matthews Johnson, *The First Charity: How Philanthropy Can Contribute to Democracy in America* (Washington, DC: Seven Locks Press, 1988), 149.

21. Jim Wallis, *The Soul of Politics: A Practical and Prophetic Vision for Change* (New York: The New Press, 1994), 151.

22. U. S. House. Committee on Government Reform. Subcommittee on Federalism and the Census. *Poverty, Public Housing, and the CRA: Have Housing and Community Investment Incentives Helped Public Housing Families Achieve the American Dream? : Hearing Before the Subcommittee on Federalism and the Census of the Committee on Government Reform, House of Representatives, One Hundred Ninth Congress, Second Session, June 20, 2006.* Serial No. 109-218. (Washington, D. C.: Government Printing Office, 2007), 23. Statement of George Moses, Chair, Board of Directors, National Low Income Housing Coalition. http://www.nlihc.org/doc/062006test.pdf.

23. Background Information for participants in the Second National Low-income Housing Conference, held June 24–28, 1984 (Washington, DC: National Low-income Housing Coalition, 1984).

24. These and subsequent comments on the Coalition's organizing on this issue are from a memo written by and in the possession of the author, dated August 9, 1994.

25. Nyden and others, *Saving Our Homes,* 1.

26. James E. Crowfoot and Mark A. Chesler, "White Men's Roles in Multicul-

tural Coalitions," in *Impacts of Racism on White Americans,* ed. Benjamin P. Bowser and Raymond G. Hunt, 2nd ed. (Thousand Oaks, CA: Sage Publications, 1996), 206.

27. Cynthia M. Gibson, "In Whose Interest: Do National Nonprofit Advocacy Organizations Represent the Under-represented?" *Nonprofit Quarterly* 12, no. 2 (Summer 2006), 16, http://www.hudson.org/files/pdf_upload/NPQ_Dissertation.pdf.

28. "The Center's purpose has been to help establish and develop community organizations across the country, 'bring attention to major national issues related to poverty,' and 'help insure that government programs are responsive to community needs.'" Center for Community Change, http://www.cccfiles.org/about/history/

29. "Since launching the first online network for activists in 1987, HandsNet has aggregated current human services and community development information important to low-income communities and communities of color. We seek to foster comprehensive thinking on approaches to improving the lives of people living in these communities." HandsNet, http://www.handsnet.org.

30. U.S. House, *Housing and Community Development Act,* 132. Testimony of James Fields on behalf of the Coalition to Save Subsidized Housing, Chicago, IL.

31. Gibson, "In Whose Interest," 16.

32. Sheila D. Collins, *The Rainbow Challenge: The Jackson Campaign and the Future of U.S. Politics* (New York: Monthly Review Press, 1986), 285.

33. Mary Beth Rogers, *Cold Anger: A Story of Faith and Power Politics* (Denton, TX: University of North Texas Press, 1990), 184–185.

34. Matt Schudel, "Cushing Dolbeare, 78, Fair-housing Crusader," obituary in *Washington Post,* March 20, 2005.

35. Activities Report, National Anti-Displacement Project, July 1991. A copy is in the author's possession.

36. Nyden and others, *Saving Our Homes,* 19.

37. Emily Paradise Achtenberg, "Federally Assisted Housing in Conflict: Privatization or Preservation?" in *A Right to Housing: Foundation for a New Social Agenda,* ed. Rachel A. Bratt, Michael E. Stone, and Chester Hartman (Philadelphia: Temple University Press, 2006), 169.

38. Nyden and others, *Saving Our Homes,* 9.

39. U.S. House, *Housing and Community Development Act,* 163. Statement of Charles Edson, Counsel, National Leased Housing Association.

40. J. Craig Jenkins, "Social Movement Philanthropy and the Growth of Nonprofit Political Advocacy: Scope, Legitimacy, and Impact," in *Exploring Organizations and Advocacy: Strategies and Finances,* ed. Elizabeth J. Reid and Maria D. Montilla, Nonprofit Advocacy and the Policy Process: A Seminar Series, vol. 2, no. 1 (Washington, DC: The Urban Institute, 2001), 56, http://www.urban.org/url.cfm?ID=310226.

41. Crowfoot and Chesler, "White Men's Roles," 228.

Chapter Five

Burning Deep Inside: Anti-racist Accountability in a Faith Community

Gillian Burlingham

This chapter is dedicated to the memory of Margaret Rush Gottlieb, 1918 – 2007, a true friend and Friend who was there from the beginning.

Accountability is a heart connection first, a head connection or philosophy second. The relationship, the love, the human connection are primary. Secondary is the theory supporting why it's important. Practice first, preach second.

When you're in a relationship with a friend, family member, spouse, partner, or other loved one that's built on mutual love, respect, and understanding, you want the best for that person — as you do for yourself. That's the basic foundation of accountability. You want your loved one to succeed, to have ample resources, support, and love. You want them to be treated well and have access to all the stuff of life that goes toward meeting our basic human needs: food, water, shelter, health care, education, employment. Also, since it is their life, they know in what form and in what way they can best receive and use those basic necessities. Self-determination is a key component of accountability. There's no charity involved, no patronization or superiority. It's not giving anything except your own commitment to yourself and your fellow humans to equalize power and access to resources. Commitment to these ideals is a fire burning deep inside me, energizing my every thought and action. This is the story of bringing a tiny bit of this flame out into the world.

Beginning Sparks

For years I felt I needed to prepare myself for…something. I didn't know what that something was, but there was an internal urge, a drive, a push and pull that were all too clear. From college onwards, I sought opportunities to observe, read, learn, and organize in ways that exposed me to understanding dynamics of power, race, and racism. I studied African-American history, made friends across racial and religious lines, learned from the movement at my college intent on forcing the school to divest from apartheid South Africa. After college I organized with low-income people in several cities, which provided hands-on learning about power and justice. A few years later, a friend and I gathered a small informal group of white women to look at whiteness, culture, and race. In graduate school, I focused on understanding cross-cultural conflict. I joined a spiritual community without hierarchy or clergy — the Religious Society of Friends, known more commonly as Quakers — because the circularity and equality of Friends' practice made sense to me. Friends' practice is to sit in expectant silence together until anyone who feels moved to speak shares a message with all present; there are no official clergy or sermons. I knew about Friends' history of challenging slavery and that, too, was a draw. I became a member of University Friends Meeting in Seattle (which I'll simply call "Meeting"), a thriving community of more than 150 members.

Over the years — often randomly, but persistently and in nearly every setting — I explored, learned, organized and thought about racism, culture and power. Always, I felt a need to prepare for some endeavor or work that would develop or emerge.

Circuitously, through my connection to Friends and other anti-racism work I'd begun on my own, I found my way to the Commission on Racial Justice — a working group of the Church Council of Greater Seattle. There, I met compatriots and friends who were equally committed to undertaking anti-racism work within a spiritual context. I also found a leader who inspired and pushed me to deepen my anti-racism work within my own faith community, and who helped bring me to the moment I felt I had been preparing myself for years.

Kindling the Flames

The Church Council represents over 400 congregations and fifteen denominations in the Seattle area and works for interfaith collaboration, primarily on issues of justice, peace, and economic equity. University Friends Meeting, to which I belonged, was an established member of the Church Council. The Church Council has numerous programs, projects, and committees focused on issues such as youth training, racial justice, promotion of local and international peace, and homelessness and housing support for low-income people. According to a Church Council description sheet from October 1996, the Commission on Racial Justice was "created by the Board of Directors...to address issues of racial and ethnic justice, both within the Council and throughout the greater Seattle community." The Commission was charged, with among other things supporting diversification of the Church Council staff and board; helping build relationships among congregations and faith communities across racial and ethnic lines; organizing or sponsoring community education to promote dialog, awareness, and justice; and involving religious leaders of various faiths in all of the above.

Shortly after I joined the Commission, Paula Harris-White, a new member who assumed the role of co-chair, took these guidelines to heart. She galvanized the Commission to undertake a "Year of Challenging Racism and White Privilege" which we organized for months then launched on September 7, 2001. We invited leaders of diverse faith communities to meet quarterly over the year to share challenges, successes, and commitments to continue or begin anti-racism work within their own communities. Dialogues were held privately to facilitate a greater level of trust among leaders, and there was also time after each dialogue when those leaders were available for a public conversation and questions from the press. In a September 8 editorial, the *Seattle Times* applauded the efforts of "Puget Sound religious leaders who yesterday launched a year-long campaign against racism" and encouraged those leaders to look into their own hearts to accomplish the work set before them. "religious leaders are used to making others squirm with exhortations about converting good intentions to action. That's exactly the challenge for themselves in the campaign they've boldly and rightfully embraced."

As Commission members, we were charged with bringing this focus of "challenging racism and white privilege" to our own faith communities. I had previously brought ideas to the University Friends' Peace and Social Concerns Committee, of which I was a member, and I'd organized a weekly series of anti-racism discussions in May 2000. Several other members or attenders had sought, over prior years, to spark anti-racist awareness at Meeting — but we had not yet undertaken any sustained work to challenge racism or educate Friends.

I began by bringing the Commission's call to action first and foremost to Friends or Meeting attenders of color. At Meeting there were few members or attenders of color, but I reached out to each of them to broach the idea of challenging racism and white privilege at Meeting. Each person was generally supportive of my efforts. Some agreed to continue in dialog with me as I proceeded. I also made stronger connections to a Friend of African descent,

Vanessa Julye, whose personal ministry focused on undoing racism on a national level within the Religious Society of Friends, and a white Friend from New Jersey, Jeff Hitchcock, whose primary anti-racism work is outside the Society of Friends, but who is embedded in both. I wanted their feedback and insight, and I wanted them to help me see the broader picture and context in which I was working. I knew that they each knew more about national Quaker anti-racism work and structures than I did, and I wanted to coordinate my work with national efforts as much as possible.

The next step in outreach was to so-called "weighty Friends" at Meeting — Friends who by reason of long-time membership or innate clear-headedness were respected or had influence within the Meeting. I wanted their assistance to clarify the next steps to "grow" the "Year of Challenging Racism and White Privilege" at Meeting.

Accountability to me meant forming these ongoing relationships to keep information flowing; to encourage or support work of the others in a collaborative way and to ask for the same; to receive guidance and advice on how to approach my work; and to make my efforts transparent, integrated into the work of the community, and in line with the needs of people of color. As part of this effort, I created a listserv for Meeting anti-racism work, and began posting updates and information about meetings and events there, and on a national Quaker ending racism listserv. Transparency and sharing information are key elements of accountability, as well as being good organizing techniques. I did my best to make sure I kept people informed of what we were doing at each step.

In the work I was doing at University Friends Meeting, there were multiple levels and forms of accountability: informal and formal, personal, interpersonal, group, and community levels. I saw and felt my accountability as a series of concentric, intertwining or overlapping circles: most centrally, to members of color within Meeting and other Friends of color; to the Commission co-chairs (who were two women of color) and to the other Commission members; to people of color in the greater community; and to Meeting members.

It would be helpful at this point to distinguish between two forms of accountability — *formal* and *informal*. For any white person or white group undertaking anti-racism work, either or both forms need to be in place. If there is no clear existing accountability structure or relationship, ultimately it's the responsibility of the white person or white group to seek it out, set it up, or do whatever it takes to develop. Whether it's informal or formal depends on the context and the wishes of the people of color to whom one is accountable.

Formal accountability is a structured relationship with a defined process. It might involve membership in a group to whom one reports regularly, or it could be a council or advisory board set up specifically to monitor the work being done. It could also be accountability to one's boss, if the work is being done through one's employment. For accountability to be real, the board, council or group should be a majority membership of the group to whom one is accountable. In the case of anti-racism work, the council or board should be more than half people of color.

Informal accountability is just that — more casual, less clearly defined, and based on informal relationships. This could be with a friend, a community member one sought out, or someone who sought you out to offer advice, feedback, support, or a kick in the pants. Informal should still be regular, transparent, respectful, ongoing, and real. It just doesn't have to be on a set schedule or with a set process or structure. It could look like regular, though unscheduled, phone calls or discussions over coffee; occasional emails when something is on your mind or you have news to share; catching up when you run into each other at community events; or any combination of the above.

Neither of these is necessarily about having someone tell you what to do. Someone may tell you, but in my work I assume that I'm bringing my years of experience and skills, my common sense, and my long time knowledge of white culture to bear in figuring out how to undo or end white privilege. I'm not looking for someone to give me orders. I may get direction, advice, feedback, criticism, or praise, but that is up to the person I'm connected to in an accountable relationship. I'm not laying myself out and saying, "Here I am, ready to fight racism, tell me what to do." That would put the responsibility and burden on people who have carried the forceful weight of racism for too long. Instead, I'm following through on my own sense of what I need to do next to challenge white privilege and racism. The accountability part is keeping people informed so they can tell me "sounds good, keep going" or "whoa, what are you up to?" or "that sounds weird" or anything in-between. I'm taking responsibility for my actions as I move ahead to dismantle the privilege I've been given in this lifetime as a white person.

As a member, I was formally accountable to the Commission and to Meeting, as Meeting was to the Church Council. Membership comes with responsibilities, obligations, and opportunities for the group and its members. Though I never explicitly stated this, I was able to use the leverage of Meeting's membership in the Church Council to advantage in holding Meeting accountable to doing anti-racism work. I believe Meeting members implicitly understood and respected this accountability and responsibility on their part. While Friends were receptive to my ideas and energy in general, with the leverage provided by an "outside" group calling for action, I was able to bring my own passion and commitment forward. Meeting had long been a member of the Church Council. The Church Council's call for action provided an added legitimacy to my own drive, effort, and desire. Membership provided mutual accountability of Meeting to the Church Council, and vice versa.

Formal accountability also involved answering to the Commission co-chairs who were people I respected both as spiritual and community leaders, and as individuals.

Lines of informal accountability were based on relationships I formed or drew upon, particularly with Friends of color at Meeting or other Friends of color, including Friend Vanessa Julye.

Primary accountability for me was to Quakers of color who were members of Meeting and to Paula Harris-White of the Commission. I felt a responsibility to weave my anti-racism work more deeply into the Meeting fabric. That need especially came out of my relationship with Paula — contributing my part toward what she asked of us individually and collectively.

I also anchored my work to long-standing values of Friends — in particular, that of equality which evolves from the Quaker belief that there is "that of god in each person." As stated in Pacific Yearly Meeting's *Faith and Practice* (a guide to Quaker practice developed by each yearly meeting for itself):

> Friends testimony on equality is rooted in the holy expectation that there is that of God in everyone, including adversaries and people from widely different stations, life experiences, and religious persuasions. All must therefore be treated with integrity and respect…Friends recognize that unjust inequities persist throughout society, and that difficult work remains to rid ourselves and the Religious Society of Friends from prejudice and inequitable treatment based upon gender, class, race, age, sexual orientation, physical attributes, or other categorizations. Both in the public realm — where Friends may "speak truth to power" — and in intimate familial contexts, Friends' principles require witness against injustice and inequality wherever it exists.[1]

Anti-racism work at Meeting was a collaborative and creative effort emerging from a non-hierarchical structure that nurtured equality. My work and the Meeting's work co-evolved. Quakers' centuries-old peace orientation in a war-filled world goes bone-deep. It is a rich compost out of which activism grows consistently as Friends recognize "that of god in each person." True recognition of this most Quakerly insight often leads to actions or ways of life intended to equalize power and resources for all people.

Leverage is a critical component of organizing work and systems change. As Archimedes said, "Give me a place to stand and with a lever I will move the whole world." Leverage is the potential to make change; the lever is the tool used to instigate change. A leverage point is a connecting point, a soft spot, a sweet spot, at which the lever can be inserted to exert pressure for movement.

In my work, leverage came in several forms. In addition to the leverage point of membership (mine within Meeting and Meeting's membership in the Church Council), there were the relationship of national Quaker groups to local ones; the community influence through local media and leadership; and the use of Quaker values as both a foundation and a lever.

The Fire Spreads

On the evening of September 19, 2001, I sat alone in Meeting's social hall meditating prior to our first anti-racism meeting. As I sat in silence, a small voice inside said, "It's begun." With that short message, I knew that all my years of preparation were reaching fruition. Of course just a little over a week before, events of September 11 had changed the course of our nation's history. I'd set the anti-racism meeting date a month ahead but as it happened, the Church Council organized a peace march at the same time to respond to calls for violence after 9-11. A Friend asked if I planned to reschedule the meeting, but I felt strongly that I needed to hold the space and energy for challenging racism within the Meeting, and I declined to change it. I knew this would mean a low attendance and, subsequently, two Friends came for the meeting. With that seeding, we began.

Each month we held meetings on topics ranging from reparations, white anti-racist leadership and the history of Quakers and anti-racism to addressing institutional racism. We also sponsored a month of discussion hours on Sunday mornings, and began to look for ways to integrate and institutionalize anti-racism within the Meeting itself.

After a few months had passed, I felt a need to gather a small committee around me to clarify my role and give shape to the work that I was undertaking. (This would also serve as part of the structure to hold the Meeting and me in a mutual bond of accountability.) I invited a handful of trusted Friends and community members to meet with me in a process similar to what Friends call a "clearness committee." Friends use this process to help clarify feelings, choices, or next steps at times of personal cloudiness or uncertainty. Through gentle, goal-less questioning and probing, a small group focuses attention on the dilemma or puzzle facing the person for whom the committee has been convened. In this case, I convened my own committee to help me see clearly what next steps I needed to take to bring anti-racism work to a deeper level within Meeting. What emerged from this process was an ongoing support committee for my work, and ultimately a Meeting subcommittee called the Committee for Ministry on Racial Justice, which supported our work within Meeting. Following the conclusion of the Commission's "Year of Challenging Racism and White Privilege," this committee continued to sponsor evening education sessions, brought anti-racism events to the attention of the Meeting, and organized a two-week-long Friend-in-residence program with Vanessa Julye in May 2004.

In December 2003 I became the first anti-racism coordinator at a small non-profit agency — my dream job! The work I did at Meeting and for the Church Council helped to qualify and prepare me for the position. I continued to do both for some time, but as the pace and pressure of my paid employment picked up, I felt a need to step back from leading Meeting's anti-racism work. My partner and I were also preparing to leave the country due to the fact that she was a Thai non-US citizen with a student visa that was running out. With that in mind, I began to turn leadership of the Committee for Ministry on Racial Justice over to other committee members. I saw that as part of my accountability — to leave a structure in place for the work to continue after my departure.

Illuminations from the Fire

I learned much during this three-plus-year journey at Meeting that started with a push to action by my friend Paula and our Commission. If I were to go back, I would listen more deeply to

Friends. I'd also try to learn more about the existing Quaker structures and use those processes and structures to move the work along. I did this to the extent that I could, but as a "convinced" Friend — a Friend by convincement or conversion, not by birth — my understanding and knowledge of Quaker process was more limited.

Some of the challenges I faced were personal, some institutional. An example of the latter: Once I began speaking with "weighty Friends," a dynamic that quickly became apparent was the "ping pong effect" — being bounced between the Peace and Social Concerns and the Worship and Ministry committees. When I would meet with one committee, they would say, "Well, this is really a matter for the other committee; you should talk to them." I should have asked for a joint meeting of representatives of the two, but at the time I became disappointed with committee members who were seemingly not feeling the issue as urgently as I did, or simply couldn't find the right pigeonhole to place it in. The response felt bureaucratic and slow, as if the committees preferred to avoid involvement and have the other committee step up instead. Furthermore, while there was some resistance to anti-racism work, it's also true that Quaker process moves slowly and deliberately. I wasn't always patient with that.

One thing that frustrated me was a tendency among Friends to bring up John Woolman, a legendary eighteenth century Quaker who challenged slavery in a very gentle manner. Friends faced with my urgency would suggest that I use Woolman as a model. They thought I would be more effective in my work if I approached them and Meeting with gentle inquisitive love rather than what they experienced as self-righteous conviction. I realized, after the fact, that their analogy placed themselves and other Meeting members in the role of the slaveholders — without acknowledging the role. I now see that I could have pointed out their need to take responsibility for educating themselves, rather than grooming a modern-day Woolman to do it for them. My response to them at the time was simply that I was not John Woolman and I had my own style, approach, and thoughts. Asking me either to rise to the level of a legend or to refrain from speaking until I did was, in essence, moving toward shutting down my message and voice. It came across as "say it this way or we won't listen or hear you." Needless to say, while I tried to speak and present myself in ways that could be heard, filling the shoes of a long-gone, famous forebear was impossible. I didn't try. All praise to John Woolman...*and* we need present-day models and change agents.

A personal challenge that sticks in my mind more than any other was one incident involving Commission members and the Church Council staff. I can't remember the full context, but what remains etched in my memory is seeing clearly that part of accountability is about whom you choose to be loyal to, and from whom you don't keep secrets. This is what I recall: Three or four of us — two or three commissioners and one top-level Church Council staff person, all white — were waiting for our chairperson to arrive to begin our monthly Commission meeting. While waiting, the staff person, a leader within the Church Council, began criticizing and complaining about the chair in a highly emotional way. A Commission member joined in. As I listened I became upset, and though I'm often very quiet in groups, I felt I had to speak up and challenge what was being said. It upset me so much that I cried. When the chair arrived, I asked to speak with her privately. I told her what the other members had said. She seemed less surprised or bothered by it than I had been. She took it in stride and went with me back into the meeting room and called us into session.

In choosing to tell the chair what had happened, I was trying to give her fuller access to information that directly impacted her. As other members shared their thoughts and opinions freely in front of me, it felt as if I was expected to participate in a conversation with other white people that relied on my complicity — based on our shared race — to keep their views private. I felt this internal expectation and conflict to the point of tears, though I never doubted or questioned my response or loyalty. In fact, my distress was most likely the result of the assumption that my whiteness would keep me a willing and silent co-conspirator in a highly critical complaint session about a woman and leader of color whom I deeply respected. To be assumed to be that *kind* of white — the kind of white who would hold their tongue or even join in — was deeply upsetting to me. My relationship and deep sense of responsibility and accountability to our chair wouldn't allow it.

I'm as imbued with and embedded in US culture as the next white person. But I had to speak up and name the dynamic I saw in the room that day, just as I expect other white people to hold me accountable when I'm not acting with full integrity. Otherwise our work might look good on the surface, but be meaningless or inconsequential at the levels that matter. We have to get real to get the job done.

Greater by far than these challenges were the overall successes of the Meeting's and the Church Council's anti-racism work. Meeting held monthly educational meetings that drew anywhere from two to thirty-five people; we facilitated a month of Sunday morning discussions; we organized a two-week visit with Vanessa Julye that included a day-long workshop, interfaith lecture and dialog; and we visited multiple local Friends meetings and worship groups. We participated in the Church Council's "Year of Challenging Racism and White Privilege" events, including sending members to converse with other faith leaders at the quarterly dialogs. The Commission for Ministry on Racial Justice, which began as a "clearness committee," turned into a support committee — and then became an anti-racism committee unto itself. We brought proposals to Meeting's business meetings to sponsor and participate in community anti-racism events, and also asked Meeting to move toward de-institutionalizing racism in its structure.

While no community can currently say they have undone every bit of racism within their bounds — and University Friends Meeting is no different — I believe Meeting rose to the challenge. It might have been in an uneven manner, but we did rise as a community to do what we could individually and collectively to end racism when and where we saw it. Meeting responded as a primarily white community, so perhaps there was not as much fire and urgency as I hoped and wanted — but the sparks within me were nourished there. Ultimately, University Friends Meeting was, in some measure, accountable to the core belief that there is "that of god in each person." I pray that each of us continues to heed that still, small voice and the flame inside that burns for global justice and equity. Together as a species we will burn up the falsity of racism and cleanse ourselves for new growth to come. May that time come soon.

Postscript

I spoke with Paula Harris-White recently about her reflections on our work together on the Commission. We didn't achieve all we set out to do in our "Year of Challenging Racism and White Privilege," she said, but she's occasionally reminded of the impact we made, perhaps indirectly or unexpectedly. For example, the Commission sponsored a workshop and speech by Tim Wise on white privilege and someone asked permission of Paula to videotape it. Recently, a man told Paula that he had seen that videotape in a class and learned from it. It's hard to quantify how change happens, but part of it is the incremental nature of these moments of learning that Paula and other Commission members facilitated through our work together.

I've wondered about my choice to tell Paula immediately about the Commission meeting at which the staff person and Commission member complained about her so vocally and emotionally. I asked Paula if I made the right choice. Yes, she said. The energy was already there in the group. There was resistance, undermining, a lack of support and follow-through — but nothing was being said directly. The information I shared confirmed what she already felt. It allowed her, as a leader, to reassess our work together, to recalibrate, pull back, and set reachable goals given the level of support (or lack of it) within the Commission.

The Commission member in question stopped coming to meetings either immediately or shortly after that session. I can't remember now if I reached out to follow up with her, though that would be my tendency. We weren't close, and we didn't get closer after this. On the other hand, our work together on the Commission cemented my friendship with Paula. She is still a trusted friend, and a community member for whom I feel respect and affection.

On a personal note, my partner won the US green card lottery a few short months after repatriating to Thailand, and we returned to the US a little over a year after leaving.

While the Commission gradually disbanded after our year of applied action, it re-formed again several years later under the guidance and leadership of a man of color very dedicated to social justice and change. He subsequently became the first non-ordained director of the Church Council. Perhaps our previous work sowed seeds that grew in the garden he came to tend.

NOTE

1. Pacific Yearly Meeting of the Religious Society of Friends, *Faith and Practice* (n.p.: Pacific Yearly Meeting of the Religious Society of Friends, 2001). http://www.pacificyearlymeeting.org/fp/pymfp2001pg009.html.

   University Friends Meeting (UFM) is formally a part of North Pacific Yearly Meeting (NPYM), an annual regional gathering of local Friends Meetings in Washington, Oregon, Montana, Idaho, and northern Wyoming. Pacific Yearly Meeting, from which NPYM was born in 1973 as part of a natural growth process, includes Friends' groups from California, Hawaii, Nevada, Guatemala, and Mexico. Though University Friends Meeting is not a part of PYM, PYM's *Faith and Practice* expresses Friends' beliefs more plainly than NPYM's, and so I've chosen to borrow their phrasing because the underlying beliefs are equivalent.

Chapter Six

White Antiracist Organizing in a Social Service Agency: Lessons Learned and Unlearned

Benjamin G. Kohl, Jr. & Lisa V. Blitz

Who We Are

While we had worked in the same large, decentralized metropolitan social service agency for years, we did not know each other very well. Our professional paths rarely crossed. Ben worked in community-based services with families and youth, and Lisa worked in milieu-based and residential programs. Lisa knew of Ben's interest in race and racism through his work in developing agency-wide multicultural training programs. Lisa's work around institutional racism and culturally responsive mental health practice had been localized to her program, so Ben was less familiar with her perspectives.

We are both white. Experience in antiracism work, unfortunately, had dampened our enthusiasm for other white people's social justice ideals. By that time, we both held some suspicion about others' ability or willingness to address their white identity and privilege. We liked and respected one another, but maintained a polite wariness that limited our curiosity.

We were brought together by a senior member of the management staff, an African American woman who was organizing to address systemic racism within the agency. She believed that we could be effective in co-facilitating a group of white agency leaders as part of a comprehensive antiracism initiative. The commitment and mentorship of this senior colleague was compelling, and we both agreed to meet and begin the work.

Our collaboration in antiracist work began with a simple, initially unspoken, question: "I see that you're white — but do you know what 'white' means?" We were asking each other to be vulnerable and share our struggles around understanding and disavowing the invisible, unearned privileges of being white in a racist society. And so began our complex odyssey of personal growth and professional action. During the process, questions about identity and accountability were often revisited, reexamined, and retested on both personal and organizational levels. We share our journey here hoping that others will be inspired to take similar action in their workplace and that our experience will help guide and inform that effort.

The group we facilitated was composed of white agency managers, supervisors, and program directors who had attended an Undoing Racism™ & Community Organizing Workshop offered by the People's Institute for Survival and Beyond (PISAB). Like us, these co-workers were committed to applying what they had learned from the training to their work. We facilitated the group together for two years. Lisa continued with another co-facilitator for an additional year after Ben left the agency. Lisa then left the agency, but the group continues under different leadership to this day.

We focus here primarily on the first year of establishing the group and moving toward defining and implementing antiracist practice within the agency. We will share lessons we have learned — and unlearned — over the course of that year and beyond about professional and racial identity development and the reification of white privilege in the social service milieu. We will discuss our efforts and struggles in creating systems of accountability within the organization, where even naming the identity of "white" drew criticism, suspicion, and anger, and claiming "antiracism" was sometimes construed as a racist act.

Establishing Accountability and Trust

The tension between white people in power who maintain unconscious assumptions about the superiority of their organizational culture, and "others" — who are aware they are being "appreciated for their diversity" yet are not being given any real voice in decision making — is one manifestation of racism we came to recognize in our agency. Recognition alone will not create change, however; change only comes through action. With this knowledge we understood that our growing consciousness about our white racial identity, and how it manifests itself in our work, was going to be crucial to our endeavor. It also became clear to us that our tendency to intellectualize and to *understand* was inhibiting our ability to be fully accountable to implementing change. As co-facilitators, we saw a need to move beyond understanding into action, and discovered a mutual commitment to unpacking the meaning of whiteness in our lives and applying what we learned to our work.

We came to understand that no one can effectively work for social justice change without clear methods of accountability to the group they are hoping to support. Accountability requires working in partnership with members of the oppressed group — in our case, people of color. This partnership must include an articulated agreement that both parties will confront or question actions that appear to promote or enact privilege. Accountability to other members of the agency's antiracist initiative was also crucial. We will discuss this in detail later in this chapter.

Lisa's personal accountability centered around two primary groups: close professional colleagues from her program and a small group of friends of color who shared her socio-political and historical understanding of race and racism. She had spent several years in close collaboration with an African-American woman developing and implementing a framework for antiracist practice in the domestic violence shelter where they both worked.[1] Throughout that process, they worked diligently to maintain an honest dialogue about race that included confrontation, challenge, and questioning. The staff members of the shelter, primarily people of color, were also encouraged to openly discuss issues of race, institutionalized racism, and personal prejudice. They were encouraged to identify and confront enactments of privilege, and Lisa was part of many meaningful discussions that brought her into a cultural world she might not otherwise have been exposed to. Friends helped her sort through her emotional reactions and confronted her on blind spots. With both groups — professional and personal — Lisa had explicitly asked to be held accountable and made a point of asking for feedback on a regular basis.

Ben's accountability grew from a gradual recognition that despite decades of human service work in communities of color and a commitment to cultural competency, he was often unaware of, or ignored, the depth to which race and racism impacted his practice.[2] Several clients, colleagues, and friends helped him more fully realize the central role race played in his life and the lives of others. As he became more self-aware and attuned to the issues of white identity, Ben became committed to helping other social workers integrate an analysis of race and racism into their practices. He developed a training partnership between the agency and a graduate school of social work that included experiential training groups for interns, field placements with opportunities for cross-racial practice, and race-focused colloquia.

Although Ben's training project did contribute to the antiracist organizing within the agency and the academic community, it did not have established or defined systems of accountability built into its design, and that was a problem. Ben's efforts to create and launch the project continued to be influenced by his own internalized racial superiority. Over several years, and through the mentorship of colleagues, he began to understand how his socialization as a straight white male was a liability that limited his effectiveness as an antiracist organizer. It was during this time that he and Lisa began the white antiracist caucus work.

To be effective in our partnership, trusting each other was essential. We established this by talking openly and honestly about racial identity, but also about other aspects of identity that impacted our relationship. Our different genders provided us with unique experiences within the agency, and differences in personal background meant that we each experienced the social world in ways that were not readily understood by the other. We acknowledged the need to challenge each other on enactments of privilege, and strove to accept these confrontations as positive invitations to growth. Occasionally we just disagreed and had to learn to incorporate these differences into our partnership.

The Context of Our Work: Agency, Clients, and Staff

At the time we began the white antiracist group, our agency was in the beginning stages of addressing systemic racism. As a large mental health and social service agency in a very diverse urban area, it met the needs of children and adults through a multitude of programs including community based counseling, milieu-based therapy and case management, outreach services, and residential treatment facilities. The initial mission of the organization, set many generations ago, was to serve a specific white cultural group that included many poor European immigrants. Over the many decades of the agency's existence, its mission expanded to include the mental health and social service needs of children, adults, and families of all cultural and racial groups within the geographic range of its services. As clients became more racially and culturally diverse, the organization began to develop a commitment to culturally competent practice.

At the time our work began, approximately 65 percent of our clients were people of color, many of them poor and living in racially-segregated neighborhoods. In parallel process, staff members at the lower levels of the agency's hierarchy were generally men and women of color, many of whom lived in those very same neighborhoods. The jobs most commonly held by the staff of color paid the least and had the least amount of decision making authority. These positions included direct care/mental health workers with high school educations, janitors and maintenance staff, and clerical workers. In these programs, especially residential services, this staff most closely resembled the clients served by the program. These similarities often led to a sense of kinship and understanding, where direct care staff held critical knowledge about the lives of the clients that was not acknowledged or valued by the clinical or management staff.

The clinical staff of the agency was about 75 percent white, most of who held graduate degrees and lived outside of the culture and neighborhoods of their clients. These therapists and case managers had considerable influence on the functioning of the programs and decisions about client care. Many programs reported tensions between the direct care and social work staff, with each group claiming that the other did not understand or value its work.

The middle managers of the agency, e.g., senior supervisors, program directors, and department heads, were approximately 80 percent white. These were the most powerful gatekeepers in the agency, responsible for hiring, firing, and promoting staff. They had direct influence over every aspect of their programs and also had a voice in the overall agency administration. Many of the people in this group had been hired as social workers, and assumed more responsibility in the agency over time. They often had extensive knowledge about many aspects of the work.

The senior and executive managers of the agency were almost exclusively white. This group had the most powerful influence on overall agency direction, but less direct influence on the day-to-day functioning of programs. These individuals often had many years — often decades — of experience within the organization, drawing upon professional knowledge, experience, and traditions that often had not taken cultural competency or the power disparities of racism into account.

From Culturally Competent to Antiracist

Fifteen years ago, a diversity task force was established to help the agency meet its goal of increasing its ability to hire, retain, and promote staff of color. Typical of organizations at this stage the diversity task force focused on advocating for best practice and organizational equity for specific racial, cultural, and marginalized groups.[3] It did not, however, confront the overall culture of the agency or include an analysis of the distribution of gate-keeping and decision-making power within the organization. As more people of color began to have a voice in program functioning, it became clear that diversity and cultural competency initiatives alone were not going to meet the evolving needs and demands of the workforce and clientele.

Our agency had made symbolic change in the direction of multiculturalism and was moving toward cultural competency in its approach to clinical work. It had not, however, examined or made any changes to its own organizational culture.

In 2003, a group of senior and middle managers, including those of us who had been working in the diversity/cultural competency initiative, attended an Undoing Racism™ & Community Organizing Workshop. This two-and-half-day training, offered by PISAB, was pivotal in helping us to identify three central concepts that transformed our work: the role of race in the history of the United States; the creation and dominance of white culture, specifically white organizational culture in American institutions; and the unconscious perpetuation of institutional racism by well-intentioned people, usually whites. The workshop challenged us to understand race as a social construct, and recognize racism as a system that privileges those who have come to be called white, placing people of color at a disadvantage. By moving beyond the view of racism as simple prejudice or bigotry, this knowledge clarified for us that unless an organization is intentionally antiracist everything it does will disproportionately benefit white people. Our challenge, therefore, was to understand exactly how this was playing out in our agency.

The Agency's Antiracist Commitment

To provide context for our white antiracist caucusing work and the group's struggle with accountability, it is important to understand some aspects of the institutional changes during this time. Within the first year and a half following the initial group's attendance at the PISAB Undoing Racism™ Workshop, several other middle and senior managers also attended and became motivated to address organizational racism within the agency. As a result, a number of changes were implemented that reflected the agency's growing commitment to becoming antiracist. Some of the advances described below are indeed innovative and may present a picture of an agency unified in its desire to change. It is important to bear in mind, however, that many of these changes were viewed as highly controversial and were met with considerable resistance throughout the organization.

The agency created the position of Director of Multicultural Practice and Research, and Ben was appointed to this job. In this role, he was responsible for implementing a training series for program managers, overseeing the dissemination of antiracism information, sustaining an antiracism training project for social work interns, and tracking staff and client demographics.

Experts in the field were hired as consultants to educate all agency staff on the role of race and racism in mental health and social service practice. Additional consultation was obtained for senior and executive management regarding organizational culture and institutional racism. Each senior manager was required to include goals related to antiracism as part of their annual strategic plan, and every meeting of the agency's managers included an agenda item related to race and racism. Program directors were also encouraged to address antiracism in their annual plans and to facilitate dialogue about racism with the staff in their programs.

Ben was also charged with staffing and chairing an Antiracism Task Force which replaced the diversity task force. The Anti racism Task Force was a multiracial and multicultural group, most of whom had administrative responsibility at the agency and who had also attended the Undoing Racism™ Workshop. This committee was charged with identifying and prioritizing measurable recommendations related to race in four areas central to agency functioning: best practices to clients, staff training, staff relations, and research.

Finally, the executive management of the agency called for the development of race-based caucuses, or racial affinity groups. The purpose of these groups was to focus on how racism manifests within the organization and to develop recommendations for change.

Racial Affinity Groups or Race-based Caucuses

Knowing little about racial affinity groups or caucusing at that time, we turned to the literature and consulted with colleagues experienced in antiracist work for guidance. We found significant support there for the concept of doing a white-specific antiracist group. Most noted that the nature of institutional racism is to downplay the role of white culture, pull towards a supposed ideal of color-blind fairness, and discourage talk about white racial identity.[4] Thus, those of us who engage in intentionally white antiracist organizing are violating one of the fundamental, unarticulated "rules of whiteness." In many subtle ways we are warned: Do not talk about white people as a group; do not focus attention on their experience in society; do not speak of white culture. Rather, focus on people of color, make note of their particular needs or difficulties, and highlight how they are different from us. Indeed, we found quickly that the idea of a group of white people meeting alone to discuss race and racism was one of the most controversial and hotly debated components of our antiracism initiative.

The basic purpose behind white antiracist caucusing is for white people to come together to better understand our role in the dynamics of oppression we are committed to dismantling. As this process evolves, we come to understand better how we, too, have been hurt by being indoctrinated into an oppressor position. Ultimately, this self-awareness can lead to our becoming effective partners with the oppressed or marginalized group in advocating for social change that advances fairness for all. Race-based caucusing can function to promote antiracist practice, advance organizational change, and support the personal and professional growth of the caucus members. It is also valuable in fostering accountability and validating multiple perceptions of institutional racism within the organization.

Launching Race-based Caucuses

With the help of consultants, a core group of the Antiracism Task Force carefully considered who to include in the group and how to extend invitations. It was decided that staff of color, because they had such disparate experiences of racism in the agency, would have gender-specific groups, at least during the beginning phases of the project. In considering whether to have separate groups for white staff members it was acknowledged that although white men and women also had different experiences in the agency based on gender, those differences could actually contribute to the group's discussions about power and oppression within the organization. Therefore it was decided that white men and women would meet together. Co-facilitators were identified for the three caucuses, with us co-leading the white one.

The leaders of the three racial affinity groups established accountability by meeting regularly as a group, as well as frequently meeting with each other informally. The seven leaders — two women of color, two men of color, the two of us, plus the executive (an African-American woman) charged with overseeing aspects of the antiracism work — formed a steering committee. Consultants from PISAB — a white man and a white woman — worked closely with us and attended many of the steering committee meetings. Their input was invaluable to the development and productivity of the caucuses. Accountability was built into the meeting structure through formal discussions that gave all participants permission to question and challenge any of the caucusing work. Of particular importance for us was the steering committee members' feedback on how they viewed the white caucus group process and action — or lack thereof. Steering committee members and the consultants were very astute at highlighting subtle enactments of privilege that were impeding aspects of the work, and helped us to problem solve and move to the next steps.

This steering committee maintained, and eventually formalized, a line of communication with the executive management of the agency. Establishing other formal systems of accountability to people of color employed or served by the agency had been identified as a goal for the white caucus. But, due to many factors, progress toward that goal was minimal during our time with the antiracist initiative. Before the members of the white caucus became ready to see themselves as accountable to another group, they needed to form their own group identity and agree upon the purpose of the caucus. Although there was support for all three caucuses from within the organization, the white caucus also received significant resistance from staff members who did not understand or agree with the need to focus on the role of white people in developing racial equity. The white caucus, therefore, needed to develop a more complex response to the internal resistance to maintain accountability to people of color without sending a message that we were forming an alliance against other white people.

An agency-wide memo from executive management announced the groups' formation, encouraged attendance, and provided guidelines on releasing employees from their regular work assignments so they could participate. The men and women of color groups extended an open invitation to all people of color in the agency and had an initial attendance of fifty and ninety-nine respectively.

Beginnings of the White Antiracist Caucus

The first meeting of the white caucus was by invitation only and consisted of twelve people. We invited both men and women, all of whom had attended the PISAB Undoing Racism™ Workshop. The decision to initially limit membership of the white caucus to those who had completed the workshop was based on our desire to form a strong base of people who shared a similar socio-political and organizational analysis of race and racism. By inviting only white people who already understood that our antiracism work was about something more complex than anti-prejudice work or cultural competency, we hoped to clarify the role of white people in analyzing and confronting racism within the organization. Unfortunately, this decision may also have contributed to the air of mystery that later caused others in the agency to question the purpose and utility of our group.

The twelve people invited to the first white caucus meetings were all from the middle and senior management tiers of the organization. About a year into the process, the agency executives mandated and sponsored all managers and executives to attend the People's Institute training. At that point, the list of potential participants grew to over seventy, most of whom attended at least one caucus meeting. Eventually, there was a core group of about twenty-five people who consistently attended meetings which were scheduled monthly and held at the agency's central office.

Five central concerns emerged at the first meeting that recurred throughout our history with the group. From the beginning we struggled with: group purpose; difficulty in knowing whether or how to make room for other social group identities; concerns about enacting white privilege even in our attempts to confront it; building in of consistent group accountability to the other caucuses; and finally — and persistently — the finding of a name for our group.

Group Purpose

From the beginning, we struggled with the question of group purpose. Were we a group formed to process issues of white identity and internalized racial superiority? Were we a problem-solving group charged with discussing program management issues related to race and privilege? Or were we a task group designed to institute organizational change? Even we could not agree on each point all the time. While various members never did completely agree on our purpose, ultimately there was general agreement that all three goals were important. In the beginning, however, passionate discussion around these questions created tension between us as co-facilitators, which in turn, threatened the sustainability of the group as a whole.

These discussions brought out unconscious competition (Who was the most dedicated antiracist in the room? Who was the most racially 'evolved'?) as well as deeply felt philosophical differences. As a collective, we felt a persistent confusion about ourselves, our antiracism work, and the agency we felt proud to work for. Staying with this confusion — as our consultants and the caucuses of color gently pointed out — is a peculiar privilege of whiteness. None of the people of color were the least bit confused about the purpose of caucusing, nor were they confused about what work they wanted us to be doing! Our purpose was to confront and dismantle institutional racism. Period. It was up to us to figure out what we needed to do, personally and professionally, to make that happen.

Incorporating Diverse Social Group Identities

Through this early work, members of the white caucus also learned that, regardless of the focus on organizational change, the work itself is highly personal, often in unexpected ways. We faced complex negotiations regarding the other social identities of caucus members. Many of the core members identified with groups marginalized in American society. Although white men held the highest positions of authority in the agency, the majority of influential gatekeepers were white women. Many of these women also identified as lesbian and/or belonging to marginalized religious or cultural groups. For our antiracism initiative to be effective, we needed these women to be invested in the work.

Motivated white people are often able to set aside their other social group identities to focus on race for a limited time. Engaging them as partners in a long-term process of working toward systemic change, however, required that we also validate their experiences of prejudice and marginalization within the organization and in society. Understanding and responding to the intersections of various forms of oppression without diluting the significance of race and white privilege became a critical task. We needed to find the place for gender, ethnicity, religion, sexual orientation, class, and other social identities, while maintaining a clear and unambiguous focus on race, privilege, and power.

We understood that validating people's unique identities and experiences allowed us to use the social hierarchies that emerged within the group to inform our learning about hidden and unearned privilege. At first, however, these were very precarious negotiations that added to our general confusion about the work. Those members least identified with marginalized groups — particularly straight white men — were the most likely to insist that focus on anything outside of race was a distraction from our work. Women, gays and lesbians, new immigrants, and non-Christians were often likely to disagree. Sometimes the straight men were right, and we acknowledged that and redirected the discussion. And sometimes it was the straight men's unwillingness to recognize heterosexism and male privilege that was derailing our process, and that also needed to be validated. Ben became an effective role model for how to acknowledge male privilege, and he skillfully integrated that awareness back into our discussion about race. Similarly, Lisa's disclosure that she was bisexual was helpful in diffusing the defensiveness of some members who identified as lesbian, gay, or bisexual. She was able to honor their experiences of marginalization, while keeping racism at the center of the discussion.

The caucus, like any group, developed its own dynamics. Members took on various roles and, at times we as the leaders became the focal point for our group's collective distress. The relationship between us became an important factor in learning how to address this tension. As co-leaders we recognized that our ability to work through our differences in perspective, borne out of our different social identities and life experiences, was crucial to the overall health of the group. Through consistent and sometimes difficult dialogue, we developed a trusting alliance that we could draw on to more effectively facilitate the group. Ben sometimes needed coaching from Lisa to recognize how he could be more inclusive when moving forward with administrative aspects of the caucus or facilitating group process. Lisa needed coaching from Ben to effectively work with the straight male members of the group around addressing patriarchal group dynamics. Our ability to maintain this dialogue, especially during times when the group was polarizing or losing focus, was crucial to keeping the process going and maintaining the spotlight on racism.

Enactments of White Privilege

We learned that enactments of white privilege are inevitable and efforts to avoid them confounding. As we struggled with group purpose, some members became increasingly compelled to take action beyond their home program or department in the agency. At the same time, they were not using the group to discuss or explore how institutional racism was being addressed in the areas of the agency over which they had the most influence, nor were they discussing how they struggled personally with these issues. We became concerned that caucus members were locating the problem externally, and not looking at themselves or becoming vulnerable with other group members. Since the caucus members were middle and senior managers, we were concerned about their use of power in initiating action in other programs or departments. We questioned what an appropriate use of power would be, especially when the power is granted through unearned advantage.

Group Accountability with People of Color Caucuses

The white caucus' difficulty in defining its role in the organization was partially a result of the inability of all three caucuses to come together for a large, joint meeting to discuss our shared work. There were logistical obstacles, such as where to hold and how to facilitate such a large gathering, and how to get so many people released from their jobs simultaneously. More importantly, there was also resistance within our group that we did not fully understand. Caucus members realized that to depend on people of color to define our work, or to defer to them as authorities on race issues, was an avoidance of responsibility that could be offensive to people of color. Therefore we remained uncertain about how to work in harmony with the other caucuses and cultivate accountability. When the dilemma around cross-caucus collaboration was presented in one of the regular meetings with the other caucus leaders, a leader of the Men of Color group suggested that we do something fun together, rather than meet formally. The white caucus group's reaction was to worry that a party — or some other activity — would dilute the seriousness of our efforts to develop a system of antiracist accountability within the agency. There was concern that this might seem like a "celebration of diversity" and be perceived as a step backwards in our organizing.

What's in a Name?

The ambivalence of many managers and administrators in the agency towards the white caucus can be captured in the reactions to its name. We had initially chosen the name White Allies Caucus. This label reflected our understanding that we were working to eliminate the institutional racism from which we benefited. The caucus' name was inspired by Andrea Ayvazian's 2001 article "Interrupting the Cycle of Oppression: The Role of Allies as Agents of Change," which was distributed to program and department managers with the hope of providing context for the name and the work we had undertaken.[5]

Although we will return to the problem of white antiracists self-identifying as allies in the discussion of accountability later, it is interesting to note how strongly many white colleagues reacted specifically to the use of "allies" in our name. One senior departmental manager responded to the term by stating, "This is a terrible name, it makes me think we are at war." Another commented "We (white people) should be leading this struggle, not *allied* with people of color."

More troubling was the reaction of some to the inclusion of the word 'white' in the caucus name. One white program director noted, "I don't want to be involved in anything named white. It makes me think of white supremacy." Despite our explanations, many colleagues were unable to overcome their negative reactions to the name. The steering committee discussed the matter and agreed that the term 'allies' was negotiable, but the term white must remain. We eventually settled on White Antiracist Caucus (WAC).

Unfortunately, this too created controversy among people — white and of color — who adhered to ideas of 'color-blind' fairness. For them, any mention of 'racist,' even in a word with 'anti' in front of it, was threatening and suspect. More than once we were accused of being racist and projecting our internal conflict (our "white guilt") onto those who sincerely believed they had no issues or problems with race.

Additional Aspects of Accountability

White people initiating a role in antiracism efforts may encounter problems with self-identifying as allies to people of color. As discussed by the Safehouse Progressive Alliance for Non-violence, the position of "ally" to people of color is an earned title, and being identified by one person of color does not guarantee ally status with all people of color.[6] Through learning about white culture and our own racial identity, however, we came to take on the fight against racism for personal reasons. As we recognized the costs of oppression to ourselves and other whites, racism became personally offensive. We came to understand that being pulled into the role of oppressor is another form of oppression. At that point, our work became allied with people of color in the fight against oppression, working toward genuine equity and freedom for all members of society.

People of color in our agency were curious and sometimes cynical about our involvement in antiracist initiative. Over time we were consistently asked some version of the question: "Why are you doing this?" We came to understand these questions as profoundly important invitations to trust and to heal. We learned to listen to the stories of pain and resiliency shared by people of color, and to communicate our experience of being white in a racially structured society. Through our personal relationships with people of color, our understanding of racism was expanded and this further enhanced our effectiveness in the work.

We Benefitted Disproportionately

One interesting development of the white caucus was our own growing status and visibility within the agency as a result of our leadership in the group. As change agents in a multi-functional organization, the two of us developed relationships with executives, program directors, departmental managers, as well as clinical, direct service, and support staff. We became sounding boards for those who were curious about the agency's antiracism initiative and for those who felt safe enough to share their belief that racism should not be discussed in the workplace. Our roles within the antiracist initiative put us in positions where we were noticed and recognized as effective and trusted leaders by those in upper management positions. As this process unfolded, our careers within the organization advanced. We were both given professional opportunities that highlighted our strengths. Subsequently we received promotions in title and responsibility, and increases in salary. It is noteworthy that with one exception, the same was not true for the people of color involved in the initiative.

The attention our antiracist work brought to us became yet another example of our white privilege. It was essential that we maintained an awareness of how we benefited professionally from our participation, while others did not. In addition, Lisa struggled with how the changes in her position limited the time she was able to devote to white caucus and the agency-wide antiracist initiative. While she appreciated her promotion, the added responsibility reduced her ability to participate in the antiracism work within the agency. The question remains: To what extent was her promotion actually a promotion out of antiracist organizing?

Progress and Difficulties Encountered in the Work

In spite of the fact that the white caucus had received formal sanction from the agency's executive management, it became marginalized in the agency's overall antiracism efforts. The men and women of color caucuses were invited to make formal presentations at meetings of the agency middle, senior, and executive management teams. These presentations included updates on the progress of the caucuses, outlined specific goals the caucuses were working toward, and included suggestions regarding potential agency changes. The white caucus was never invited to make a similar presentation, nor was it mentioned in announcements that highlighted other antiracism activities within the agency. We came to understand this to be linked to leadership's reluctance to address white identity and privilege and its role in perpetuating racism. It became clear that there was a division between whites in the organization who understood the importance of exploring white privilege and internalized racial superiority, and those who held a 'color-blind' perspective.

As the work progressed, many white caucus participants reported significant changes in their worldview. For some it was shocking, painful, and at times disorienting to see the ways they unconsciously perpetuated racism. Most developed a more sophisticated understanding of power dynamics, and began to question traditional philosophies and styles of management as potentially racist. During this time the agency was undergoing a significant strategic planning process and leadership shift. For the first time, many of the white caucus members were examining their position in this process through an antiracism lens. During this transition, however, other white managers began to forcefully challenge the value and relevance of focusing on white privilege.

Although senior leadership continued to communicate its commitment to antiracism, other whites recommended that the initiative focus on developing measurable outcomes related to cross-cultural and cross-racial best practices. Caucus members agreed that although this was an important aspect of the work, exclusive focus on this area was too limiting. Unless best practices related to working with people of color are anchored in a comprehensive examination of power distribution within the institutional system, modifications in practice will not necessarily change the system. We became concerned that the structurally focused efforts of the antiracist initiative were shifting back to cultural competency.

Before we both independently left the agency for other jobs, the three caucuses were asked to develop a list of manifestations of white privilege perceived or experienced in our agency. The two caucuses of color were able to compile their lists in one meeting. It took three meetings and much contention for the white caucus to develop ours. In the end, however, all three lists were remarkably similar — and in this we found some hope.

We have remained in touch, and understand that there are still no plans for a formal meeting of the general membership of the caucuses. The people of color caucuses took the lead and organized a social gathering to honor all of the consultants who have contributed to the agency's antiracism work over the past five years, and they invited the white caucus members to this event. Furthermore, additional white caucus groups are forming within the agency to accommodate white staff members whose program sites are geographically removed from the agency's central office. The organizers of these regional caucuses include an increasing number of middle managers who were initially resistant to the idea of white antiracism caucusing. We see this as an indication that more people are now responding positively to the agency's ongoing antiracism work.

Final Thoughts

We learned many invaluable lessons in leading this caucus, and we both continue our antiracism organizing in new positions. Most importantly, we learned that in caucusing, as with any form of antiracism work, the heart and dedication of the people involved is fundamental. We found it essential to maintain a sense of humor, a sense of honor, and faith in humanity. We also learned to navigate a delicate equilibrium between goal-focused action and insight-oriented processing. Both are necessary, and both can become reifications of privilege. Vague processing and good intentions that are not anchored in a commitment to institutional or systemic change do nothing to move the organization toward antiracism. A rush to action without sufficient understanding of one's own internalized superiority, however, can become an enactment of racism. Only through the development of clear systems of accountability — anchored in solid and trusting relationships — could we work toward a productive balance between process and action.

Authors' Note

The authors would like to extend our sincere gratitude to Margery Freeman and David Billings of the People's Institute for Survival and Beyond for their thoughtful guidance, keen insights, and warm support in our antiracist organizing efforts.

NOTES

1. See Lisa V. Blitz and Linda C. Illidge, "Not So Black and White: Shades of Gray and Brown in Antiracist Multicultural Team Building in a Domestic Violence Shelter," *Journal of Emotional Abuse* 6, no. 2/3 (2006): 113-134.

2. Benjamin G. Kohl, Jr., "Can You Feel Me Now? World View, Empathy and Racial Identity in a Therapy Dyad," *Journal of Emotional Abuse* 6, no. 2 (2006): 173-196.

3. Samuel D. Johnson, "Classic Defenses: A Critical Assessment of Ambivalence and Denial in Organizational Leaders' Responses to Diversity," in *Addressing Cultural Issues in Organizations: Beyond the Corporate Context,* ed. Robert T. Carter (Thousand Oaks, CA: Sage Publications, 2000), 181-192; Madonna G. Constantine and Derald Wing Sue, "Effective Multicultural Consultation and Organizational Development," in *Strategies for Building Multicultural Competence in Mental Health and Educational Settings,* ed. Madonna G. Constantine and Derald Wing Sue (Hoboken, NJ: John Wiley & Sons, 2005), 212-226.

4. Jeff Hitchcock, *Lifting the White Veil: An Exploration of White American Culture in a Multiracial Context* (Roselle, NJ: Crandall, Dostie & Douglass Books, 2003).

5. Andrea Ayvazian, "Interrupting the Cycle of Oppression: The Role of Allies as Agents of Change," in *Race, Class and Gender in the United States,* ed. Paula S. Rothenberg (New York: Worth Publishers, 2001), 609-621.

6. Safehouse Progressive Alliance for Nonviolence (SPAN), "Qualities of an Anti-Racist Ally," in *Tools for Liberation Packet 2007 - Abridged Version: For Building a Multi-Ethnic, Inclusive & Antiracist Organization* (Boulder, CO: Safehouse Progressive Alliance for Nonviolence, 2007), 6. Document in PDF format can be downloaded from http://www.safehousealliance.org/download.cfm?DownloadFile= B97F67C7-D614-E19E-2C2C73560930E09E. "Qualities of an Anti-Racist Ally" is on page 6.

Chapter Seven

Resistance in Brooklyn:
Accountability for Anti-Imperialist Action

Matt Meyer

When one hears the letters R-N-B, hopefully, they trigger a little shake of the hips, a smile, and a nod of the head, as we are reminded of that amalgam of musical forms which has been the basis for so much good rocking and dancing, crossing of cultural lines, and overcoming of political barriers. However, in Brooklyn, NY since 1992 "RnB" has come to stand for something else as well: Resistance in Brooklyn. This variation on RNB started off without a name; it began as a group of friends who liked working together and whose own organizations were going through periods of decline and transition. Attracted by our affinity for each other's commitment to lasting social change, a dozen of us decided to sit down and reflect on how to build something new.

Back then, our vision involved creating a space on the left for strident and committed struggle against racism and imperialism while avoiding the dogmatic and sectarian errors of those who had preceded us. We wanted to convey a sense of energy and possibility, a willingness to reflect upon the world even as we worked to change it, and a spirit of flexibility and openness, even as we put forward strong positions about the role of white people in com-

bating oppression. We wanted to create an organization where we
— as white folks self-consciously struggling in solidarity with the
internal liberation movements of Black, Puerto Rican, Mexican,
and Native nations — could challenge old structures of rigid "leadership" while remaining accountable to those same movements
and leaders. Our early flyers and the Principles of Unity we formulated talked of the Red and the Black, of Roses and Bread, of
Rice and Beans, and of Revolution and Beyond.

Fewer white people professed a concern for an explicitly
antiracist practice in 1992 than seem to be doing so today. And
back then, as now, gaining clarity about what that practice might
look like was a major challenge. Accountability to organizations
and people "of color" was certainly one guiding principle often
discussed, but the specifics and practicalities of what that
meant differed in every locale or situation. RnB's founding story,
as recounted here, reflects some of this lack of clarity. A mobilization in commemoration of 500 years of indigenous resistance
was taking place at the time of the 500th anniversary of Colum-
bus' voyage across the Atlantic. Replicas of the Nina, Pinta, and
Santa Maria were approaching the New York harbor as part of a
recreation of that fateful day in 1492. Several coalitions, including many groups and individuals one or another of us had long
histories with, were calling for militant action. At some point, a
number of us answering this call noticed increasing tension
among the assembled demonstrators — and between us and
the New York City Police Department. Instinctively, we gathered together, recognizing that we felt safer in proximity to those
we trusted, even if we weren't from the same organization or
ideological faction of the Left.

We quickly noticed that a number of the leading Black and
Puerto Rican activists we were friends with, who made up a nu-
meric minority at the demonstration, had no "security" working
with them — no folks who would help or act as witnesses if the
cops tried to single them out. In response, we came up with a plan
to divide into two small groups, check in with our comrades from

the Black and Puerto Rican movements, and stay close to them and each other as the mobilization proceeded.

In fact, at one point, as thousands marched across a narrow street, the police did cut off about half a dozen people. It was of little surprise (and some relief) that those arrested included half our number along with the Puerto Rican representatives. The rest of us noted what had happened, contacted sympathetic lawyers, let the other protesters know about the police "sting," and met our arrested allies at the precinct. We pressed for — and got — immediate release without further incident.

In retrospect, those of us who founded RnB soon after might have described our actions that day as being borne of a "sense" of accountability. Though we had no direct responsibility to or relationship with the groups we reached out to support, our own histories and antiracist perspectives alerted us to what might take place at the demonstration, who might be targeted by the police, and how best to protect our movements. Without a prior working relationship with those targeted leaders, however, our "sense" of accountability and protection could well have come off as paternalistic, arrogant, or misplaced. How, then, to build long-term, antiracist accountability that is neither rigid and formulaic nor disorganized and unplanned?

Predecessors and Principles of Unity

During the early days of RnB, wrestling with accountability and what it means for people of diverse backgrounds to work together were instrumental concerns in shaping the approach of our fledgling affinity group/collective. Given this ongoing struggle, it is worth looking at the positive and negative examples set by the organizations which RnB's founders belonged to previously. In the late 1980s, six of us (most in our twenties at the time) started a study group interested in looking at race and colonialism from multiple perspectives. Two of us had been part of the New Movement in Solidarity with Puerto Rican Independence and Socialism; one had even done jail time for refusing to collaborate with a grand jury investigation of the Black liberation movement. The New Movement and the organizations involved in its formation had a decidedly Leninist world view, yet the activists from that group wanted to learn more about anarchist theory and radical pacifist practice.

Two other RnB founders were leading members of the War Resisters League (WRL), a nonviolent direct-action group founded in 1923 and committed to Gandhian principles. The WRL encompassed both socialist and anarchist tendencies; we battled out our differences at baseball games played at our annual national conferences. The final RnB founders, two Vermont-based anarchists, had been involved in environmental and anti-militarist protests and have always proved willing to put their bodies on the line. Early in our discussions, they reported on a friend who was part of a local Catholic Worker group, who had just spoken at a rally in support of the Palestinian Intifada and called for a support of the use of Rocks and Bottles in bringing about change. Inspired by this, our preliminary name was hatched and our discussions about strategy and tactics — and about the convergence of revolutionary nonviolence and armed propaganda as part of a people's war — began in earnest.

While we had gained our early experience in the Reagan era, we were all students of the movement of the Sixties — the period from 1952 until around 1978. Three men and three women, we were straight, gay, and bi-identified, working and middle class — and aware of ourselves as white people in a white supremacist society. We understood that organizing in the 1990s was — and would likely continue to be — more difficult than it was in 1968. But we also knew that strong movements were built in small increments over long stretches of time — and that the struggle must continue even during repressive and reactionary times.

The New Movement — and its related Free Puerto Rico Committee (FPRC) — had a formal relationship with and direct accountability to the organization that helped create it: the Puerto

Rican Movimiento Liberacion Nacional (MLN). An explicit all-white group pledged to work "under the leadership" of the MLN, the FPRC was a solidarity organization committed to building support for the initiatives of the MLN and the broader Puerto Rican independence movement. FPRC members were strongly encouraged to travel to Puerto Rico only on study trips led by MLN members and their island-based colleagues, and not to travel elsewhere in the region. At a time when it was fashionable and commonplace for progressives to take vacations and work trips to Central America, Cuba, Grenada, and elsewhere, this rule reflected the expectation that FPRC members would devote their whole lives, their money and other material resources, and their labor and creativity to the cause of the Puerto Rican people and the campaigns of the MLN.

This direct leadership model addressed some of the basic issues related to accountability. Regular meetings with local MLN representatives would review the work of FPRC individuals and the organization as a whole; people would be held responsible for the work they had taken on and for their commitment to the cause. If a person's behavior or actions were deemed lacking, they were criticized in the hope that they would improve their practice and strengthen their discipline and organizing. The FPRC could develop its own projects only if they were designed to broaden work among white people — and only with direct approval by and oversight from the MLN. Accountability was a one-way street and was regularly measured, evaluated, and judged.

Hoping for impartial assessment by the MLN and with an eye on building ever-stronger ties between peoples, many whites in the FPRC (including those who helped form the early RnB study group and RnB itself) did gain great skills, a deep understanding of the situation of Puerto Rico and of Puerto Ricans in the US, a deep commitment to life-long radical work, and deep and long-lasting relationships with people still in leading positions in the Puerto Rican movement.

On the other hand, this formulaic work was not particularly sustaining. Many whites interested in helping to end US colonialism in Puerto Rico, or at least the US bombing of Vieques, were unwilling to make the life changes necessary to become members of the FPRC. Furthermore, as the MLN was only one of several organizations on the Puerto Rican left, it was hard not to fall into the middle of partisan battles. This was also true for some of the FPRC's sister organizations, including the John Brown Anti-Klan Committee (JBAKC), which was similarly structured and under the leadership of the New Afrikan Peoples Organization. Finally, the special access to "heavies" in the Puerto Rican and Black movements led some whites within FPRC and JBAKC to a predictable arrogance toward other whites struggling against racism.

The lessons which the FPRC founders of RnB brought to our early conversations included an understanding of the racism inherent in multiracial structures. In many such groups, whites claim to be committed to anti-racist principles, but hold greater power than their Black or Latino counterparts because of their access to funding sources and other forms of white-skin privilege. A whites-only group offered a strong basis for developing both criticism and support as individual members worked on their personal and political issues of privilege and prejudice. Accountability to, and critiques from, an outside group of radicals drawn directly from the oppressed movements provided a constant check on racist allocations of power and resources.

Much of this analysis is based on the New Left understanding of the politics of contemporary imperialism. In its thirst for power, the US, it is argued, is an empire imprisoning whole nations of people. Puerto Rico, the northern half of Mexico, all Indigenous American Indian nations, and the Black nation of New Afrika are all part of the capitalist machine, which requires white supremacy and imperialism in order to survive. National liberation movements, therefore, and not One Big Union of workers, will be the leading force in eliminating oppression and injustice in our time. Part of this thesis is developed in the work of J. Sakai, author of *Settlers: The Mythology of the White Prole-*

tariat (1983), which posits colonialism as an ongoing phenomenon. This definition of imperialism and the US state continues to shape RnB's work.

The War Resisters League members among RnB's founders were less rooted in specific anti-racist movement paradigms. But WRL's strong support of the anti-nuclear Mobilization for Survival (MFS) coalition brought us into direct contact with two other MFS member organizations. The Puerto Rican Socialist Party (PSP), and more significantly, the All-African People's Revolutionary Party (AAPRP), had committed several members of their leadership cadre to the staff and boards of MFS in the early 1980s. This put them in key positions to teach the new generation of resisters (of which we were a part) their own lessons about movement building.

The AAPRP had been founded, in conjunction with Pan African statesmen Kwame Nkrumah of Ghana and Sekou Toure of Guinea, by Black Power advocate Stokely Carmichael, known by then as Kwame Ture. Not only had Stokely popularized the phrases "Black Power" and "Hell No, We Won't Go" — bridging, in his own way, the civil rights and anti-war movements of the Sixties —, he had led the Student Nonviolent Coordinating Committee (SNCC) as a close ally of Dr. Martin Luther King, Jr. While at the helm of SNCC, Carmichael demanded that whites leave the organization and take up anti-racist organizing in their own communities — a call that disturbed many of those who had gained knowledge, comfort, and camaraderie working among Blacks in the south and were less excited about working among "our own kind," literally much closer to home.

The AAPRP's representatives to MFS and WRL, Bob Brown and Mawina Koyate Sowa, offered broader instructions about what white folks should do to bring about change in the 1980s. They provided daily suggestions and inspiration for building outside the "boxes" of traditional Left structures. Convinced that young people could and should play a leading role in developing new formulas for struggling against racism, they remained neutral on the question of all white or multiracial organizations, but steadfast in their understanding that revolutionary "Third World" and indigenous struggles would bring the empire to its knees.

For those of us from the WRL tradition, accountability therefore became much more personalized and individualized. We were led to understand that while anti-racist caucuses, teach-ins, or trainings might all have their value, these tactics would hardly be decisive in bringing about lasting change. Ironically, despite the person-to-person nature of tutoring between a few folks in the AAPRP and a few folks in the WRL, it was made clear that only by building strong organizations would the revolution be won. The fact that some groups, such as WRL and MFS, were predominantly white didn't bother our comrades in the AAPRP or PSP. In their view, white groups, if appropriately anti-racist in their politics and deeds, could work within their cultural norms and communities. If principled multinational coalitions could be built, the interests of all the people would be served.

Accountability, in this scenario, was very loose indeed: History itself would condemn to irrelevance any white organization unwilling or unable to work with its counterparts among indigenous peoples. On the plus side, we were discouraged from the sometimes brutal criticism/self-criticism that our RnB cofounders occasionally had to deal with. We did — and continue to — try to advance principled, anti-racist politics within the larger peace and pacifist communities, seizing upon any opportunities or allies that arise. However, a major problem persists: Almost by definition, there is little consistency in this work — and limited ability to measure how we are doing or where to proceed.

Some might appropriately suggest that this model provides very little accountability at all. Despite this, some of our predecessors — such as Chicago Eight icon Dave Dellinger, feminist (s)hero Barbara Deming, Anne Braden and Ralph DiGia, Jim Peck, Jean Zwickel and Ruth Reynolds — are among the white elders most respected by Black and Latino radicals.

After RnB's formation, when it became clear that we might stick around for awhile and should therefore develop principles of unity, we were careful to reflect back on our various histories. We were not ready then — and are still not ready today — to say that there is only one best way to build a radical organization. Our community-based interconnectivity is seen in our agreement to maintain creative tension in our work by leaving some fundamental questions unanswered. This openness is reflected in the section of our principles concerning race, history, and ideology. "With a strong consciousness of the power of white-skin privilege," we wrote, "some of us have worked in primarily white groups under the leadership of people of color, while others have worked to build multiracial organizations." One thing we remain most proud of about our Principles of Unity is our ability to remain open about some vital issues that require ongoing struggle.

Though we concluded our Principles document with a list of questions we were challenging ourselves and others to remain open about, we also acknowledged that our answers and actions must always be informed by, and accountable to, our long-term goals. "In the process of fighting for change," we stated, "we must change ourselves, our relationships to each other, and the ways we work together." RnB set forth that it is particularly incumbent on men to struggle with other men to change sexist views and behaviors, for whites to work with other whites in trying to eliminate racism, for straight people to take on fighting heterosexism among themselves, and for the economically privileged to fight classism. Furthermore, while not outlining specific organizations or individuals we'd be accountable to, we affirmed the general understanding that "we respect the right of all oppressed groups to define their own struggles, agendas, and processes. Given the fundamental role of racism in US society, we recognize the leading role that communities of color play in fighting for fundamental change. Material, financial, social, and cultural resources must be redistributed in the course of struggle to ensure that all communities have equal access."

Practical Work: Enemies of the State and the Legacy of John Brown

RnB members are involved as organizers in many unconnected groups. Some members have a continuing presence on WRL's staff and board and continue to work on contemporary Puerto Rican solidarity efforts. Others support the local Pacifica radio station, organize for prison and drug law reforms with the Drug Policy Alliance, work on immigrant rights, and/or are active in neighborhood block associations and in building educational alternatives in our city and county. One of our most consistent ongoing projects, however, carried out publicly and self consciously under the aegis of Resistance in Brooklyn, is our work around US political prisoners.

For all of us, even with our diverse points of view, political prisoners represent an unfinished part of the Sixties legacy. They are revolutionaries locked up because their beliefs and actions have been criminalized by the government. If we are to build strong fighting movements in this new political moment, we must stand together in defending our organizations against attack. Prisoners from the Black Panther Party, its offshoots and allies, the American Indian Movement, and others are, we believe, the most powerful symbol of our weakness. Freeing them all is our most urgent task.

Based on this view, discussions in 1996 began between a few RnBers and David Gilbert, a white (North American) political prisoner. David was a leader of the Columbia University chapter of Students for a Democratic Society at the height of the anti-Vietnam War movement. During his decades of respected anti-racist activities, David also took part in organizations (mainly underground) under the leadership of Black liberation groups. By the 1990s, accountability for those on both sides of the prison wall was applied with as much flexibility as RnB's operating stucture could provide. But we all felt the need to generate more public dialogue, not only concerning political prisoners, but also on questions of the meaning of accountability and anti-racism in a new era. The idea of a self-published booklet came up as a way in which three white political prisoners could review their histories, comment frankly on the mistakes they made and lessons learned, and open up questions for anti-racists on "the outside."

Enemies of the State came out in 1998. Much to our surprise, it became such a major "hit" that we had to immediately re-publish (photo-copy!) and mail it to friendly distributors. Ten years later, *Enemies* has gone through more printings than we can keep track of and has been revised and re-published by at least three small presses in the US and Canada. With tens of thousands of copies in print, *Enemies* was not only more influential than we ever expected, it also affirmed our sense that an emerging generation of activists was taking the question of anti-racist practice very seriously. In addition to David, prisoners Laura Whitehorn and Marlyn Buck were included in the booklet. Marilyn, also an SDS member, was renowned for her precocious criticisms of male privilege and sexism in the organization — and had also worked with radical Black groups from the mid-Sixties on. Laura, a member of the Resistance Conspiracy Case that tied together the trials of six white anti-imperialists, cited as a primary inspiration the words of assassinated Chicago Black Panther Chairman Fred Hampton: "You can jail the revolutionary, but you can't jail the revolution."

Buck and Whitehorn, serving time together at California's Federal Correctional Facility in Dublin during *Enemies'* initial publication, answered several questions jointly to show their shared politics. Not surprisingly, the question of accountability came to the fore. "Some of our errors," they admitted, "included being unclear about what we meant when we said our strategy was carried out 'under Third World leadership.' At times, we interpreted what the leadership of any given struggle was arguing for to suit our own politics. At other times, we became involved in debates inside other movements that were inappropriate for us to be actively involved in. It's fine to have opinions and positions about the liberation struggles of other peoples whom you support, but it was and is wrong to intervene in the middle of debates within a national liberation struggle."

The question of how anti-racist whites should appropriately and respectfully work with these movements is left somewhat vague. When, whether, and how it might be acceptable to enter into substantive discussions with comrades in these movements remains an unresolved question for many current activists. Whose "permission" among movement leaders makes such dialogue acceptable? If there is ongoing disagreement between two organizations within the same movement and with similar activities, is it appropriate for anti-racist white allies or organizations to simply stand aside and do nothing? How can one's accountability to and relationship with one organization satisfy other sectors of the movement, which might view the very same work as privileged, unprincipled, or unaccountable?

A further "big problem of our work," Buck and Whitehorn continued, "was our inability to organize larger numbers of white people to work with us. While many people over the years attended activities and events that we held, our standards of commitment were so stringent that people wouldn't join our groups. Internally, other misuses of 'criticism/self criticism' and our strict methods of leadership served to weaken rather than to strengthen members. These methods also militated against wider recruitment. A revolutionary organization should build its members, becoming stronger in the process." While RnB's own experiences suggested that some strengthening within those strict structures did go on, our work took place more than a decade after the activism of Marilyn and Laura.

Following the publication of *Enemies of the State,* RnB initiated intense civil disobedience, direct-action projects on behalf of incarcerated Black journalist Mumia abu-Jamal and fourteen imprisoned Puerto Rican patriots. Attempting to reach out to broad groups of predominantly white activists in progressive churches and peace groups, we tried to bring together folks who had not worked closely before. On the heels of the Mumia and Puerto Rico campaigns, RnB laid the groundwork for a conference to bring together white anti-racists involved in different organizations and campaigns across the country.

May of 2000 marked the 200th anniversary of the birth of John Brown, the radical abolitionist. Our plan was to hold a conference in collaboration with the multiracial, Black-led Student Liberation Action Movement at New York's Hunter College. We'd hear updates and rousing speeches from leaders of US national liberation movements and hold sessions to discuss the meaning of solidarity, the role of white people in anti-racist organizing, and the issues of leadership and accountability. John Brown had long been a symbol of white anti-racist commitment and was held in high esteem by leaders as diverse as W.E.B. DuBois and Malcolm X. Our take on Brown was that his importance wasn't based solely on the fact that he was a white person willing to take strong action and devote his life to the cause of freedom. He also saw it as vital to work in partnership with the oppressed Africans whose lives were at stake. Brown was willing to put his own life on the line and was interested in working alongside of the likes of Harriet Tubman and others. In addition, his work also involved organizing members of the white community — including his own family — and encouraging them to devote themselves to the cause.

In preparation for this conference, we convened conference calls with groups from Chicago, San Francisco, Los Angeles, New Orleans, Washington DC, and elsewhere. Groups still intact from the New Left, such as Prairie Fire Organizing Committee and Fireworks, participated alongside younger activists from Anti-Racist Action. Several Catholic Worker friends helped out, as did several former political prisoners who had spent most of their pre-jail time organizing clandestinely. It quickly became clear that we had as many differences as we had points in common, but we persevered build a successful event and stronger movement.

Ultimately, we were able to bring together an impressive array of presenters, including South African poet Dennis Brutus, Puerto Rican Cultural Center founder Jose Lopez, former Black Panther Party leader and political prisoner Dhoruba bin Wahad, recently released Puerto Rican political prisoner Alicia Rodriguez, noted Black feminist activist-publisher Barbara Smith, League of Indigenous Sovereign Nations representative Chief Billy Tayac, Native American poet Crystos, and Puerto Rican human rights attorney Luis Nieves Falcon.

Author Terry Bisson reflected on the team of people assembled by John Brown, noting how much organization was needed to carry out the dramatic work he led. Rita Bo Brown of the Out of Control Lesbian Committee to Support Political Prisoners gave an impassioned speech about the need for white people to struggle across class lines in order to fulfill their anti-racist commitment. Finally, Safiya Bukhari of the political prisoner support group known as the Jericho Amnesty Movement closed the conference with a challenge to us all. "John Brown is important," Bukhari stated, "because he took political action in the form of militant action. You can't just talk about revolution; you can't just talk about what needs to be done; you've got to take the steps to make sure it happens. This is also why Mumia is so important. If we don't champion the issue of political prisoners and don't build a movement that recognizes the contributions of these people and the fact that they're in there because of the work they've done, then they'll try to silence us all."

Contemporary Concerns

RnB at the end of the twenty-first century's first decade has three annual events. Before the height of the holiday season in December, we invite friends, family, comrades, and colleagues to join us in an arts and crafts adventure: making and writing cards to all the political prisoners in the US. Often, we'll include the list of prisoners of conscience put out annually by the War Resisters International in conjunction with Prisoners for Peace Day. Lately we've been working with the Anarchist Black Cross Federation to bring diverse generations and nationalities and ideologies to our own brand of holiday party.

In March, the women of RnB, along with a few cohorts in the Black, Puerto Rican, and Dominican communities, hold an open microphone International Women's Month Poetry event. Every year a featured poet — including, in past years, Sonia Sanchez, Amina Baraka, Nawal el Saadawi, asha bandele, Alix Olson, Bev Grant, Mariposa, Susana Cabanas, and Kimiko Hahn — joins newcomers to raise funds for some group selected by the women on a rotating basis. Finally, RnB's annual Anti-July Fourth B-B-Q brings together scores of community members in an effort to raise funds for different groups each year — and to raise some hell as well.

RnB has not sought definitive answers to the questions confronting us about accountability. Our annual events, however, clearly suggest a consistent understanding of the need to put our material resources where our political commitments are. Accountability to one another has meant space within the collective to challenge and support each others' attempts at putting anti-racist and anti-imperialist perspectives into practical and enjoyable action. Accountability to the people and organizations in the movements in which we work has come to mean different things in each different situation. Within the WRL, it means support for an informal grouping of staff and national committee members. At WBAI Radio in NYC, it means support for a more formal justice and unity caucus. In our work with the Black and Puerto Rican liberation movements, it means continuing some of the relationships and commitments that some of us have held dear for decades, while pursuing them in less sectarian, static, or rigid ways.

Internally, it has meant continuing conversations about who we are. Some of us now define ourselves as bi-racial or multiracial; others are raising multiracial children — all the while remaining committed to a politics centered on fighting against white supremacy and for people's self determination. Externally, accountability continues to mean ongoing conversations with our Black and Latino comrades about "when and where to enter," even while understanding that some within those movements can and will never accept the validity of our work.

We must fight against paternalism, complacency, arrogance, a sense of our own rightness, hopelessness, and cynicism. We must move forward with the realization that anti-racism for white folks — individually or institutionally — is a never-ending project, while still maintaining our belief that nothing is impossible.

Nothing short of revolution will change the course of globalized capital or of an empire dependent on racism to divide and conquer people, nations, and land. No one looking carefully at the current crisis we face can believe that the revolution, with all its phases, processes, and sub-components, is just around the corner and about to win victory over all bad things. There are substantial cracks in the empire, however, and we must work together to exploit them. If we begin with basic steps, struggling against racism and for greater accountability within the context of the larger battles ahead, tomorrow will surely be a better day.

Chapter Eight

'Passing It On':
Reflections of a White Anti-racist
Solidarity Organizer

Sharon Martinas, cofounder of the Challenging White Supremacy
Workshop with CWS Workshop cofounder Mickey Ellinger

> The purpose of this chapter is to share reflections on the goals,
> strategies, pedagogies, and challenges of practicing different kinds
> of accountability during the 13 year herstory of the San Francisco-
> based Challenging White Supremacy Workshop.
>
> The perspective is that of its cofounder and coordinator, so the nar-
> rative will use a lot of "I" statements. The discussion will not attempt
> to present perspectives of workshop participants on the workshop's
> effectiveness, which is a story for another time.

About the CWS Workshop

The mission of the CWS Workshop was to 'train principled
and effective grassroots anti-racist organizers.' Typical workshops
were called 'Becoming an Anti-Racist Activist,' 'Becoming an Anti-
Racist Organizer,' or 'Introduction to Grassroots Anti-Racist Organizing.' The workshop began in the spring of 1993, after its
cofounders were inspired by participating in the People's Insti-

tute's Undoing Racism™ Workshop. The CWS workshop closed in June 2005.

Each workshop lasted from ten to fifteen weeks, and met three hours per week. Participants were expected to complete reading assignments of 100–150 pages per week, to volunteer in a prearranged racial justice organization for six to eight hours per week, and to raise funds to pay the honoraria for organizers of color who presented to the workshop.

Workshop participants were mostly white, college-educated, working- and middle-class grassroots social justice activists between the ages of twenty and thirty. Approximately 90 percent of each workshop class of thirty was women; and 60 percent was lesbians, gays, bisexuals and transgendered activists. After 2001 all applicants had to have at least one to two years prior experience as social justice activists in order to participate in the workshop.

In its last five years the CWS Workshop developed a program for more experienced grassroots anti-racist activists called 'The Workshop as a Lab.' Prior workshop participants took on various workshop roles as preparation for their anti-racist community work. They learned to become Small Group Organizers (aka facilitators). They adapted certain workshops focused on challenging white privilege and facilitated these workshop sessions. They mentored workshop participants who were volunteering with local racial justice organizations in some basic principles and practices of accountable behavior. They trained other participants in grassroots fundraising tactics. They recruited and interviewed potential workshop participants, and they organized all workshop logistics. This group of anti-racist organizers-in-training became known as the workshop's Organizing Crew. They spent four months in intensive training preparing for their workshop roles.

CWS as a 'Solidarity' Workshop

The CWS Workshop was an anti-racist solidarity workshop. Its cofounders, Mickey Ellinger and I, came from a political tradition of white anti-racist solidarity activists who, from the late 1960s through the 1980s, practiced our belief that the role of US white revolutionaries was to win other white activists to support national liberation movements on both sides of the US borders.

Mickey and I grew up politically in the era of SNCC, the Black Panther Party, the American Indian Movement, the National Liberation Front of Vietnam, the Young Lords Party, the Puerto Rican Independence movement, the Farabundo Marti National Liberation Front of El Salvador, the Pan African Congress, and the African National Congress of South Africa. All of these organizations and movements were fighting for land, justice, and self-determination.

We believed that the struggles for justice of racially and nationally oppressed communities in the United States — Black, Puerto Rican, Mexican and Native people — were or could become national liberation movements, and that these movements, along with struggles abroad, could bring down US imperialism. White activists had a specific role to play in organizing other white activists to see that anti-racist struggles were central to defeating U.S. imperialism.

Mickey and I created the CWS Workshop as a political education project to pass on to a new generation the revolutionary tradition which had grounded our political lives. 'Back in the Day' — 1960s through 1980s — this tradition was called 'solidarity politics.'[1]

Goal #1: Passing on the Theory and Practice of Anti-racist, Anti-imperialist Solidarity Politics

The first and most important form of accountability of the CWS Workshop was to the ideology and political practice of 'solidarity politics.'

Winning people to this definition of accountability presented enormous challenges throughout the herstory of CWS: How do we make a vision and a politic that came from a different time and worldview relevant and meaningful to a young generation of white activists who were growing up in profoundly different political, social, and economic times?

The early 1990s were very different from the late 1960s. By the time the CWS workshop opened its doors, the US had crushed most national liberation movements worldwide. Most white activists had no experience working with revolutionary movements led by people of color. They probably had never heard of the term 'solidarity,' and they lacked the experience to be able to discuss 'accountability' in doing 'solidarity work.' Nonetheless, we believed that it was still true that U.S. white supremacy was fundamental to the staying power of the U.S. system, so we searched for ways to translate that understanding to different movements in a different world.

Working with Multiple Meanings of 'Accountability'

Through my study and reflections on the ways that the People's Institute for Survival and Beyond, and its affiliated anti-racist white organization, European Dissent, used the term 'accountability,' I began to see relationships between the practices of 'accountability' and 'solidarity' that I knew from experience but for which I did not have the language.[2]

I also learned that there are multiple meanings of 'accountability' for social justice activists today. For example, here are just a few of the multiple meanings I learned from CWS workshop participants through the years:

- For some, 'accountability' means the practice of doing what you say you're going to do, when you say you're going to do it, and calling if you can't get it done. In this meaning, 'accountability' is a synonym for 'dependability,' and connotes 'reliability' and 'ethical practice' of an individual activist.

- 'Accountability' may also mean the process of building trustful, authentic relationships with others, both white and of color. Used in this sense, 'accountability' connotes 'relationship building,' especially between two people.

- An activist may hold herself 'accountable' to a particular community organization, or specific group of people. 'Accountability' here may involve a feeling of 'loyalty,' and a practice referred to as "I've got your back." Trust built day by day, for a long period of time, is a key factor in this aspect of accountability.

- A group of social or racial justice activists may hold themselves accountable to a particular social justice movement. In this meaning, 'accountability' combines general agreement with the political praxis (analysis, practice, evaluation, goals, visions) of that movement, as well as with the implicitly or explicitly shared cultural values and norms of that movement. When this meaning of accountability is experienced, participants often use the term 'community' to describe their participation in that movement.

In an anti-racist solidarity workshop, 'accountability' can and does involve all of the aspects mentioned above. But how can the *learning experience of a workshop* (which as Catherine Jones points out in her powerful article, 'The Work is Not the Workshop: Talking and Doing, Visibility and Accountability in the White Anti-Racist Community' is not *the work*) be utilized in some ways to frame the values and ethics of 'accountability' in the politics of 'anti-racist, anti-imperialist solidarity?'[3]

Goal #2: Practicing Anti-Racist Solidarity with Local Racial Justice Organizations

Mickey and I understood that, even though we could share our solidarity stories with workshop participants, we could not 'teach' solidarity. All we could do was to organize a political program that offered participants the opportunity to practice solidarity with organizations led by people of color so that they could experience how it might transform their lives as it had ours. No, we could not 'teach' solidarity, but perhaps our workshop program could 'model' it.

It took CWS years to develop an effective and accountable racial justice solidarity program for white workshop participants. However, by the time the workshop closed its doors in 2005, CWS's solidarity program was the strongest and most effective component of the workshop's curriculum.

I learned through error and trial, in that order, how difficult it is to use a workshop to prepare mostly white participants to practice accountable solidarity relationships with organizers and organizations of color. Here are some of the lessons I am still learning about how to do this work in an accountable and effective way:

> *It helps to have a definition of 'solidarity' to provide a political foundation for the workshop's anti-racist solidarity program.*

CWS's definition of 'solidarity' was 'an act of bonding with a people struggling for their liberation.' The definition was influenced by Mickey's and my political experiences as anti-racist, anti-imperialist organizers in solidarity with national liberation movements of the 1960s through the 1980s.

Most workshop participants tended to use the term 'being an ally' rather than 'standing in solidarity.' But 'being an ally' connotes an individual relationship to another individual, whereas 'standing in solidarity' assumes an organization-to-organization relationship in the context of a movement for self-determination of thousands of oppressed people — even whole nations — struggling to free themselves from the system of US imperialism.

It wasn't until 2001, eight years after CWS began, that a young activist, politicized in the Bay Area racial justice struggles of the 1990s, asked in a workshop session, "Sharon, what does 'solidarity' mean today?" I responded, "I think you are already practicing it, because you have the experience to ask that question."

> *To practice anti-racist solidarity work, I think we have to understand what 'respecting the leadership of organizers of color' means. White workshop participants need to be given the opportunity to experience it for themselves. That experience has the capacity to transform their lives, if they are open to that transformation. But if they only read about 'leadership' in a workshop reader, the experience may awaken their anti-racist consciousness, but not move them to making a life-time commitment to solidarity work.*

Therefore, a workshop anti-racist solidarity program must prioritize developing firm, accountable relationships with community organizations of color that are strong, guided by principles and practices of self-determination and accountability in their own communities; and whose vision, goals, strategies, and practices can inspire, educate, and motivate white anti-racist activists in the workshop.

The Bay Area is blessed with having many powerful grassroots radical organizations of color. But that development has not happened overnight. US government attacks on national liberation organizations from the 1960s through the 1980s decimated our local movements for justice. Many of our elders were imprisoned, murdered, or alive but of the 'walking wounded.'

A new generation of radical and revolutionary organizers of color emerged in the early '90s, in response to the Los Angeles uprising of 1992 after the trial of Rodney King and also the first US war against Iraq. These organizers developed their leadership capacities in the struggles for immigrant rights (fighting Prop. 187) and defending affirmation action against Prop. 209.[4] They honed their organizing capacities through training programs like SOUL (School of Unity and Liberation).[5] They led fierce demonstrations and grassroots electoral campaigns which CWS workshop participants participated in and supported. But their grassroots institutions, their community organizations, were still new and developing their own local leadership. Most of these organizations were not yet ready to consider taking on white volunteers, and many organizations were politically unwilling to do so. Their experiences with the racism of white social justice activists made them understandably distrustful of working with us.

In the years between the path-breaking Critical Resistance Conference at Berkeley in 1998 and the Bush regime's wars against Iraq and the so-called 'war on terror' in 2001, the new generation of organizers of color had strengthened their grassroots institutions to the point that many were willing to experiment with taking on 'racial justice volunteers' from the CWS workshop. Our Racial Justice Volunteer program began in the Fall of 2001.[6] It was coordinated by an experienced and accountable solidarity organizer named Brooke Atherton.

> *While the <u>experience</u> of solidarity cannot be taught in a workshop, I believe that the <u>practice</u> of accountable behavior can be taught.*

A story of how CWS's racial justice volunteer program got off the ground might illustrate this point. In 2001, a coalition of organizations of color held a community forum to discuss, in a global justice framework, our movement's response to Bush's wars. CWS was invited to the forum and asked to help with childcare and logistics. Brooke headed up the volunteer coordination effort. When twenty-five mostly white volunteers who had signed up to work came on time and did what they were asked to do with precision and humility, some organizers of color were so impressed they asked her to set up childcare for the weekly meetings of their organizations' membership.

One racial justice volunteer placement rapidly expanded to fifteen as the word spread that CWS could provide organizations of color with accountable volunteers, mostly for routine tasks that overworked organizers of color were glad to share.

The Racial Justice Volunteer Coordinator did meticulous phone and personal followup with each CWS volunteer, checked regularly with the volunteer's supervisor at the host organization for feedback on the volunteer's work, developed a basic 'accountability check list' for volunteers, personally mentored the new Volunteer Coordinators for the next CWS workshop session, and contributed to writing the workshop's 'Racial Justice Program Booklet,' which each workshop participant received as part of the CWS orientation program.[7] In all her work, Brooke modeled what it looked like in real life to practice accountable behavior as an anti-racist solidarity organizer.

As CWS Workshop coordinator, I prioritized supporting the Racial Justice Program Coordinator's work, since I had already decided that the racial justice volunteer placement program was the core of CWS's programmatic work. This support involved sharing with her all my own experiences and lessons learned as an anti-racist solidarity organizer, and sharing her work load because she spent hundreds of volunteer hours as Racial Justice Program Coordinator. And it was up to me to do the heart-breaking work of having to ask a workshop participant to leave the workshop if, after numerous discussions, the participant was still practicing unaccountable behavior — like not showing up for her volunteer work shifts or not calling her supervisor ahead of time.

Even with two organizers putting in so much time for the racial justice placement program, lots of vital work still fell through the cracks. Perhaps most important was that sometimes we did not learn about a participant's unaccountable behavior till the end of that workshop session, or when we were calling the organization the next season to see if they wanted CWS volunteers. It became obvious to me that the 'Workshop as a Lab' program, in which CWS trained the 'Organizing Crew' for the next 15 week workshop needed to prioritize training new anti-racist solidarity activists to become solidarity organizers who could help coordinate the CWS Racial Justice Program.

Becoming a Racial Justice Program Coordinator: reflections on some early steps

In the last three or four years of the CWS workshop, we offered a workshop called 'Becoming an Anti-Racist Organizer.'[8] When that workshop was no longer offered because of the workload of trying to coordinate two fifteen-week workshops each year, we focused on a four-month training program called 'Workshop as a Lab.'The program was geared to orient volunteers whom I had recruited from prior workshops to become the 'Organizing Crew' for the next workshop.[9]

Among the 'Organizing Crew' were activists whose primary anti-racist experience was in doing volunteer solidarity work with local racial justice organizations led by organizers of color. Out of this group came the new group of volunteer coordinators of the 'Racial Justice Volunteer Placement program.'

The efforts of these three to five Racial Justice Coordinators, working collaboratively together each workshop session mentoring and supporting no more than eight workshop participants each, vastly improved the accountability of the whole program, as well as strengthened their own skills and commitment to anti-racist solidarity organizing.

I began to dream of expanding CWS's racial justice volunteer program to include an intensive training curriculum for anti-racist solidarity organizers, grounded in twenty to thirty hours per week of volunteer internship with local racial justice organizations, mentoring from elder solidarity organizers in the community, and a new curriculum focused on developing their capacities as anti-racist solidarity organizers. Unfortunately, the CWS Workshop ended unexpectedly in the spring of 2005, so that dream was never realized.

CWS tried to create a coordinated workshop curriculum and program that models what solidarity work looks like, on a daily basis, and sustainable for a lifetime.

While the Racial Justice Volunteer Placement program was the core of the workshop's curriculum, it was not the only way in which participants learned what it might mean to do solidarity work. Other aspects of the work included:

- Reading about the histories and contemporary struggles of national liberation and racial justice movements as a core part of the readers specially edited for the workshop. In practice, this meant about 150 pages every other week. Alternate reading weeks focused on the history of white supremacy and white privilege, and different essays by activists of color and white activists experienced in challenging the white privilege and political and cultural expressions of social justice activists.

- Inviting guest organizers of color, many of whom coordinated the organizations with whom participants were volunteering, to speak about their racial justice organizing work. This part of the program, in conjunction with the readings mentioned above, was called 'Legacies of Liberation.'

- Training workshop participants to do grassroots fundraising to make sure that guest trainers of color received a respectful honorarium for their willingness to share their wisdom with a predominantly white group through the panel presentations.

- Learning how to invite their friends to the presentations by organizers of color, and to debrief with their friends after the workshop.

- Setting up a weekly calendar of racial justice events and encouraging participants to go to these events and to invite their friends.

- Training workshop participants in the art of 'practicing active listening,' so that when organizers of color presented to the workshop, participants were focused on what the organizers were saying, rather than jumping immediately to how, as white activists, they *felt* about the organizers' presentations.

- Training Small Group Organizers in the art of respectfully refocusing small group discussion so that it started with what the presenters had actually said, before requesting participants' reflections. In a tiny way, this activity modeled how we white activists can 'decenter our whiteness' while learning to do solidarity work.

- Making sure that small group discussions focused on connecting participants' experience in their racial justice placements with their readings, and their experiences within the workshop setting: i.e., modeling 'the work is not the workshop.'

- Organizing special small group discussions exclusively for discussion of racial justice volunteer placement experiences.

Goal #3: Learning the Real History of the US White Supremacy System, Especially Its Negative Impact on White-led Social Justice Movements

In 1983, Robert Allen, an African-American editor of *The Black Scholar,* in collaboration with Pamela Allen, a white feminist who had been politicized in the Mississippi freedom struggle of the 1960s, wrote *Reluctant Reformers: Racism and Social Reform Movements in the United States.* It's a history of how racism in white-dominated movements — from Abolitionism in the 19th century through the Central America Solidarity movements of the 1980s — have undermined and disrespected movements of peoples of color, and prevented the building of multi-racial alliances that might have ended systemic oppression and created new worlds of social justice for everyone in the US. The book blew my mind!

Mickey and I used the lessons from the book and our own experience with white social justice movements to create a curriculum on white privilege that was grounded in the history of the US white supremacy system. We focused on the impact of the politics and practice of white privilege in social justice movements: how white privilege frames our movements' agendas, limits our choices of allies, harms equitable leadership development strategies, undermines resource-sharing, and prevents the development of relationships of mutual respect and trust with organizations and movements led by grassroots organizers of color.

We created interactive history exercises like 'How Mother Earth Became a Piece of Real Estate' — focusing on the theme of land struggles, land loss of communities of color, and land grabs by European descended 'pioneers' backed up by federal government laws and policies — and 'Family Herstories,' during which participants interviewed their own elders for the hidden histories behind how European immigrants became white people. Great stuff!

But when we looked at contemporary white-led social justice movements, especially those in which participants were actively involved, people complained about 'stereotyped role plays' and that 'their organizations' were being targeted, even though the rules of the exercises prohibited mentioning any groups by name.

I learned some tough lessons about challenging white privilege. White guilt can pop up in unexpected ways. Just because nothing is said personally, doesn't mean that folks don't take it personally. I also learned that I was a poor role model for practicing accountability toward white social justice movements, since I don't even believe they are practicing 'social justice' if they're doing their work in a racist way. My attitude came through, and frequently (and often justifiably) pissed people off.

Some Strategies: 'Creating an Anti-Racist Agenda'

In spite of its hard edge, and the 'no passing the hankies in this workshop' feel to it, CWS had a very optimistic strategy. To challenge white privilege in social justice movements, white activists can 'Create an Anti-Racist Agenda.' The 'Agenda' is grounded in six principles, which I called 'moral, spiritual, and political rudders that can guide individual and collective transformation of anti-racist activists.'

The Principles Are:

- Act on your principles (Do the right thing. Practice and model respectful behavior. Challenge white privilege);

- Create an anti-racist culture of resistance (language, group dynamics, study of history);

- Stand in solidarity (with radical racial justice struggles);

- Prioritize the issues of radical organizers of color;

- Respect the leadership of radical organizers of color;

- Hold on to your visions (of a world without white supremacy).

The principles are based on learning to analyze, strategize, and practice anti-racist political activities. It does not focus on emotional release, nor on delving deeply into personal stories.

The principles also suggest that the workshop is only a place to practice what we want to do in the world. It is not a substitute for that world. 'Workshopitis' doesn't help us become stronger anti-racist organizers.

But often when I came home exhausted on Sunday nights after the workshop, I wondered, "How can I keep accountable, as a solidarity organizer, to radical organizers of color in the Bay Area when I'm spending sixty hours a week working almost exclusively with white activists?" In this period it was not possible for me to have a structured solidarity relationship with an organization, such as CISPES was able to have with the FMLN or the John Brown Anti-Klan Committee had with the New African Peoples Organization. My own moral, spiritual, and political rudder often felt very much off its keel.

Creating an Anti-Racist Pedagogy for the Privileged: Many Unanswered Questions

Even though I had been an anti-racist solidarity organizer and a grassroots political educator for nearly 30 years, I was ill prepared to create anti-racist curriculum for white social justice activists in the 1990s.

Sometimes participants and I miscommunicated because I didn't speak 'workshopese.' Consider these examples of linguistic challenges:

- When young white workshop participants called me a 'facilitator' of the CWS workshop, I looked up the linguistic roots of 'facilitator' in my dictionary. Sure enough, 'facilitator' comes from 'facile': to make something easy. "Hell No!" I protested. "I don't want to make anti-racist work for white folks easy. I want it to be the most difficult work they've ever done in their lives. People of color are regularly murdered for doing racial justice work. Making it easy for white folks to do the same will just reinforce our white privilege, and strengthen the white supremacy system."

- Small groups in the workshop operated on the principle of self-determination for participants of color: Activists of color could join groups with other people of color and bi-racial people, or they could join a white group if they wished to. White participants, on the other hand, could join only white small groups.

- Once, an all-white small group criticized the work-shop for not allowing them enough time for pro-cessing. Their spokesperson was a young woman with blond, curly hair. I looked at her in confusion after she offered her criticism. "Processing?" I repeated. "Excuse me, but this is a workshop, not a hair salon. And I don't see any African-American women in your group who might want their hair processed!"

But there were far more serious challenges in the curricu-lum creating activity. Here's a beginning list of questions that I grap-pled with, often unsuccessfully, during the herstory of the CWS Workshop:

1. *How can CWS pass on the anti-racist solidarity poli-tics that emerged in the era of strong national liber-ation movements in a very different world?*

   a. 'Back in the Day' we learned our politics by first looking at global power relations, then US power relations, followed by power relations in our com-munities, and finally, what work we as activists should take up to help change these power imbal-ances.

      Today most workshop participants start their work with an "I" statement: How do I feel? What are my particular experiences? What are my skills and chal-lenges? And then they slowly build their analysis out to a global world view. What impact does this have on exercise creation?

   b. 'Back in the Day' most Third World national libera-tion struggles that were winning against U.S. impe-rialism around the world were governed by Marxist-Leninist political analyses and strategies. Most white anti-racist solidarity activists took our revolutionary cues from these winning movements, and believed we were 'correct' to do so.

Today most college-educated white workshop participants have learned to view the political and ideological world through the lens of 'post-modernism,' which was founded by anti-Marxists and based on a belief that there are no political truths, only individuals' diverse perspectives. What impact does this culture clash have on curriculum?

c. 'Back in the Day' many white solidarity activists tended to organize ourselves in democratic centralist organizations with strong leadership and high expectations of discipline. We tried to mirror the strengths of national liberation movements, which were involved in open warfare with US imperialism.

Today many or most young white social justice activists have been strongly influenced by feminist and anarchist organizational structures, which often value peer learning, collective decision making, and collaborative leadership. How can we create curriculum that is respectful of this democratic culture while challenging the cultural arrogance of some of the white movement's assumptions and values?

d. 'Back in the Day' political alliances and other organizing strategies tended to put more weight on having a similar political line: analysis and strategy. We focused more on results and effects.

Today many white activists put as much or more weight on personal relationships with individual organizers. They tend to put as much or more emphasis on the process by which decisions and actions are made as on the results of those decisions and actions. What kinds of curriculum can challenge participants to evaluate both processes and results equally as needed?

e. 'Back in the Day' white middle class anti-racist solidarity activists were often able to do our work
without worrying about paying huge debts to
banks for our college education; and white working class folks were still able to guarantee that their
children would have a better life financially than
they did.

Today though white activists still have far more
financial flexibility and access to networks of
white class privilege than activists of color, their
time of relative financial 'freedom' is much
shorter. And white working-class folks have seen
dramatic losses of jobs, income, and homes, with
no basis for hoping that their children will have
a better life.

How can our curriculum take account of the
shrinking material benefits of white privilege in
this neo-liberal era of global imperialism?

f. 'Back in the Day' white activists and activists of
color believed that the revolution was around the
corner so our pace of activity was frantic. Many of
us felt we weren't serious revolutionaries if we
worried about 'taking care of ourselves.'

Today many white activists prioritize taking care of
themselves as revolutionary work, a way to stay in
for the long haul. They prioritize having a more balanced life, with time for friends and relaxation, as
well as paid work and political activities. How do
we develop a rigorous, tough curriculum which
also respects the desire for a balanced life?

2. *In the work of training white anti-racist solidarity
organizers, how can CWS follow the effective organizing strategy of starting where people are at while*

maintaining strong anti-racist principles of keeping white people focused on the task of challenging our white privilege?

a. CWS analyzed the social location of non-ruling class (i.e., poor, working and middle class) white people as being both oppressed and privileged. We are oppressed by class, gender, sexual orientation, age, politics, and physical ability, but we are privileged by race in relation to all peoples of color.

   Many white social justice activists come into political consciousness through the experience of their own oppression. How can an anti-racist pedagogy of the privileged be created which can respectfully move activists from identity politics to solidarity politics?

b. CWS had a race-centered analysis. Like the People's Institute which inspired CWS, we saw racism as a major (not the only) barrier to building grassroots multi-racial alliances that could bring fundamental change to this country.

   Many white participants in the workshop held an intersectionality analysis. They saw racism, patriarchy, classism, and heterosexism as interrelated and equally powerful systems of oppression in the US. How can an anti-racist pedagogy of the privileged respect different political analyses of workshop participants while holding fast to the workshop's fundamental political frames?

c. CWS's solidarity principles talked about 'respecting the leadership of people of color.' We distinguished 'respect' from 'following the leadership of people of color.' What kinds of tools can we use to create a pedagogy of solidarity and accountability that fosters respect of white activists for organizers of color, while also supporting the crucial role of critical thinking on the part of young white activists?

3. *CWS strongly believed in the importance of modeling effective, accountable, and solidarity-practicing leadership as a part of the leadership development of a new generation of solidarity organizers.*

   a. Effective leadership necessitates one-on-one relationships with participants. But CWS was never able to carry this out because for most of its herstory, CWS had one workshop coordinator and up to 40 participants.

   b. Accountable leadership requires being able to address daily problems that arise in a workshop on the spot. Because CWS had only one coordinator for most of its herstory, momentary decisions never had the crucial backing of several experienced souls collaborating together.

   c. Accountable leadership for young white activists necessitates having leaders who are both grounded in historical solidarity politics and practice, and in contemporary white activist sub-cultures. CWS tried to function without that real multi-generational leadership for most of its existence.

   d. Solidarity-practicing leadership is probably best modeled by a multi-racial team of workshop coordinators. CWS had that for only one of its thirteen workshop years.[10]

In spite of these serious, long term leadership problems, this coordinator made the decision, year after year, that it was better to have a CWS Workshop available, with all its problems, than none at all.

As I reflect on the many amazing, committed white anti-racist solidarity organizers who participated in a CWS workshop, and are now themselves modeling accountability and solidarity in grass-roots movements around the country, I believe that I made the right decision.

Transitions

In the spring of 2005, CWS held its last workshop.

I can now reflect somewhat calmly on the workshop's inability to meet the multi-faceted challenges of trying to create an anti-racist pedagogy for the privileged. At the time, I felt like my life as an anti-racist solidarity organizer was finished and that I was a failure. This self-definition as a 'failed revolutionary' was not a particularly functional place from which to ask the obvious question, 'So what do I do now?'

Katrina Solidarity Work

Katrina answered the question for me. Glued to my television in September of 2005, I sat in 'shock and awe' as I saw New Orleans nearly destroyed by a government-made disaster. I shook with rage as I watched desperate New Orleanians abandoned on their rooftops simply because they were Black. I sobbed when I heard Malik Rahim, cofounder of Common Ground, tell a KPFA radio interviewer that the police had turned away a whole carload of health workers and all their supplies because the emergency workers were African Americans.

At the same time, my email box was filled with messages from mostly white activists asking for others to join them to go to volunteer in New Orleans. Thousands of white activists have made that journey, and they've worked with grassroots groups, not with the Red Cross. They came with big hearts, wanting to help, some perhaps wanting an adventure. They came because they were able to. 'Have knapsack, will travel on a moment's notice' is a particular capacity that white and class privilege provides, especially to young adult activists who are healthy and do not yet have children.

These activists provided important relief services. Concentrating much of their work in the devastated Ninth Ward, they gutted houses, organized medical clinics, provided nourishing food and drinkable water, ran errands, set up computer communication systems, and created innovative child care and education projects. But for the most part they carried out their community work in total ignorance of the rich history of resistance to racism in New Orleans. They did not stop their work to listen to the stories of African-American residents. They did not respect the centuries-old African-American culture of New Orleans. And they often acted as if they knew what needed to be done, without first asking community residents what residents wanted to do.

Many grassroots activists of color in New Orleans began to express concerns about the behavior of white social justice volunteers. In response, experienced anti-racist organizers in New Orleans — mostly from the African-American-led People's Institute for Survival and Beyond and their white anti-racist collective, European Dissent — began to network with their counterparts around the country. Many of the national activists knew each other from CWS Workshops in San Francisco and from the national anti-racist movement building activities of the Catalyst Project, also based in San Francisco. In the language of the People's Institute for Survival and Beyond, these anti-racist organizers networked; they built a 'net that works.'

Out of dozens of cross-country phone conversations emerged a new anti-racist organizing strategy.

We would act in solidarity with the growing grassroots racial justice movement in New Orleans that was working for the 'right of return' of all 'internally displaced persons' to their home communities in New Orleans and the Gulf Coast.[11]

We would recruit experienced white anti-racist organizers to go to New Orleans to partner with local anti-racist organizers, and we would provide political support for these solidarity organizers in New Orleans.

We would collaborate closely with the People's Institute and European Dissent in their efforts to provide anti-racist political education and mentoring to white social justice volunteers, so that these volunteers might learn to do their work with accountability to the African-American community, and solidarity with local racial justice organizations led by organizers of color.

We would encourage these 'outside' anti-racist solidarity organizers to continue doing Katrina solidarity work when they returned to their home and campus communities.[12]

Out of this national anti-racist solidarity effort has emerged a new generation of white anti-racist organizers in New Orleans. This new generation gives me great hope for the future.

Learning from History:
The Legacies of the Black Liberation Movement
and the 'First,' 'Second,' and 'Third Reconstructions'

Many organizers affiliated with the movement for the right of return called this movement part of the 'Third Reconstruction.' They hoped that a Black Liberation Movement for justice, dignity and self-determination, led by residents forcibly displaced by US government policies, would bring on a new era of justice and democracy in the US, as did their ancestors in the eras of the First and Second Reconstructions.

The First Reconstruction (1865 – 1877) was initiated and inspired by the mass movement of formerly enslaved African Americans, in alliance with free African Americans and progressive whites, north and south. Together, this alliance created southern legislatures with substantial Black representation, built the first comprehensive free public school system in the US, and brought social welfare programs to both African Americans and poor whites for the first time in US history.

In 1877, the federal government abruptly ended this experiment in multi-racial grassroots democracy. They withdrew the US army from the south, disarmed all Black soldiers, and ignored — even supported — the vicious violence of the KKK, the lynching of thousands of African Americans, and the construction of almost a century of legal apartheid in the South.[13]

The Second Reconstruction (1955 – 1975) was the period of the Civil Rights and Black Power movements. Once again, African-Americans led a mass movement for dignity, human and civil rights, and self-determination. This time they built a broad multi-racial and multi-class alliance of millions of people: Latinos, Puerto Ricans, Asian-Americans and progressive whites. Once again, this alliance pressured the government to enact broad measures of racial and social justice. And it inspired new social justice movements: women's liberation, LGBT justice, anti-war, students and locally based grassroots organizing against poverty and for human rights.[14] Many people believed that it was possible that the U.S. could actually be radically transformed. As the title of a book on the period declared, there was "Revolution in the Air."[15]

Sadly, history repeated itself. Once again, the US government and its allies in the political parties and corporations crushed this liberation movement with betrayal and murderous violence. In 2009, we are still living through the aftermath of the near destruction of the Black Liberation Movement.

Learning from History?
The Roles of White Anti-Racist Solidarity Activists in the Third Reconstruction

Reading the tangled histories of racism and anti-racism in white social justice movements after both the First and Second Reconstruction periods suggests to me that many white activists in those movements at first worked in solidarity with African-Americans struggling for freedom. These activists learned vital organizing skills from their solidarity work, and then went back home to organize in their own communities.

Most of these white activists proceeded to build strong movements against their own oppression (class, gender, sexuality, social location or issue) at the expense of the concerns of the Black Liberation movements which had taught them what it means to fight for justice, inspired their work, and opened the political space in which to win their own demands. The tiny minority of white activists who remembered their political roots were mostly marginalized and silenced.[16] The politics of the Challenging White Supremacy Workshop — its concept of 'Creating an Anti-Racist Agenda' and its emphasis on solidarity with radical grassroots organizations of color — was a direct response by its cofounders to our first-hand experiences of these betrayals in the aftermath of the Second Reconstruction.

Nearly three decades later there is a new white anti-racist movement in this country. It is young and fragile, but it is national, growing, and one of its epicenters is New Orleans. Another is the Bay Area, where the Catalyst Project is beginning the second season of its path-breaking 'Anne Braden Training Program' for white social justice activists at the time of the writing of this chapter.[17]

I believe that the new generation of white anti-racist solidarity activists has both the tools and the demonstrated commitment to make a new history as part of the Third Reconstruction. They have the capacity to stay with the struggle as long as it takes.

That's why I am so hopeful. The work has been passed on.

NOTES

1.   See Dan Berger, *Outlaws of America: The Weather Underground and the Politics of Solidarity* (Oakland, CA: AK Press, 2006); *Enemies of the State: Interviews with Anti-Imperialist Political Prisoners Marilyn Buck, David Gilbert and Laura Whitehorn* (New York: Resistance in Brooklyn, 1998). Reprinted as *Enemies of the State* (Montreal: Abraham Guillen Press, 2001); *Prairie Fire: The Politics of Revolutionary Anti-Imperialism,* the *Political Statement of the Weather Underground; Breakthrough,* the *Political Journal Of Prairie Fire Organizing Committee;* and *No KKK! No Fascist USA!,* the newsletter of the John Brown Anti-Klan Committee.

2.   The People's Institute for Survival and Beyond, an anti-racist training organization based in New Orleans, defines *accountability* as:

> "... a position by which one will be held in check or account for one's decisions and actions...the acceptance of a role fits within a cultural, political, and social perspective that leads to the liberation of peoples of color from racism, oppression and cultural subordination. It requires a commitment to the vision of African Americans and other oppressed peoples to assume self-determination over those areas deemed by them to directly affect their lives."
>
> (Definition heard at an Undoing Racism™ Workshop by the People's Institute.)

European Dissent, the anti-racist white organization affiliated with the People's Institute, reminded me - through their newsletter *The Journey of European Dissent: A journal dedicated to building an anti-racist white culture in the United States; Volume 1, Issue 1* (New Orleans, May 1997) and working drafts of their *Mission Statement of European Dissent, New Orleans;* (November 1996 and May 1997) — that a key aspect of 'accountability' is *commitment.* Some expressions of commitment are:

• Among a group of white anti-racist activists, taking a stand against racism, in both personal and public lives; being honest, trusting, respectful and caring of each other; and supporting members of the group on their anti-racist paths;

• Supporting and respecting the group by coming to meetings regularly, carrying out assigned tasks, bringing in new members, and working to maintain the group's integrity;

• Working with other white people to respectfully challenge racism, promote anti-racist culture and networks;

• With people of color, accepting leadership of people of color while defining within the allied group what precisely accepting 'leadership' really means.

3.   Read Catherine's essay at
     www.cwsworkshop.org/katrinareader/node/404.

4. Proposition 187 asserted that immigrants without papers could not get health care or receive an education, and would have made health workers and teachers into immigration cops, reporting immigrants to the Immigration and Naturalization Services for deportation. Proposition 209 made it illegal to utilize affirmative action programs for people of color and white women to challenge inequities in jobs, education, and public contracts in California.

5. SOUL's website is www.schoolofunityandliberation.org.

6. Critical Resistance's website is www.criticalresistance.org.

7. For a copy of CWS's 'Racial Justice Program' booklet, please email cws@igc.org.

8. For a typical workshop agenda, see www.cwsworkshop.org.

9. For more details on the agenda for this training program, please email Sharon at cws@igc.org.

10. Elizabeth 'Betita' Martinez co-coordinated the workshop for the Spring session of 2001. As a co-coordinator of the Institute for MultiRacial Justice, she recruited activists of color, and CWS recruited predominantly white activists. We planned our agenda topics collaboratively, but with different emphases. The two groups of participants met together every other week. Alternate weeks featured separate meetings with separate emphases appropriate to each group's participants.

    At the end of the workshop session, CWS participants evaluated their time spent with the Institute's participants as vital to their learning experiences. But the participants of color in the Institute's workshop evaluated their time spent jointly with the white activists as mostly wasted. They requested an entirely separate workshop for the coming fall. This was one more lesson for us as coordinators about the challenging work of attempting to build and strengthen multi-racial relationships that involve white activists!

11. 'Internally Displaced Persons' is a United Nations Human Rights designation for people displaced by war or natural disaster from their homelands, but who are still in their country of residence. Under the UN Treaty, to which the U.S. is a signatory, Internally Displaced Persons have the right to return to their home communities, and to receive adequate restitution from the central government. For more information, please check out the website of the U.S. Human Rights Network: www.ushrnetwork.org.

12. For some eloquent accounts of this work, see www.cwsworkshop.org/katrinareader. Click on 'Anti-Racist Solidarity: Perspectives and Tools.' Check out the organizational accounts by European Dissent, the Catalyst Project, and the Anti-Racist Working Group. For individual reflections by members of these organizations, read the essays by Ingrid Chapman, Catherine Jones, Rachel Luft, Molly McClure and Pamela Nath.

13. The classic account of the Reconstruction period is W.E.B. Du Bois, *Black Reconstruction in America, 1860 - 1880* (New York: Atheneum, 1973).

14. The term 'The Second Reconstruction' is taken from Manning Marable's *Race, Reform, and Rebellion: The Second Reconstruction and Beyond in Black America, 1945–2006*, 3rd ed. (Jackson: University Press of Mississippi, 2007). Books on the 1960s are too numerous to mention here. I have my favorites and would be happy to share a bibliography with you. Email me at cws@igc.org.

15. Max Elbaum, *Revolution in the Air: Sixties Radicals Turn to Lenin, Mao and Che* (New York: Verso Books, 2002).

16. For a history of this phenomenon, check out Robert and Pam Allen's *Reluctant Reformers: Racism and Social Reform Movements in the United States* (Washington, DC: Howard University Press, 1974). See also the path-breaking analysis and strategy developed by SNCC, the Student Non-Violent Coordinating Committee. In 1966, SNCC became an organization advocating Black Power. In an illuminating article, SNCC chairman Stokely Carmichael explained the multiple aspects of Black Power as SNCC understood it, and why they had asked white activists and supporters of SNCC to go organize against racism in their own communities, where racism is located, in order to be able to help build the kinds of multi-racial alliances that could effectively challenge the white supremacy system in the U.S. See Stokely Carmichael, "What We Want: SNCC Chairman Talks about Black Power," *New York Review of Books,* September 22, 1966.

17. The Catalyst Project's website is www.collectiveliberation.org.

Chapter Nine

Liberated Narratives: Being Accountable for Self, Friendship, and Community

The Alliance for Racial and Social Justice

> *The power and privilege of whiteness is rooted in coloniza-*
> *tion and the colonizing process of de-culturization*
> *renders white privilege invisible to white people.*
>
> Nocona Pewewardy and Margaret Severson, "A Threat to Liberty"

> *Colonization is embedded in our institutions*
> *and is a powerful psychic navigator*
> *of personal and social relations.*
>
> (ibid)

The ever evolving story of accountability for self is a cornerstone of our organization. We see it as critical to creating the fairness and equity we seek in the world. We are pleased to share how this concept has developed with our grassroots collective through a multi-layered process of dialogue, reflection and action. We are convinced that accountability is at the heart of social justice as well as our own "permanent liberation."[1]

In this chapter, through the narratives written by our members, we will describe our process of developing an internal system of accountability. These accounts are not linear or chronological in the sense that one happens after another in a neat order or that one member somehow evolves out of the process of accountability. Our experiences and challenges happened over months and years and involved a dialectical process beginning with confrontation and always culminating in action. And we know those experiences and challenges will begin again with another confrontation and unfolding process of reflection, dialogue, and action — looping around to similar pitfalls. This trajectory of learning and responsibility is more like a dynamic spiral than a line.

The Alliance for Racial and Social Justice (ARSJ) is a diverse, liberation-based, anti-racism organization founded on the principles of restorative justice.[2] Our primary purpose is to form a collective across the spectrum of power, privilege, and oppression to work toward justice for all through political actions. The group uses the principles of critical consciousness;[3] restorative justice; Freirian theory; models of power, privilege and oppression; accountability; and action. In this chapter, among our narratives, we will offer the language, theory, and process that formed and continues to sustain ARSJ. We believe that our model for social justice work is both powerful and replicable.

The Recipe: Accountability as It Could/Should Be

As a social justice organization our mission and processes are manifest in our public work. For example, when Don Imus attacked the Rutgers University women's basketball team on his radio show, we followed as the media trivialized and whitewashed the assault. In response, we wrote an open letter to the local paper that suggested the accountability we wanted to see him take. In it, we included the reparations we thought fit his assaults:

While Don Imus viciously assaulted the Rutgers women's basketball team in PUBLIC, he was afforded a very PRIVATE and speedy apology (one in a long string of apparently unredemptive apologies) and subsequently awarded a judgement of $20,000 dollars for losing his job on the radio. This process robbed the women, the public and, incidentally, Mr. Imus, of an opportunity for a more authentic and healing process of accountability. Of course, for that process to take place it would have meant devoting time, something our "sound bite" culture is rarely willing to afford any process, even one that involves the taking of lives, and a public dialogue in the spirit of the Truth and Reconciliation Tribunal. Had Mr. Imus been required to submit to such a process, with authentic reflection and the help of a healing community to guide him, the following REPARATIONS might have been the result:

- Attend an anti-racist workshop (such as the Undoing Racism™ & Community Organizing Workshop created by the People's Institute for Survival and Beyond)
- Attend the White Privilege Conference to be held in Springfield, MA, in April 2008
- Donate $100,000 annually to a charity of the team's choice
- Underwrite 200 scholarships per year for girls of color to attend summer sports camps
- Finance graduate school for the entire Rutgers women's basketball team
- Use "my power and popularity for social justice moving forward in my career"

From this public representation of ARSJ's worldview, what is not so apparent is the humbling, ongoing accountability we learned to expect of ourselves. It is our collective's internal accountability that enables us to demand the kind of accountability we laid out for Don Imus and others.

Let the Games Begin

Our grassroots group did not start out as a collaborative collective with the critical consciousness and social justice agenda that we have now. We began as a diverse group formed to liberate ourselves from legacies of dominance and violence in our families. Our membership spanned the full range of socio-political identities around race, socioeconomic class, gender identification, and physical ability. We met regularly for mutual support and consciousness-raising around power and control in gender oppression. We shared our experiences of being assaulted by our partners and the biased, ineffective court systems.

In 2003, several of the white women in the group created a separate caucus to study and begin taking responsibility for our unearned white privilege. We had experienced first-hand how avoiding accountability for white privilege hurt our sisters and brothers of color and derailed our collective work. In our effort to understand institutional oppression and power, we started reading and discussing articles and books,[4] viewing videos, and attending lectures and demonstrations.

We brought what we learned back to the collective, engaging in dialogue and inquiry, coming to understand where we stood as individuals with respect to race, class, gender, and sexual orientation.[5]

Following is a partial narrative from a white woman participant describing her growing understanding of the larger context and complexity of domestic violence outside the Euro-centric, dominant discourse:

> I was starting to receive an education about male power, privilege, and domination as I learned about the domestic violence in my family. (In the group) I learned that a young African-American teenager that I had befriended had also endured the same experiences. This amazed me since I had never been exposed to anyone other than white, Christian families in my life, and for the first time I realized that I was white. Most importantly I learned the

human experience of those different from myself. It was the total opposite of what I'd been told all along. The whole secrecy and shame of domestic violence is shared by many, and each of us has very different lasting effects.

We began to see that to hold those in power accountable we needed to understand oppression and accountability on multiple levels.

In addition to diversity across socio-political identities, we have worked to maintain a wealth of expertise in our membership — e.g., education, training, law, domestic violence, fundraising/friend-raising, public relations, social justice, community organizing, mental health, evidence-based policy making, teaching/education, organizational psychology, accounting, nursing, ministry, and web-based communications. Through collaborating in this diverse group with its rich social capital we began to appreciate how our own liberation is linked to the liberation of those who are both similar and different from ourselves.

For example, after attending an anti-racist training given by the Peoples Institute for Survival and Beyond, one of our Asian sisters, an upper middle class social worker who was pursuing a Ph.D. in Psychology, described herself within the context of this diversity in this way:

> When I was first with the women, I was seeing them so far away from myself. I was in a one-up position and arrogant. But after looking at the P & C Wheel[6] and reading 'Letter to Ma'[7] I realized that I was one of the oppressed women, just to a different degree... then [I began] experiencing more compassion towards them. During the Undoing Racism Workshop™, the whole panoply of institutionalized racism exploded before my eyes. I was really enraged. Until then, I had looked at racism as a personal thing...

Holding the universality of domestic violence while, at the same time, not minimizing the devastating consequences of white privilege and racism — in the world, and within our group — was not, and is not, easy. As Pewewardy and Severson explain, "Advocates for social justice can perpetuate oppression if they fail to recognize their privileges and their social location and function in society."[8]

As we sought to hold individuals and institutions accountable for gender oppression in the world, the white members began to understand the importance of openly challenging each other for abuses of white privilege and bringing these challenges back to the larger group. Stepping out of the collusion of white privilege by challenging other white people is difficult, and it is an obstacle we continue to face in our work. One story in particular illustrates a crossroad we met in the beginning of developing our process of internal accountability.

Sarah and Marcia, both white women and victims of domestic violence and active in challenging gender oppression, enjoyed a close friendship outside the social action group. One day, upon hearing a story of some young white men terrorizing black neighborhoods by driving by and throwing bananas out the window, Sarah off-handedly joked, "It should have been watermelons." Marcia, who had been supporting Sarah through her struggles as the victim of domestic violence and class discrimination, struggled with whether to ignore the assault, confront Sarah in private, or come back to the white caucus collective with the story. Marcia chose the last option, taking an important step in our process of internal accountability as a group.

As part of her accountability process, Sarah was supported to research slavery and the significance of watermelons in African-American history. This is what she brought back to the group to report and get support more publicly:

> You asked me to research the history of people of color and the connection to watermelon. I have since learned that watermelon was one of the only sources of water for the slaves working in the fields of the plantations in the south. The climate was very hot. The slave masters did not give out water freely to the slaves. The slave masters were very stingy, and from time to time they would give a watermelon to a family of slaves to share. It was a source of refreshment from the heat, yet many slaves were killed

for trying to take anything more than what they were given by their masters.

Sarah's reparations, engaged in for her own healing, included agreeing to go to her children's school to share this piece of history.

This story underpins our first steps in operationalizing awareness of white privilege. We asked ourselves to examine our actions with these fundamental questions in mind:

1. Do you hold yourselves accountable? How?

2. When there is collusion or derailment among the powerful at the expense of others, how do you move forward?

3. How do you move beyond the fear of looking bad or ill-informed or simply wrong?

4. With all the pitfalls in doing white privilege/anti-racist work, how do you still move forward and promote equity and fairness?

One white man described his experience of publicly examining his privilege:

> At an ARSJ meeting the leaders placed a large replica of the Hierarchy of Power, Privilege and Oppression on the floor.[9] Everyone in the group was asked to place themselves in the sections of the triangle that best represented their social, political, and economic standpoint at that time. The group included some youth of color with whom we frequently collaborate on social action activities; the adults of color who are variously connected to us; and those of us, white women and men, who had been examining our social and political status as part of our work in ARSJ. As a white male I put myself at the top of the pyramid. The ARSJ facilitator asked me, "Where are you facing?" I realized that I was looking ahead. Toward nothing. Toward other "imaginary white males" – white males perhaps with more power than me, those that I had to compete with. All the while, I was completely oblivious to the 30 other people in the room with less power. All of whom were standing below me.

Getting Serious

After two years meeting as a white caucus (which we called the Euro-American Privilege Group), we moved to create ARSJ as a non-profit organization. Guided by Almeida's work, and Freire's focus on praxis,[10] we made social political action central to our personal work toward liberation.[11] We launched individual projects in our communities and institutions — local PTAs, a Unitarian Universalist congregation, and in several of our workplaces, to name a few. We used our regular meetings to support one another in these efforts. Met by resistance on many levels, we soon became frustrated. We found that social action based on these personal agendas had limited impact and minimal potential for sustainability.

Ultimately, we found ourselves stymied by the overwhelming hurdles presented in doing anti-racist work piecemeal. As one white lesbian participant explains:

> Being part of a diverse collective was challenging at first. I was familiar with doing things by myself and challenging power by myself. I also was not familiar with collaborating, and acted impulsively and in isolation. I thought that collaborating was slow and painstaking and not potent or efficient. Slowly I began to unravel how my isolated choices and impulsive actions were useless, dangerous, and self-serving.
>
> In my privilege, I often took action to make me feel better; to elevate myself. Pretty twisted, huh? In ARSJ we learned to see and name and challenge this kind of privilege. We learned that it's a choice to act with privilege. I learned a lot about replacing traditional male norms with more collaborative efforts in doing social justice work. For example, our GLBTI student college group came up with a proposal to have a large doorway in the student center for folks to walk through on National Coming Out Day. As the advisor to the group, I was asked to approve the proposal. I quickly signed it without considering the ramifications for safety on a campus without any real welcoming culture for GLBTI folks.

> With challenges and support from ARSJ, I rescinded my
> approval of the coming out door and we had an infor-
> mational booth instead.

In 2005, having a clearer understanding of the necessity of responsible collective action, we decided to work together — sometimes in the homogeneous white caucus, and sometimes in the
diverse collective — on future projects. Further, through participation with the collective we were seeing that diverse coalitions
are exponentially more powerful than those with a homogenous
membership. Expanding this principle outward we began to seek
like-minded but differently situated groups to ally with.

For instance, we launched a voter registration drive in a poor,
racially diverse section of our county seat in collaboration with a
group of formerly incarcerated black youth. This collaboration gave
each of our groups credibility in various communities, and through
this alliance ARSJ gained authentic access to a population socially
distant from ourselves.[12]

Not Me! I Wasn't There When All That Went Down!

We began to acknowledge personal accountability for unearned
privileges that were predicated on the oppression of others, past
and present. We also saw the acts of holding others accountable as
part of our own liberation from the role of colonizer.

As part of our reparations for the unearned privileges we
leveraged throughout or lives, we wrote letters for external audiences, such as "letters to the editor" that challenged racist incidents
when we encountered them. Among other actions, we joined a
campaign aimed at *Vanity Fair* when, in their "Dame Edna" column, they printed:[13]

> Forget Spanish. There's nothing in that language worth
> reading except Don Quixote, and a quick listen to the CD
> of *Man of La Mancha* will take care of that. As for every-
> one`s speaking it, what twaddle! Who speaks it that you
> are really desperate to talk to? The help?

We demanded an apology and challenged the ignorant statements about the value of the Spanish language and contributions to civilization made by people from Spanish-speaking cultures. We labeled the column's content as racist and expressed our outrage and disdain.

Some of our efforts were directed at the following gaps in the child welfare system. We articulated our observations and concerns in a letter to representatives of Children's Rights Inc., a non-profit in New York overseeing the settlement that forced New Jersey's Division of Youth and Family Services (DYFS) to overhaul its services:

> Like you, we are invested in real change for New Jersey's children and families. We are concerned that children are caught in the crossfire of serious systemic dysfunction and neglect by the systems that have been created to help them. The current DYFS structure of wrap-around services and in-home therapy poses these issues to be addressed in the process of revamping services:
> A. Major players around the policy-making table have not changed.
> B. Services are not culturally competent, and are based on Eurocentric models.
> C. Batterers are not referred to ethical treatment.
> D. Domestic violence victims are referred to shelters while their children are usually referred to the mental health system and seen in individual therapy fracturing the treatment and the families.
> E. Referring to court appointed evaluators who employ the Parental Alienation Syndrome (PAS) diagnosis although it is discredited as junk science by the APA and barred as evidence in the Massachusetts and New York courts.
> All of these conditions threaten to further destabilize families already traumatized by violence.

Reversing the Mirror

Ongoing collaboration with those with different privileges than we individually enjoyed increased our awareness and reinforced our thinking that to hold larger systems accountable we needed to maintain a rigorous, well articulated-system of accountability among and over ourselves. Incorporating the principles and tools gleaned from our expertise in domestic violence and male privilege and readings on restorative justice, we asked our members of color to function as an advisory board. In this role, they could, at their discretion, be part of our broader social action without feeling the sole burden of accountability often felt by people of color in heterogeneous groups out in the world, and historically. They agreed to monitor and mentor our progress and inform us of opportunities for anti-racist work that we may be missing. They also remained integral to the internal accountability of our group, again, without feeling the sole burden of holding white people accountable for our abuses of privilege. In other words, ARSJ's mission came to include creating and sustaining within our group the meaningful change, liberation, and accountability we wanted to create in the world.

The Better We Get, the Worse It Looks

As our friends and allies of color saw us become more aware and willing to challenge each other on our white supremacy and misuse of white privilege, they were more willing to confront us when we offended against them. We were creating a safer space for them to point out our abuses of power and privilege, and they could count on us to start from the premise (often reversed in the larger world) that if they saw racism — even if we didn't — they were more likely to be right. This assured them of further dialogue, inquiry, and action. Although some of these challenges looked like things were getting worse, in fact we came to see we were being exposed to the truth of how deep privilege and its underbelly — oppression — are in our lives.

We continued to collaborate across socio-political identity lines while attempting to make inroads on the larger society. But we were — and are — not immune from making mistakes. Ignited by missteps and personal assaults toward the members of color, ARSJ's white members broke off from the diverse collective to reflect, take action, and construct reparations when appropriate. The white members learned to support one another to view these challenges as a sign of our growing sophistication about our privilege and its harmful effects.

We saw that more rigor was needed, particularly in identifying the elusive intersections of institutionalized racism, homophobia, and white supremacy. We began formalizing our system of internal accountability. We already understood that "accountability begins with acceptance of responsibility for one's actions and the impact of those actions upon others."[14] This meant moving beyond trying to avoid making "mistakes" that would offend or exploit our colleagues and friends of color to a more robust construct.

We admitted to ourselves and each other that in one way or another — and because of the deeply rooted and historical structures of colonization, patriarchy, capitalism, and Christian hegemony — we assaulted our friends of color every day. There was never a time, we realized, that NOT extending the dialogue and inquiry about white supremacy and accountability to ourselves would be an option or something to deprioritize in our work. We were understanding at a deeper level what Crenshaw described in her "Mapping the Margins": "Ignoring the differences within groups frequently contributes to tensions among [the original] groups."[15]

Drawing from the experience of activists in the field of domestic violence, we knew the need for "going public" when holding others accountable.[16] We chose to create equity among us by publicly challenging those who assaulted members of our circle. We also contextualized the assaults in a social and political context. We used letter writing in our meetings as documentation of our accountability and as partial reconciliation for our assaults.

Creating this structure for internal accountability is a cornerstone of our process: "It moves beyond blame and guilt. It results in reparative action that demonstrates empathic concern for others by making changes that enhance the quality of life for all involved parties."[17] One example that crossed racial and gender boundaries can be traced in Brad's story of accountability as a dialectical process of critical consciousness, reflection, and action, moving to increased critical consciousness:

> I felt I got a lot out of the traditional diversity trainings I received at work. However, I did not see anything I needed to do differently in my life. I think the only thing that I took away is the need for me to actively seek out diverse candidates for jobs. I went on with my privileged life, feeling better about myself because I was aware.
>
> Then I met my wife, Juanita. Juanita is Columbian, and at first I did not think that was anything to care about. In fact, the first time someone referred to us as an interracial couple I was surprised! This lack of awareness and lack of support disconnected me from what she was going through in life as a Latina woman. It entitled me to assault her with a potpourri of comments. It came to a head when I shook the hand of a former boss of hers whose sexual and racial harassment at work caused her to have panic attacks so severe she required hospitalization.
>
> Slowly — very slowly — I felt the need to do something different. I reached out to our Unitarian Universalist congregation. I was really excited about joining an anti-racism group and hoped to make some changes. I soon found out that while I had found a place of people who were liberal and agreed in principle with anti-racism work, they were not really ready to fully tackle their own privilege.
>
> I was doing most of the work in isolation, cherry-picking my projects and being the one to judge how it was going. It was also easy for me to use time as a defining factor; this justified dropping projects when other things in my life were too hectic.
>
> Still it was a comfortable place to be for me. Then I assaulted my family again. I was on the beach with my wife and kids and a close friend. I made a racist joke about a group of white guys, saying that they were part of a "Mexican drug cartel." Immediately, I knew this was off, but it took a while to see how these patterned assaults were more likely

to occur if I remained isolated and not truly connected to racial justice. I needed to be connected to a group that would challenge and continually hold me accountable.

Sometimes, we made mistakes that were either patronizing and/or dangerous to our allies of color, as illustrated by the following example:

> When that white woman — who had been part of our collective for several years, and benefited personally from her participation — decided not to join the ARSJ or do any work around white privilege, I was hurt and angry. I laid into her and revealed a mutual friend of color's disappointment in her without letting the woman of color know that I had done that. The collective helped me not to stand in judgment or cast out those who don't want to do the work but rather to stay in the discomfort and recruit others. The fact that I have a choice is a privilege.

While this example fell into the category of patronizing, as we reflected on the incident, we saw that the white woman had been standing on the back of her sister of color and placed her out front in the challenge instead of taking sole responsibility for how she was impacted by the other white woman's choices.

In addition to deepening and expanding our understanding about white privilege and intersecting oppressions, we began to systematically include reparations as part of our own accountability. Current writings on restorative justice define it as "repairing the losses suffered by victims, holding offenders accountable for the harm they have caused, and building peace within communities."[18] All the parties with a stake in a particular offense come together to resolve the impact of the offense and its implications for the future by identifying and taking steps to repair harm.[19] Sometimes repairing harm is limited to public acknowledgment of the offense and an apology. But we knew that true healing on both sides of the offense requires an exchange of concrete goods or services. It is easy to see how repaying stolen (or withheld) money or beginning to take responsibility for making the meals in a family where you have expected to be catered to would be healing for the victim. But for true healing, reparations are a necessary component for the perpetrator, as well.

In keeping with our understanding of reconciliation, we are committed, as we move forward, to keeping alive the tenet expressed by Wole Soyinka in *The Burden of Memory, The Muse of Forgiveness:* "Reparations are the missing link between Truth and Reconciliation."[20] Reparations came in the form of making meals, helping with construction projects, learning about and volunteering time to the communities and causes that represented those we hurt, and becoming active members of non-profit groups formed for the empowerment of marginalized people, to name a few. These reparations came — and must come — no matter how busy our lives, or our track record for "good" work in the world, even deadlines associated with our anti-racist work. There is no short-cut for true healing, no excuse for not making meaningful and responsible reparations.

Big Picture/A Million Small Wounds

We continued to read and engage in dialogue and inquiry while intervening with larger systems. We analyzed how they undermined any real systemic change and looked for parallels in our own interactions. We began examining our own impulse to colonization. As we worked together, ARSJ members became sensitive to the subtle ways that we marginalized and exploited the women of color who had stood by us for so long. We wrote letters, as historical documents, when there was a pattern of assault for which we were responsible. We included incidents in which we made those who were "other" and their histories of oppression and exploitation invisible, and noted ignoring when our privilege was the inverse of that exploitation. We interrogated the multiple identities that we all represented around class, race, gender, ethnicity, and religion. We interrogated our misuse of heterosexist privilege when appropriate.

For example, a heterosexual woman in the group, Maureen, had recently been challenged about marginalizing the experience of one of her lesbian friends, Alice. Attempting to repair that friendship, Maureen made plans to join Alice and others at a performance by Kate Clinton, a lesbian comedian. Maureen had started dating a man. The night of the performance, she declined Alice's invitation to join her and her lesbian friends for coffee after the show, saying that she had to rush, that she was looking forward to having sex with her boyfriend. The ARSJ circle asked Maureen to consider how her heterosexual privilege dictated her decision to prioritize her liaison over joining Alice and her lesbian friends to discuss the comedy act. Her choice in this context was emblematic of her heterosexist lack of respect for the significance of her friendship and her lesbian friend's connections.

In another case, Sandra, a highly educated white woman from a working-class background, demonized one of our members of color, Juliet, her long-time friend. Juliet, a successful Latina physcian with her own practice, traveled extensively and went out dancing regularly with Sandra. Sandra began to disparage Juliet among their mutual friends. Through ARSJ's internal accountability, Sandra realized this demonization was rooted in colonization. Her accountability included writing a letter publically taking responsibility for her actions and dedicating time to a local Latina group in her region. She also wrote a narrative reflecting on her process:

> The vicious rumors I was spreading about Juliet (in the guise of wanting to help her) were all founded in a colonial analysis of Latinas and served to leverage my status in the group. I was saying she couldn't manage her money, was overly sexual with the men we met, and was prioritizing getting connected to men (others of power) at the expense of our connection — all ways that Latinas are frequently disparaged in the white canon. Juliet challenged me and made her challenge public in the ARSJ collective. I had been doing anti-war demonstrations and had shifted from a corporate job to getting a Ph.D. in public health (a very social justice oriented context). Given my self concept, I was stunned that I did this to Juliet.

> I felt I was done with my white privilege work. No way could I have been acting racist! Juliet had told me privately that I sexualized her…and was getting really racist toward her. I dismissed her feedback. I totally misused my whiteness to mishandle it. I filtered it through my experience, disregarding hers I wrote a letter of apology and read it in community. It made me sit with myself. I needed to get humble again. And holy cow, it was like I lit a fire. I realized, "Oh, my g_d, I have the power to destroy someone."

The collective helped Sandra to see the connection between her personal assaults and the long history of colonization of Latinas. At the same time they pointed out that these assaults could not "destroy" this resilient woman who had thrived in spite of multiple assaults from every quarter. Sandra's narrative continues:

> One of the easiest steps is writing the apology letter. The hardest thing is to show up and not to be victimized, to not default to "I feel so guilty…" or "I can't do this work…" or "I am not competent." And also, to deal with the reaction of the white community, let alone the community of color. I learned we are a collective. Some of us started in different spaces and we all feel it. I think about that scene in the movie *Crash* when the policeman kills the youth of color: He would never have had that access if he hadn't presented himself as an ally.

Through our process, we came to understand how critical it is that our consciousness go beyond recognition of black and white and into an analysis of complex identities of class, ethnicity, and sexual orientation — the multiple and layered intersections of access and oppression.

Larger, Ongoing Reparations

It is important here to acknowledge our ongoing, social justice effort — WATCH NJ — as it exemplifies our commitment to reparations to the larger community. WATCH NJ is a Participatory Action Research (PAR) collaboration between volunteers monitoring domestic violence (restraining/protective order) hearings in Middlesex County, and other concerned advocates and citizens who have been working against significant odds to end domestic violence in NJ and elsewhere.

Many of us had experienced gender bias in the courts. As we worked with men and women of different socio-political and economic status, we came to understand the multiple layers of oppression they encountered in the family court system. As part of our own healing, resistance, and reparations for our unearned privilege, we decided to launch a court watch in the NJ courts. Launched in 2005, WATCH NJ was created and advanced by ARSJ as part of its mission to increase public engagement to collaboratively transform systems of oppression and injustice, and to do so in a responsible and sustainable way through collective reflection and action across difference.

WATCH NJ's intentions for dissemination of what we have learned from Court Watch are:

- To duplicate the critical consciousness of the WATCH NJ process in other communities — making the public aware of its rights and providing a forum for learning about the limitations of the justice system.

- To create a process of accountability with the public which can then hold the judicial system to a higher standard of legal and statutory compliance — using a public health (environmental) model in which information and morality is reshaped at the individual, family, community, policy, and global levels.

We attribute sustaining the court watch to our commitment to continued trainings that provide critical consciousness — dialogue and reflection on the inherent complexities of power and privilege for our volunteers and ourselves. We are not there just to collect data or to influence small, temporary changes. Our goal is systemic change and liberation for ourselves and all people.

Conclusion

A great deal is written about restorative justice as a response to crime.[21] ARSJ embraces these principles, and operationalizes them within its nonprofit structure. ARSJ's activities and programs respond to social injustices by involving diverse membership, engaging stakeholders and evaluating their intentions and commitment to social justice, and identifying and taking steps to repair harm. ARSJ's mission is grounded in the morality of restorative justice — transforming the traditional relationship between communities, their governance, and responses to injustice. ARSJ's unique contribution is a highly developed process of accountability as viewed through the lens of multiple intersecting disparities of power.

In doing this work, ARSJ members have endeavored to mitigate the "tension within groups that arises from tension among groups at a deep and subtle level."[22] We have come to understand that our work in the larger world will be ineffective and/or dangerous if we don't continue to interrogate ourselves and each other about all of the insidious ways we have been socialized to rank, despise and exploit others with impunity. We have come to realize that our personal liberation is intrinsically tied to those whom we had been socialized to think are different. We now see that our work as the ARSJ collective will be sabotaged if we do not understand the power of misogyny, white supremacy, and homophobia. And we know that our own healing and liberation are inextricably entwined with the work to repair the injustices at every level perpetrated in the past and maintained in the present. It is our mission to align ourselves with those whose access to power and resources is curtailed and to work to resist the forces that maintain an unjust system of allocation.

Notes

1. Paulo Freire, *Education for a Critical Consciousness* (New York: Continuum International Publishing Group. 1974)

2. Prison Fellowship International, Centre for Justice and Reconciliation http://www.restorativejustice.org/university-classroom/01introduction

3. Paulo Freire, Pedagogy of the Oppressed (New York: Continuum International Publishing Group, 2000), 51. Critical consciousness refers to the development of an awareness of the sociopolitical context of daily life; i.e. power, as distributed in its simplest terms, between the oppressor and the oppressed, conveying an awakening among the oppressed and their allies to praxis or "reflection and action upon the world in order to transform it."

4. Works by Paolo Freire, Rhea Almeida, Audre Lorde, Arundati Roy, bell hooks, Martin Luther King, and Gandhi, among others.

5. Freire, *Pedagogy of the Oppressed;* Freire, *Education for a Critical Conciousness.*

6. First appearing in *Domestic Violence on the Margins,* ed. Natalie Sokoloff with Christina Pratt (Rutgers University Press, 2005), 301-320. The Power and Control Wheel used by ARSJ is an adaptation of work by Ellen Pence, founder of the Domestic Abuse Intervention Project (DAIP) in Duluth, Minnesota.

7. *This Bridge Called My Back: Writings by Racial Women of Color,* ed. Cherríe Moraga and Gloria Anzaldúa, (New York: Kitchen Table—Women of Color Press, 1983).

8. Nocona Pewewardy and Margaret Severson, "A Threat to Liberty: White Privilege and Disproportionate Minority Incarceration," *Journal of Progressive Human Services,* 14 (2): 53-74 (2003).

9. Rhea V. Almeida, Lynn Parker and Kenneth Dolan-Del Vecchio; *Transformative Family Therapy: Just Families in a Just Society* (Boston: Allyn & Bacon: 2007).

10. Freire, *Pedagogy of the Oppressed,* 51. Praxis is defined as "reflection and action upon the world in order to transform it"

11. Rhea V. Almeida, "Creating Collectives of Liberation," in *Feminist Family Therapy: Empowerment in Social Context,* ed. Thelma Jean Goodrich and Louise B. Silverstein (Washington DC: American Psychological Association 2003).

12. Lani Guinere and Gerald Torres, *The Miner's Canary: Enlisting Race, Resisting Power, Transforming Democracy* (Cambridge, MA: Harvard University Press, 2003).

13. Dame Edna [John Barry Humphries] "Ask Dame Edna," *Vanity Fair,* February 2003.

14. Pilar Hernández, Rhea V. Almeida and Kenneth Dolan Del-Vecchio, "Critical Consciousness, Accountability, and Empowerment: Key Processes for Helping Families Heal," *Family Process,* 44 (1), 105-130: (2005).

15. Crenshaw, K., "Mapping the Margins: Intersectionality, Identity Politics, and Violence against Women of Color" in *The Public Nature of Private Violence,* ed. Fineman, M. and Mykitiuk, R., (New York, NY: Routledge, 1994).

16. Rhea V. Almeida and Judith Lockard, "The Cultural Context Model: A New Paradigm for Accountability, Empowerment, and the Development of Critical Consciousness against Domestic Violence," in *Domestic Violence at the Margins: Readings on Race, Class, Gender, and Culture,* ed. Natalie J. Sokoloff (New Brunswick, NJ: Rutgers University Press, 2005).

17. Pilar Hernández, Rhea V. Almeida and Kenneth Dolan Del-Vecchio, "Critical Consciousness."

18. Prison Fellowship International, "Restorative Justice Online: Introduction," Center for Justice and Reconciliation http://www.restorativejustice.org/intro (accessed December 1, 2007) James Ptacek, ed., "Feminism, Restorative Justice, and Violence against Women," Violence Against Women [Special issue], 11(5): (2005).

19. Prison Fellowship International, "Restorative Justice Online"; James Ptacek, ed., "Feminism, Restorative Justice, and Violence."

20. Wole Soyinka, *The Burden of Memory, the Muse of Forgiveness,* (New York: Oxford University Press, 1999).

21. Prison Fellowship International, "Restorative Justice Online"; James Ptacek, ed., "Feminism, Restorative Justice, and Violence"; Sarah Curtis-Fawley and Kathleen Daly, "Gendered Violence and Restorative Justice: The Views of Victim Advocates,"; C. Quince Hopkins and Mary P. Koss, "Incorporating Feminist Theory and Insights into a Restorative Justice Response to Sex Offenses" in *Violence Against Women,* [Special issue], 11(5): (2005).

22. Crenshaw, K., "Mapping the Margins: Intersectionality, Identity Politics, and Violence against Women of Color."

Chapter Ten

Powerful Partnerships: Transformative Alliance Building

Shelly Tochluk and Cameron Levin, AWARE-LA/RJA

Introduction

We offer this chapter in hope that our experience can benefit others dedicated to participating in effective multi-racial alliances for social, economic, environmental, and racial justice. For clarity, we state our intentions upfront: *The purpose of this chapter is to 1) share with readers, especially white anti-racists, the way a common approach to accountability inhibits our development of a white anti-racist identity and derails social justice efforts and 2) outline a vision for how we can participate in the formation of more productive, stronger multi-racial alliances.* We would also like to mention that although this paper critiques the pattern of accountability with which we are most familiar, we in no way mean to suggest that general principles of accountability should be abandoned. We recognize that some people have been successfully creating healthy alliances that have accomplished important justice work within the context of accountability for years. Unfortunately, our collective experience leads us to believe these are the exceptions rather than the rule. Because of this, we find it necessary to offer a critique of relationships wherein white people narrowly focus on one-sided accountability to people of color and then describe a different approach leading toward what we call Transformative Alliance Building.

Who are We? AWARE-LA and RJA

AWARE-LA (Alliance of White Anti-Racists Everywhere-Los Angeles) is an all-volunteer group of white people working to combat racism within our selves, communities, and the world. The leadership team of AWARE-LA includes eight members, each with five to ten years or more experience working to understand and dismantle racism, white privilege, and white supremacy. AWARE-LA recognizes the need to maintain close relationships with people of color and build multi-racial alliances. For that reason, the group initiated the development of a multi-racial, Racial Justice Alliance (RJA) that includes AWARE-LA members and people of color from various social justice networks in the Los Angeles area.

How Does This Chapter Reflect a Multi-racial, Collaborative Effort?

Two members of AWARE-LA's leadership team took responsibility for conducting interviews and writing this chapter. The primary author spoke with three white AWARE-LA members and three people of color from the RJA, and then both authors engaged in cycles of questioning, writing, presenting, and editing to get feedback from the AWARE-LA leadership team, members of the multi-racial RJA team, and other people of color with whom they share a professional relationship. The three white people interviewed include co-author Cameron Levin, Jason David, and Susan Goldberg. The three people of color include Salina Gray, Diane Burbie, and Hamid Khan. The authors intentionally chose three women and three men to participate as well as three people of color with diverse racial/ethnic backgrounds and experiences.

The development of the model that emerged from the findings of the interviews has progressed through cycles of review in a multi-racial context, as is evidenced by the historical timeline presented below.

Why Are We Contributing to This Book?

AWARE-LA began building alliances with people of color after its first year of existence, in 2005. This first effort involved creating a multi-racial group intended to produce a one-day racial justice dialogue in Los Angeles. This group did not sustain itself and disbanded after less than one year. Following the 2006 White Privilege Conference, the leadership team of AWARE-LA agreed that it was time to build a Racial Justice Accountability Board (RJAB) to serve as a mechanism of accountability to people of color and a space to begin developing its formal, multi-racial work. However, as people of color attended initial dialogues, many were uncomfortable with the approach to accountability to which AWARE-LA members were accustomed. These people of color bristled at the idea of being an approving body and named problems with the use of one-sided accountability guidelines. Many spoke of the dehumanization they had seen it engender, destructive effects on relationships, and perpetuation of oppressive systems. They argued that we needed to build our alliance on equal footing, with *all* parties being accountable for confronting their privileges and acting as honestly and humanely with each other as possible. This, they said, is a more viable path toward productive alliances for social justice.

The RJA members called on the AWARE-LA leadership to take responsibility for holding *themselves* accountable for their own process and expressed dissatisfaction with the idea that people of color should carry the burden of monitoring white people's anti-racism work within the white community. Essentially, the people of color said they trust AWARE-LA's ability to work with white people and if the sole purpose of the RJAB was to hold AWARE-LA accountable, they wanted nothing to do with it. *(Note: We acknowledge that a group of people of color collectively vocalizing its trust in a group of white people doing anti-racism work with other white people is rare. But, this is the relationship AWARE-LA and the members of RJA have with one another.)*

Hearing from these people of color, AWARE-LA realized that in our context in Los Angeles, the accountability model within which many white anti-racists are trained — one in which one-sided accountability to people of color remains the overriding focus — was creating real barriers for us to do the work we collectively wanted to do. The AWARE-LA leadership team returned to the multi-racial group proposing to work toward "Accountable Alliance Building." Again, the people of color questioned our approach. After much discussion we understood that if white people's primary emphasis is on one-sided accountability to people of color, we will continue creating superficial relationships that lack deeply honest, meaningful dialogue.

This experience prompted us all — AWARE-LA and RJA — to look more closely at the dynamics existing within what we experience as the social justice movement's most prevalent form of accountability relationship. We now see that although many traditional principles of accountability ought to be retained as part of a trust-building process, multi-racial alliances will be stronger when they involve healthy relationships that invite each party to bring their full, honest selves to the table. With full recognition that there may be people who already create healthy, productive alliances in their own communities, we found it necessary to formally describe the development of this type of alliance relationship for ourselves. We call our model Transformative Alliance Building.

This approach, still in draft form, was originally unveiled in a workshop at the 2007 White Privilege Conference. AWARE-LA invited an early reviewer of this chapter, Jorge Zeballos, a regular presenter and co-facilitator of the people of color caucus at WPC, to be part of a dialogue whereby we would offer the model up for consideration. As Jorge was not a member of RJA during the interview and internal dialogue stage, he took on the role of critical observer within the facilitation team. Feedback from the conference work-shop was then used to refine the model and make necessary changes to better convey our essential findings.

Over the summer of that year, RJA decided that our approach should be presented anew at the following year's conference, but that this time the offering would come from a multi-racial team of AWARE-LA and RJA members in order to better represent our local-ized context. Over that next year, a team of four engaged in con-structive dialogue to further modify and refine our model and we then presented a new version at the 2008 White Privilege Con-ference. RJA later held a day-long workshop for continuing and new members in October 2008 in which we presented the model and considered how we can continue to refine the model and move the work forward. Twenty-eight individuals participated in the workshop — twenty-one people of color and seven AWARE-LA leadership members.

This chapter incorporates all feedback offered up through the October 2008 workshop. We hope that readers will recognize that we make no judgments or suggestions regarding how or why the patterns we identify have come into existence. We seek only to highlight what we have experienced and how we hope to move forward.

Principles of Accountability

It is important to re-state that we are not advocating that accountability guidelines be abandoned. The white people involved in this are *not* trying to get out of their responsibility to self-reflect and develop skills. In fact, we believe accountability guidelines are extremely valuable because white people's lack of sensitivity to race issues makes it essential that white people develop the ability to engage in relationships non-oppressively. We also believe that people of color should retain authority over naming what is racism and we recognize that trust between people of color and white people must continually be re-affirmed early in the relationship. Although we do not believe white people should be cast out and treated inhumanely when they make racist mistakes, we do recognize that people of color may understandably pull back trust when this occurs, and the responsibility falls on the white people involved to help rebuild that trust. For these reasons, accountability principles give directions for growth and are extremely useful tools.

On the other hand, the context in which many white anti-racists attempt to *live out* accountability statements can be destructive to relationships and social justice work. What we would like to highlight is that *principles of accountability are successfully enacted within ongoing relationships founded on mutual respect.* Without functional, healthy relationships, attempts to hold oneself to accountability guidelines can turn those very principles into static standards of behavior that can breed serious problems within real-life situations. For example, white anti-racists might have two respected colleagues of color asking for opposing actions simultaneously. In those situations, to whom is the white person more accountable? When is there room to question requests made by a person of color?

Unfortunately, we have seen a pattern time and time again where the ultimate goal of working toward social justice becomes lost and, instead, attention becomes singularly focused on questions of accountability. When entire relationships begin to center around this question, we find that they also tend to reinforce patterns that derive from our social conditioning within a society based in white supremacy. The shallow dialogue perpetuated by this narrow focus thwarts our efforts at building long-lasting relationships and, as a result, our justice efforts falter. With that said, we would like to offer a more complete explanation of the problems we have encountered.

When One-sided Accountability is the Sole Focus

There are many problems bred from relationships in which one-sided accountability becomes the focus. What we present here are four threads of criticism that emerged through our interview dialogues. In totality, they argue that these relationships unwittingly perpetuate our society's structures and create dysfunctional relationships that involve 1) inauthentic communication, 2) unhealthy white anti-racist people, 3) inherent inequality, and 4) ineffective collaborative practices. Although these four issues do not represent an exhaustive list, we believe they are significant enough to warrant serious questioning of the productivity of relationships wherein one-sided accountability is the overriding focus, displacing the real goal — working for social justice. We ask readers to open their hearts and minds to imagine to what degree their relationships and practices might involve some of the problematic dynamics we have experienced.

Inauthentic Communication

A primary barrier to developing productive alliance relationships is inauthentic communication. Because white anti-racists often interpret "living out accountability guidelines" as meaning that white people's attitudes and behaviors shall *always* be free of unconscious racism or enactments of privilege, white people can avoid saying anything that might reveal a lack of understanding. This translates into white people regularly holding back their thoughts and feelings within conversations — both with people of color *and* other white anti-racists.

When Susan spoke of what constitutes an unhealthy accountability environment, she said it is signaled by a sense that "there is never room to mess up" when engaged in relationships. She describes a destructive pattern that emerges when white people cannot break free from the internalized sense that they are constantly "walking on eggshells" or *"pins and needles,"* saying:

> I think unhealthy accountability has to do with this constant need to prove yourself by saying always the right thing and doing the right thing, even when those actions or words are not genuine. So, having a sense of being watched or almost a sense that the mistake is being waited on…whether it's waiting for your own self to mess up, or waiting for other people to mess up.

Essential to highlight is that this felt sense among many whites — that a mistake is being waited on — *may or may not* be supported by interactions with the people of color in their lives. Oftentimes, it is a white anti-racist who is waiting to pounce on another white person when an error occurs. Sometimes, the silencing is so profound that no verbal mistake can be made, and therefore the fear reflects only that individual's internalized anxiety. The essential point is that when white people feel that they must refrain from sharing their honest thoughts, the resulting inauthentic sharing is readily apparent to people of color and damages the potential for developing deep relationships.

Fundamentally, the sense that a "mistake is being waited on" often has a negative effect on the level of trust felt within relationships. Susan describes how white people's efforts to avoid mistakes in order to be seen as trustworthy can, in fact, end up eroding the very trust we seek to build.

> There's an assumption of the mistake and it's that "if you don't act in certain ways and say certain things, then I can't trust you." Yes, people's behavior and language is important. And yet, it ends up being twisted because then you are never being genuine. So how are you ever going to really have a relationship? So, it's a set-up. It comes from a place of trying to connect, but it ends up being an unfortunate set-up because you can't honestly connect because you're never honestly being who you are.

This lack of honest connection is disastrous for our common work of ending racism and white supremacy because these relationships are constantly on the brink of failure. Although we recognize that trust requires continuous work, we suggest that we need to consciously separate what it means to be accountable and trustworthy from what it means to make errors. If we do not do this, too many white anti-racists will continue to fear exposing their lack of understanding and therefore remain guarded and inauthentic.

Diane sums up the critique of inauthentic relationships that lack a foundation of 1) open communication, 2) deep dialogue, and 3) the acceptance that mistakes will occur with this statement:

> The list of [accountability] principles is like mom and apple pie. There's nothing wrong with the principles. But, it's not the principles that are broken; it's the relationship. It's the fact that you believe that we're going to do real changing stuff with superficial relationships with each other, and that ain't gonna happen.

Essentially, what we have found is that moving beyond superficial — and therefore fragile — relationships depends upon an approach to accountability that allows everyone to make mistakes, grow, and be challenged to further develop non-oppressive relational practices. Ultimately, all of us have been raised within intertwining systems of oppression. The degree to which each of us takes up responsibility for investigating how they have affected us and remaining accountable to non-oppressive principles is what will help us build deep relationships that allow for each person to be fully human and also retain a focus on social justice work.

Unhealthy White Anti-racist People

Within groups trying to disrupt systematic white supremacy, accountability can often mean that feelings, experiences, and perspectives of people of color should carry more weight than those of white people. This dynamic usually includes some underlying premises, such as the belief among *both* white people *and* people of color that 1) white people are inherently untrustworthy, 2) all white people will always be part of the problem, 3) white people are only legitimate allies deserving humane treatment if their anti-racist practice is flawless, and 4) white people should always defer to people of color. We acknowledge there may be many historical reasons for these beliefs to arise as well as internal psychological processes that reinforce them. However, whether they are overtly stated or subtly implied, when whites and/or people of color act in ways that promote these beliefs it encourages white people to feel more insecure, guilty, and worthless, and to avoid developing a healthy racial identity. Each of these results leads to particular problems.

A main issue is that if white people feel that they are essentially lesser partners in the fight against racism, they are not prompted to create a healthy, productive white anti-racist identity for themselves. Intending to actively work *against* the dominant white supremacist culture, many white anti-racists try to distinguish themselves from what are considered the norms of whiteness. Unfortunately, when white people lack a sense of wholeness and distance themselves from all things white, they often fall into troubling forms of cultural appropriation as they seek acceptance and validation from people of color. They often run toward the cultures of people of color they have learned to follow and this approval-seeking dynamic reinforces the sense that white people are too unstable and unhealthy to be trusted.

Salina recognizes the lack of healing involved and comments that one-sided accountability reinforces an unhealthy form of "deference." She states that she is uncomfortable with what comes with relationships wherein white people try to find personal validation by conforming to the wishes of people of color:

> I'm very uncomfortable when people walk on the proverbial pins and needles around me and do things because they feel that it's what I expect or want them to do. So, for me, I'd be more comfortable hanging out with an avowed racist than a bunch of mainstream whites who claim to be down, because claiming to be down often means to be culturally assimilated. Often it's them using language that they feel will make me comfortable, it's doing and having

> interests they feel will allow me to accept them as a black
> person instead of a white person.

Clearly, the cultural assimilation that makes Salina uncomfortable is not an expected outcome of accountability principles.
What we want to highlight, however, is that when white people
worry solely about being accountable in a way that promotes a
simplistic form of deference, they often ignore the development
of a healthy racial identity that is part of their personal healing.

Yet white people frequently feel validated when distancing
themselves from anything considered white. Cameron offers how
he experienced this dynamic:

> The whole idea when working with communities of color
> is that you should hide or minimize your whiteness. You
> want to be as thin and small as possible as a white person.
> You want to be as accepted and embraced as everything
> but for that. So, the greatest compliment is, "You're not
> really white. You're black. Or you have black bones. Or
> you have a black heart."

White people distancing themselves from their whiteness often
goes hand in hand with the belief that they are less valuable human
beings. Cameron speaks of the long road he has taken to find a way
out of this way of seeing that essentially required him to deny his
value:

> Working in many organizations run by people of color
> with majority staff of color, I internalized that my human-
> ity was of less value because I was white. Therefore I
> could be treated without concern for my humanity and the
> message was…that is the way it should be.

This is a long-standing pattern in which many people within anti-
racism circles, both white and people of color, have played a role.
Whiteness, and all things associated with it are often considered of
little to no value. Then, viewing whiteness as a something of a curse,
large numbers of white people turn away from anything associated
with their home communities. This reaction is hardly surprising.

Another feature of this pattern includes the continued presence of extreme guilt within white people. Salina puts guilt at the

top of the list of problems with this way of approaching relationship building:

> Accountability, when I think about it, is about white guilt, the notion of superiority or inferiority, this idea of answering to someone. It makes me think of a lot of contrition, certainly inequity and inequality. I think of contrition, parent-child relationship, and hierarchy. And hierarchy is inherently problematic when you talk about humans. I think that there's still a lack of healing when you talk about accountability. There's a wholeness of the individual that I think is missing.

We would like to highlight the point that we readily hear how white guilt renders white people ineffective allies and frustrates people of color. Yet, people rarely state openly that the focus on one-sided accountability can actually support the continuation of white guilt and that this guilt is a serious barrier to white people finding the kind of healing needed to do effective ally work.

Jason speaks of his experience wherein accountability structures depended on white guilt to encourage white people to continually defer to people of color:

> From the perspective where an accountable relationship is based in this idea that white people can only be accountable when coming from "I will only follow the leadership of people of color.' 'I'm only doing good work if I get a stamp of approval from people of color."… I just feel like it just requires a lot of guilt on the part of a white person or a white-led organization, either guilt or this having no sense of identity kind of place. It really requires that in order to make that work.

So far we have seen that white people perceiving themselves to be less-than-equal relationship partners can support white people in 1) maintaining an unhealthy sense of self, 2) distancing themselves from their whiteness, and 3) seeking validation from people of color. Additionally, however, the absence of a clear racial identity in relationship to anti-racism work leads to even more problems.

The lack of a healthy white racial identity also reduces white people's interest in thorough self-inquiry. One common result is that they cut themselves off from any learning that might come from their experience. Not only do white people stop themselves from fully seeing how the white supremacist culture continues to live within them, but they also deny learning that could prove helpful to collaborative partnerships.

Diane is especially disheartened by what she sees when white people feel the need to stand separate from everything related to white culture:

> I think it's detrimental to both sides...I don't think white people are motivated or encouraged to participate and offer insight. They might not even believe they have anything to offer to the process, and it's not true at all...Part of this is "I need to stand apart from my white culture, my white affiliation, and be allied to you." Well, I don't want you to do that. I want you to be able to reach into your experience from your white culture, and me reach into my experience from my black culture and do our collective thinking.

Of course, dominant white culture should be critiqued, interrogated, and transformed. Anti-racism efforts require this. But as long as white people reactively run away from all things associated with the white community, they remain less capable of mining the possibly helpful learning they have inculcated through their varied experiences.

Additionally, the premise that white people are inherently untrustworthy often translates into white people believing spending time in white caucus spaces reinforces racism. This can limit white people's ability to facilitate their own self-inquiry. Diane expresses her concern this way:

> I think the aggregate awareness of white people has been slowed because it's been led by people of color. I think it is an absolute oxymoron to say that understanding one's own culture is critical to racial relations and let me have someone outside your race tell you about your own culture, which has been far too long the model and the time spent.

An important issue is that if white people believe that "being accountable" means they should turn only to people of color for guidance, white people will continue to avoid responsibility for organizing within the white community in order to move other white people forward. While true that much about racism and white privilege can be learned through the leadership of people of color, self-examined white people are able to speak to the experience of being white. When white people have a healthy sense of self through having clearly investigated that experience, they can then speak about it with other white people and further their growth.

Ultimately, we believe the form of accountability most of the collaborators on this chapter were acculturated into, and the sense of worthlessness it supports in white people, encourages white people to run away from the very relationships that most need transformation. Only when white people find a strong internal grounding in a healthy sense of self will they effectively develop and maintain transformative relationships with the larger white community that can expand movements for justice.

Inherent Inequality

We recognize disrupting white supremacy necessarily involves challenging the dominant white power structure. However, when white people reactively enter relationships characterized by a power reversal that puts people of color in a superior position over white people, the problems inherent in any intentionally hierarchical system are bound to arise. Systems of dominance we have been acculturated into, such as white supremacy and patriarchy, are reflected in one-sided accountable relationships because one group continues to have power over another group. It may be understandable that many believe an initial power reversal is an important step on the road toward dismantling the white supremacist system. However, we believe relationships built upon this uneven foundation lead toward feelings of dehumanization and differential worth and therefore do not help us create the non-oppressive relationships necessary to create a non-oppressive society.

Further, relationships based on inherent inequity foster dysfunctional relational patterns. First, white people tend to act in patronizing ways toward people of color. Paraphrasing a lengthy explanation, Hamid describes how when white people feel they need to constantly ask "What do you need?," it is as though the person of color cannot take care of him or herself. Jason describes building relationships within this context and the questions that arose within him during times when racism emerged in a room:

> Especially as a white person, how do I come in? Because that is what I should be doing, taking responsibility for all of racism that is causing this pain in this moment. So I've got to make things better. I've got to come in and rescue and caretake…so then I act out of a place that feels really ungrounded and uncomfortable.

Ultimately, discomfort is felt on both sides and this dynamic demeans everyone in the process.

A second dysfunctional characteristic commonly experienced in relationships based in inequity involves the belief that one group cannot be trusted to do effective work without oversight by the other group. When we believe white anti-racists are *incapable* of holding themselves accountable for their own development this means that people of color *must* monitor white people's progress. This can be problematic because it 1) requires people of color to spend their time attending to white people instead of working in their own communities, 2) continues a long historical pattern of white people being served while energies are depleted from people of color, and 3) sets up a dynamic of one group "overseeing" another, as opposed to "working in relationship with" in order to provide feedback.

Certainly, many people of color remain willing to provide mentorship to white people who require help seeing issues of race and white privilege. But we suggest that these mentorship relationships are strongest when built on a foundation of mutual partnership, respect, and equality. Not only that, we believe white people can and should be encouraged to imagine they can become

sufficiently skilled so they can begin to hold themselves accountable and provide leadership within the white community.

Ineffective Collaborative Practices

A final theme that emerged involves the development of
ineffective collaborative practices that limit the social justice
movement as a whole. Of primary importance is that an approach
based in inherent inequity reduces the likelihood that we will
fully access and utilize the skills brought to the table by various
members of the lesser-valued group. Diane speaks extensively on
this subject:

> Here's the problem: The whole accountability dynamic
> doesn't invite the best thinking of the collective. It simply
> advocates blind support of the most affected. And I think that
> the most affected bring in a hugely important perspective to
> the equation. And I think great partnerships of examined
> white people do too. And those two added together, that's
> what gets positive change. But that seldom happens.

A key idea here is the acknowledgement that those who have suffered most from racism have an enormous amount to contribute.
The knowledge and experience gained from having lived through
oppressive circumstances and situations cannot be underestimated.

The trouble is that if white people who have done a lot of
internal work and have developed a sophisticated analysis of systemic racism are expected to offer unquestioned support, we lose
the possibility of co-creating more effective approaches and practices. Essentially, if we believe white people cannot contribute to
the knowledge base because of their racial positioning, we lose
whatever valuable ideas might come from a more equitable and
honest sharing.

Finally, distrust is reinforced when the "blind support for the
most affected" dynamic plays out in situations where white people become advocates and allies without becoming full partners
in an initiative. According to Diane, in the end minor battles might
be won when isolated tasks are accomplished, but the larger justice

effort does not move forward. This happens because the structure of one-sided accountability does not ask people to resolve the inner psychic issues that affect all of us raised within a culture of white supremacy. Our unresolved issues then continue to negatively impact our ability to form partnerships wherein we can look beyond a single task and concentrate on the type of long-term, sustainable effort that requires honest, real, deep relationships. On a large scale, the problematic aspects highlighted within the four themes just discussed are disastrous for the racial, social, economic, and environmental justice movements.

A Different Direction:
A Path toward Transformative Alliances

The AWARE-LA members who have been part of the creation of this model have spent many years internalizing accountability principles and building anti-racist practices. They are clear that the principles asking white people to become cognizant of the privilege and racism infused within their thoughts, emotional reactions, and behaviors are essential. They also hold as invaluable those principles that help develop 1) non-oppressive communication skills and 2) equitable relationships with people of color.

Yet, AWARE-LA is also clear that it has been a struggle to expand its thinking outside of the "accountability to people of color" box in order to claim the following: *Relationships intended to serve a racial/social/economic justice agenda will be stronger and more productive if they are founded from their beginnings in an approach that values each individual's essential humanity, offers mutual respect, and holds open the possibility for trust to be achieved.* Perhaps most radical is the contention that white people who are at the beginning stages of racial awareness should consider themselves — and be considered — legitimate allies. In keeping with this approach, new white anti-racists should also be treated with respect and consideration.

Although recognizing that some people have already been building healthy, functional cross-race relationships for years, they may represent a small minority within social justice circles. We also must acknowledge that for many people who have never experienced relationships with white people that inspire a sense of trust and/or hope, our approach will likely feel overly optimistic. For this reason, it may be helpful to see our offering as a future ideal, something to be worked toward, even if it feels out of reach at this time. We would now like to present our framework for the direction we, AWARE-LA and RJA, intend to take as we move forward.

The Transformative Alliance Building Model

We offer our Transformative Alliance Building model as an alternative to relationships focusing on one-sided accountability structures. We start by admitting that this approach asks many of us to forge a new path. We know building relationships where the highest value is placed on creating equitable, sustainable relationships that can work to uphold our common goal of advancing movements for justice is something we will need to navigate together. Here is a basic outline of the model from which we are working:

- The immediate goal is to build transformative alliances between anti-racist white people and people of color.

- To build these alliances successfully, we need to create healthy and productive relationships.

- In order to build these relationships, white people must take responsibility for how we are socialized to act out white supremacy culture and white privilege. White people are called to create a new way of being in relationship. This is where accountability principles remain important. But, the overriding understanding is that only when anti-racist white people and people of color work towards genuine relationships can both groups be free to create transformative alliances.

- Transformative alliances are the vehicles that allow us to create effective movements for racial, social, economic, and environmental justice — the ultimate goal.

We believe that this model will be instrumental in our ability to actually make good on the intentions we set for ourselves.

Where Do We Begin?

To be sure, developing healthy relationships takes time and effort. We recognize this process will neither be easy nor assured. Part of starting off in the right direction, however, involves white people helping to foster relationships with people of color by being anti-racist allies. This is done through engagement in the following:

- Anti-racist actions

- Consciousness-raising

- Learning about social justice and the history of the white supremacist system in the United States

- Honest/constructive dialogue

- Demonstrating growth over time

When white people develop these practices, opportunities are created for people of color to build trust with anti-racist white people. Not surprisingly, many of these features come straight out of the accountability principles that we find essential.

When we talked with our AWARE-LA colleagues about what it looked like for them to take up these guidelines during their beginning stages, their statements reflect the learning of essential skills. Jason explains:

> I'm constantly being vigilant in my honesty, in my self-reflection, in my willingness to take risks, in asking for dialogue around times when I am having conflict in relationship, or feeling like there's my own internalized racism playing out.

Jason's recognition that developing the characteristics of an ally is anchored in a self-reflective process is also mirrored within Cameron's experience. But, Cameron highlights the importance of approaching the work non-defensively and with an honest intent to experience change. To Cameron this means

> the ability to be engaged about issues of race and racism and having the skills and the capacities to really take in what's being said and not react from a defensive place, to take the information that's being shared and be able to integrate it into my way of being in my practice. It's not enough to just say, "Thank you. I appreciate what you're saying." But I also have to be reflective in the practice that comes from that hearing. So, for me, it is really the ability to non-defensively listen to what's being said, to be able to have a constructive engagement with how I'm being challenged and then to be able to turn around and integrate that information and have it lead to new practices.

> The most basic skill is to not get defensive. That's really hard to learn to do, but to really hear what somebody's saying, to not try to apologize too quick. Like "I'm sorry, I didn't mean it that way." But it's not about me. I had to learn that me telling them "I'm sorry" is to make me feel better.

The skills Jason and Cameron speak of take time to develop and depend on the ability to engage in relationships with people who have 1) a more advanced understanding of how racism and white privilege manifest, and 2) the time, energy, and openness to engage in this ongoing dialogue process.

We would like to highlight that the difference between the form of accountability we critiqued and the Transformative Alliance Building model is that *our approach explicitly suggests that white people deserve respect and consideration even while initially working to develop skills.* One of the guiding understandings is that white anti-racist people who are committed will undoubtedly make racist mistakes or act out white privilege and that they must be 100 percent accountable for this behavior. At the same time, white anti-racist people still need to be treated considerately as allies who are invested in — and working for — justice and not as untrustworthy white people.

As trust builds and mutual work develops, people of color should be able to ask their white allies to do the following:

- Step up and stay engaged

- Speak their truth

- Trust themselves to interact without being deferential

- Be invested in self-examination/consciousness-raising

- Engage other white people on their anti-racism

This information about what people of color should expect from their white allies was included early in our process. But as RJA took a more active role in constructing our framework, they prompted the addition of information regarding what white anti-racists should be able to ask of allies of color. This has prompted us to include the following. Allies of color who wish to create productive relationships with their white allies offer:

- Patience

- Recognition that white people and people of color need, and are able, to come together

- Investment in self-examination/consciousness-raising

- Willingness to see white people as more than simply their racial placement

- Belief in white anti-racists' ability to add value

The addition of this information required a transformative process in and of itself. Our original response was to ask our RJA members what they felt we, the white allies, could ask of them. It was not until they assured us that it was our role to courageously name what we needed that we recognized the depth of our own sense of having a lesser voice. For us, the process we have moved through has been truly inspirational and growth-inducing, opening new avenues for theoretical consideration, relationship development, and mutual work.

Where Does This Lead?

With commitments to develop our knowledge, skills, and anti-racist practices, white people can better participate in creating a foundation for functional, continuing relationships. The intentions for each person entering these relationships would include:

- Building trust as friends and allies

- Entering into alliance on an equal footing by honoring one another's humanity

- Providing leadership alongside — not over — one another

- Remaining accountable (individually and collectively) for how we act out our various privileges

- Being responsible for what it means for each of us to live under a white supremacist system and culture

The key words associated with our intentions for transformative alliances include: mutuality, partnership, sustainability, united front, common purpose, collaboration, and respect.

What Would Alliance Relationships Look Like?

Through our interview and collaborative processes, we developed some initial descriptions of what alliance relationships would entail. Important are the following characteristics. People of color and anti-racist white people would

- Have sustainable and meaningful relationships based on mutual trust and respect

- Be invested in working out problems when they arise

- Find productive solutions that are strengthened by our collaboration and collective effort

- Be committed to having one another's back through thick and thin

This last point is perhaps the most challenging. A key difference within this approach versus the common pattern of one-sided accountability relationships is that white anti-racist people in alliances would be able to expect support from people of color when the situation warrants. Cameron states that

> The biggest thing you can ask a person of color to do is stand up for white anti-racist people. That's the ultimate thing to do. I think when a person of color is willing to risk that, it's a true alliance.

As partners in alliance relationships, each individual's full humanity would be considered and honored, regardless of race.

In addition to these four main characteristics, the interviewees also commented on elements that would be expected to be present within alliance relationships. For Salina, alliance relationships would allow people to relate honestly without one person needing to continually try to please the other. She speaks of appreciating white people who are "unapologetically white," meaning those who are comfortable with whom they are as long as they are working against white supremacy. This, then, allows balance to emerge:

> When I think of alliance, first off I think of equality. I think of two whole individuals, or entities. I think of mutual respect, mutual appreciation. I think of more of a give and take. I think of balance. I think of more just and even flow between the two and I think of unity of purpose, unity of thought, unity of work.

Diane builds on the idea of mutuality, but highlights how this type of relationship also involves conscious decision-making regarding who will be a good partner:

> It is when you are willing to fully give, and that's a very discerned decision and I think, for me at least, it's a mutually invested commitment to be self-examined and then to be in partnership.

This is an essential point. We recognize that not all cross-race relationships can be alliances. Alliances will only occur when *both* parties are 1) fully dedicated to self-examination, 2) are willing to confront the privileges they receive, and 3) feel inspired to commit to the individual or group.

Some additional features include the ability to be in honest dialogue, feeling that respect is mutual, and being given the benefit of the doubt that intentions are positive. Here is what Susan said specifically about what makes an alliance relationship:

> It looks like being engaged and committed to each other in our lives within and outside of our social justice work together. The relationship isn't superficial. It is being interested in the whole story of each other's lives. In this kind of real relationship, when issues come up that need to be addressed, the relationship is there to support you and the challenge is one that helps you grow and continue learning. When an issue arises that makes someone uncomfortable, it would be talked about immediately with the understanding that we will always be trying our best and that we are always trying to be supportive and filled with consciousness. This kind of relationship would honor the fact that those of us who are engaged in this work are motivated by genuine caring and a deep desire to make the world a better place. So, when attention is brought to a mistake — either conscious or unconscious — this type of relationship allows me to immediately work on shifting the problem areas.

Susan's comments reflect a radical difference between the approaches. Whereas in the form of accountability we were acculturated into, white people's mistakes are often used to justify exclusion or harsh treatment, alliance relationships recognize that mistakes are bound to happen and are not taken as indicators of the white person's lack of investment.

But what allows us to build relationships where this is possible? We next consider the different requirements necessary for alliance relationships to occur.

What Is Required to Build an Alliance Relationship?

Several elements are required for creating and sustaining alliance relationships. First, there needs to be an emphasis on long-term commitment, seeing beyond the single issue of race when considering the effects of oppression, and both sides engaging in personal healing work. Salina speaks extensively about how each member of an alliance needs to do self-examining work to heal from the experience of living within a white supremacist system:

> For an alliance to be an alliance, and to be an effective alliance, you really have to have individuals or entities that have really done the proverbial work. If you're talking about race, I think you have to have individuals who have really gone deep within and addressed and worked out the issues and challenges of growing up in a society such as ours, where white supremacy is the overarching design. Both sides. I think the whites need to do the work. What does it mean to be white growing up in a system of white supremacy? And what does it mean to be black growing up in the system? And not only what does it mean, but how has it affected me in my life and my interactions in my relationships? And what do I need to do to move beyond the confines of white supremacy? And only once you've done that and committed to doing work to heal yourself, because whites need the healing, and blacks need the healing, then you can form an alliance...Each of us should be held to the same standards.

What we notice within Salina's statement is the idea that alliances cannot truly form until the work of healing and self-examination is engaged. We see this model as an approach to building *transformative* alliances and we believe that unless both parties are open to being transformed, a healthy dynamic will not emerge.

Diane discusses why it is so important for us all to do the work of deeply examining our own experiences and finding peace within it:

> I think the end of this is mutuality because I don't think the self-examining is different for whites than it is for people of color. It's just exactly the same. I think it is the notion of coming to terms with the fact that I am more than myself. I am part of a culture and a culture that I don't always define, but it informs and influences who I am and how I think and then secondly, to find my peace within that, to find my peace within the elements of my culture that I take pride in and I hold up and I acknowledge and I look to and I pass on to another generation and also to acknowledge the parts of my culture that I didn't craft but are real.

This idea of finding a certain kind of resolution regarding who we are within our culture and what kind of change we want to work toward in the world is essential if each partner is going to stand solidly side by side during moments of difficulty.

Three additional requirements for building alliances include understanding that 1) building trust still depends upon a significant investment of time, 2) people are bound to make mistakes if we have been recipients of certain privileges our whole lives, and 3) over time we should be able to question moments when our partner's actions appear to be based in an oppressive system. Susan explains this most clearly:

> So there is a sense of mutual respect around our needs. Again, I think it depends on the relationship whether or not I can expect [allies] to be accountable for their own growth. If it's somebody that I've known for a long time then there is the assumption that there is that accountability around a whole variety of issues, including sexism, homophobia...it's okay to struggle. In fact, it's good to struggle, especially when you're doing the best that you can to be a conscious, whole, loving person in the world and to not do harm. We are going to make mistakes. So what we're looking for in that is to really be able to talk to each other mutually and inspire each other's continued growth.

In sum, we hope that alliance relationships will be increasingly possible. We also know the challenges we face. Collectively, we have a lot to learn and a lot from which to heal. For many people, the idea of mutuality will feel premature, especially for those who have had no prior experience that validates or reinforces the idea that white people can ever be sufficiently skilled to warrant trust. For this reason we find it important to address why we feel working to build this type of relationship is so important.

What Are the Benefits of Alliance Relationships?

The success of our efforts for justice will be radically improved when we have sustainable, long-term, functional relationships. Diane speaks about how unequal accountability structures prompt short-term collaborations, but she then clarifies why we must strive to build long-term alliances among self-examined people who each hold themselves accountable to being in relationships non-oppressively:

> I think you can better serve the world when you are accountable to those principles, and those principles are applied to self-examination. Then you show up in the world differently. You show up for white people differently. You show up for people of color differently. That's when you become a change agent in the world. And I say it's to be determined because I don't think we've unleashed even a fraction of the power of what we could do if we could ever get past the constructs that prevent us from working in partnership and joining other thinking.

From our experience, this is one of the most inspirational aspects — the idea that when we combine individuals who have each done the requisite self-examination with a healthier relationship dynamic, we will tap into a deep well of power and intentionality that, so far, has all too commonly remained mired in dysfunctional relationships.

How Can White Anti-racists Increase Their Ability to Build Transformative Alliance Relationships?

AWARE-LA believes its model of Radical White Identity can help white people become more effective allies. The approach recognizes white anti-racists need a healthy, productive, and explicit white identity that involves investigating their roots, history, privilege, and organizing potential. Since space constraints limit our ability to fully explain the model here, we will simply offer some key benefits we see in building this type of identity. First, we find that with the solid sense of self this model offers, white people move away from an insecure, guilt-ridden, validity-seeking form of anti-racism work. This allows white people to have deeper and more balanced dialogues with people of color because they understand their dedication to their work comes out of their own self-inquiry and interest. Second, white people feel increasingly confident about their ability to engage in anti-racism work with the wider white community.

Most basically, AWARE-LA members learn to see themselves as valuable, invested contributors to the wider effort to dismantle white supremacy. Cameron speaks of how this model has affected him:

> I think that what's so critical is that once you have that internal sense of self based on being a white anti-racist, then you're able to negotiate a problematic role from a much healthier place. I don't feel responsible for the history of the white supremacy system but I do feel accountable to its results and how I benefit from the system. I recognize how my privilege protects me from seeing these realities. I think we don't want to stop feeling guilt or shame ever. That's not the goal...But it's not something I'm held by and guided by...I have a foundation within myself as a white anti-racist. The bottom line for me is that I have a stake in ending the white supremacist system. I'm part of the fight for justice.

Finally, this secure foundation is essential to white people's ability to effect the most change possible. It keeps them energized, motivates them to push themselves, and helps them build stronger multi-racial alliances that can propel forward the movements for justice. It is this effect on white people' anti-racist practice we find most meaningful.

What If People Do Not Want to Create Alliance Relationships?

Not all relationships between white people and people of color can be alliances in the way we discuss. The problematic dynamics described within our critique of one-sided accountability relationships will remain a common pattern for a long time because many white people and people of color will likely continue to support an unequal, hierarchical approach and/or operate out of unresolved internalized belief systems. For example, there are plenty of white people who adamantly refuse to believe that their voices are valuable or that they can become sufficiently skilled to warrant trust from people of color.

That said, what happens when the people with whom we are collaborating are interested in a relationship based solely on one-sided accountability guidelines? First, we will have to make a choice whether or not to commit to these relationships. If we do, one helpful recognition to accept is that skepticism is understandable given our country's history. For example, some people of color might have zero interest in collaborating with white people due to a history rife with disappointment and injury caused by white people and society. Others may be willing to engage in collaborative work, but they may have learned to offer trust very slowly. On the other hand, some white people are so filled with self-hatred they cannot see themselves as worthy of equal standing. In other words, we must remember each of us is an individual with differing approaches.

What this means is that we will likely struggle to remain true to our deepest beliefs when in circumstances that seem to betray our sense of equity and humanity. For example, white people may sometimes need to follow the rules of one-sided accountability even when it goes against a deeply felt sense of truth, knowing that trust may never come. This might involve taking a position of deference even when a sense of personal experience suggests the situation is dysfunctional. For people of color, this could mean engaging with white people who remain needy and deferential. With enough time and investment, work and effort, mistrust and dehumanization might give way to more equitable alliance relationships. In the meantime, we imagine we each will continue to struggle, setting our sights on creating healthy relationships and admitting when we fail.

Conclusion

Given the myriad problems with one-sided accountability relationships — including their tendency toward inauthentic communication, unhealthy white anti-racist people, inherent inequality, and ineffective collaborative practices — we need to forge a new path. We present Transformative Alliance Building as an invitation to join us in attempting to create relationships where the highest value is placed on mutual respect, partnership, equity, and the preservation of each individual's full humanity. We do this knowing we remain responsible for continuing our individual growth processes. But we believe only when the foundations of our relationships find anchor in the values of alliance will we avoid the dead ends that come with a singular focus on accountability.

Chapter Eleven

European Dissent Accountability Statement

Members of European Dissent

Overview and History

From the very beginning, Ronald Chisom and Jim Dunn —
cofounders of the People's Institute for Survival and Beyond — were
committed to organizing with, and building leadership among,
white people in the movement. Thirty years ago that was not a
popular policy to adopt, but they were determined it was the right
thing to do and the best strategy for undoing structural racism. In
1986, during a national gathering of anti-racist organizers called by
The People's Institute at a retreat center in Waveland, MS, Ron and
Jim called together those of us who were white and challenged us:

> White people who want to be effective participants in the
> movement for social justice and equity must come together
> to act as a white collective against racism. You must learn
> to speak out publicly as white people even when no peo-
> ple of color are around.

The white men and women who convened that spring
formed ourselves into European Dissent (ED), a group of people

of European descent who "dissent" from the ideology of white supremacy and organize with other whites and with people of color to undo racism. Our greatest challenge was to become an effective and sustainable collective, since all of us had been schooled to think of ourselves as individuals. As an anti-racist white collective, we recognized that even as we studied, organized and spoke out against racism, we needed to be accountable to anti-racist people of color.

Very early on we found that the creation of a statement was essential to our being able to hold ourselves accountable, even as members came and went over time. We worked on the first version soon after we formed ED, probably in 1987 or 1988. It was a very long process to create it, word by arduous word. We revisited all of those words again in 2006, when we fashioned the revision you hold in your hands now. But those seemingly bottomless discussions were crucial, since they helped us internalize not only the words but the essence of what it means to be anti-racist white people.

Ron Chisom, Jim Dunn, Barbara Major, and other PISAB leaders of color read it and gave us feedback, so that the final statement was one that could be "owned" by European Dissent and PISAB alike.

Continually returning to the issue of accountability has enabled us to deepen our relationships not only with one another but also with those organizers of color who lead the movement for justice and equity. From our work in the 1980's with the Rainbow Coalition to our post-Katrina organizing efforts in support of the right of return of New Orleans and Gulf Coast residents, European Dissent has taken direction from the People's Institute and from other anti-racist organizers of color. European Dissent's principled accountability to one another and to the larger justice community has impacted anti-racist white groups across the country.

European Dissent Accountability Statement (Revised June 20, 2006)

1. Accountability of Whites to European Dissent Organization

We accept the fact that each of us has individual racism and we understand we have privilege because we are white. With this in mind, we have made a commitment to undo racism.

a. All members of European Dissent will have attended a two-and-a-half-day Undoing Racism™ training with the People's Institute, or will have made a commitment to attend one in the next six months.

b. We agree with the statement of purpose — European Dissent Mission Statement.

c. We collectively and individually agree to work on our own personal and cultural racism and will take an active, public stance against institutional racism and report back to the group with our progress.

d. We agree to be honest with each other.

e. We agree to respect each other.

f. We will support group decisions.

g. We will create a liberated zone where individuals can and should say what is on their minds without fear. This also means that we will speak to the group, rather than outside of the group, if we have a problem. We will create the space where we talk with each other rather than about each other. This means that we will bring up problems about process, group maintenance and individual involvement in the liberated zone.

h. Each member will take responsibility for continuity of the organization through the following: attendance, staying current on decisions and activities of the group; following through on tasks we have agreed to; maintaining structure in the organization; holding meetings regularly, including committee meetings;

everyone being involved in some way beyond attendance; nurturing new members.

i.   We agree to develop and maintain trust. We should be able to trust that the group will be with us and support us when we step out against racism.

j.   We will have a commitment to struggle. We will commit to push one another to another level. We will be committed to being challenged on a personal, cultural and institutional level.

k.   We will commit to sharing information, events, and resources.

l.   We will have a commitment to being responsible to the next generation. We will educate our young people.

2. Accountability of Whites to Other Whites

a.   We commit to anti-racist work within our families, with friends, in our jobs, and our community work.

b.   We recognize that European Dissent neither invented nor owns white anti-racism, but instead is part of a national network of anti-racist whites. We have much to learn from this network and seek to create an accountable community of individuals and organizations who do this work.

c.   We believe it is our responsibility to work with and organize other whites, especially those in social justice work and those whose activity significantly impacts communities of color. We accept our responsibility to work with whites, even when we don't agree with them.

d.   We will commit to the appreciation of the whole of each other's personhood. We will respect each other's culture, class and religious differences. We will identify gender perspectives. We will be sensitive to each other's family situations.

e.   We will commit to do anti-racist problem solving with each other. We will not write each other off. We will question without a sense of one-upmanship. We will resist arrogance. We will be willing to share our weaknesses. We will question each other's accountability.

f.   We will commit to create and promote an anti-racist culture and learn to work our culture in with other cultures in a non-intrusive, non-imposing and respectful way.

3. Accountability of Anti-Racist Whites to People of Color

a.   We will commit ourselves to informing and checking with people of color about our work, both personally and organizationally. We will listen to what they say and what they are not saying. We will make a commitment to use European Dissent as a sieve, so that we can filter out some things before taking the discussion to people of color. We will share minutes and major decisions with people of color. We will share our accountability statement with them.

b.   We will engage in the struggle as anti-racist whites side by side with people of color. We will be committed to becoming a visible ally. We will be committed to action and taking public anti-racist positions. We will help build a multiracial, anti-racist movement.

c.   We will accept Black leadership and the leadership of other communities of color. We will learn not to blindly follow leadership because it is of color. Instead, we rely on PISAB principles of indigenous leadership that include embeddedness in community. In this way we will be accountable to leaders who are in turn accountable in their own communities. We recognize that we need to continue to deepen our understanding of these principles.

d.   We will learn to know when we are relying too much on people of color to do the work we should be doing.

Mission Statement of European Dissent, New Orleans

We are persons of European descent who recognize that our varying ethnic histories have been forged into a common "white community" in order to nurture and sustain racism. We work in consultation with the People's Institute for Survival and Beyond, a national multiracial network of organizers who do training workshops in leadership development, community empowerment, and Undoing Racism™. Our goal is to be a visible force in the creation of a multiracial network of people intent on building working relationships between the white community and the communities of color in the struggle for a just society.

We actively look at, analyze, change and help other whites to change the ways we as whites participate in racism personally, culturally, and institutionally. We have made a commitment to undo racism personally in our families, social life, work places, churches, and community work. To achieve this goal we feel it is our responsibility to articulate and demonstrate dissent in our communities by organizing other whites to oppose and undo racism.

We do this by organizing training seminars in conjunction with the People's Institute; through study and education; by expanding our membership and base of support; by engaging in public actions and community struggles that expose and combat racism; and by supporting one another in our efforts to undo racism in our personal and work lives.

Afterword

Bonnie Berman Cushing

We end our book by returning to its beginning and the bigger picture Ron Chisom described for us in the Foreword.

In this picture, accountability is an ever-evolving concept with a long and contentious history, and — if we are ever to succeed in ending racism — a necessarily robust future.

Racism is not simply another social issue we need to address; it is a dynamic at play through all of the issues.

And accountability is not simply one of the guiding principles essential to creating a just society — it is, itself, continually informing all those other principles: the analysis of power, the development of leadership, the pursuit of a true and complete history, the recognition of both external and internal manifestations of oppression, and the honoring of culture.

The contributors to this book are also part of a bigger picture. They are located within a larger anti-racist movement with a rich past, a vital and growing present, and a promising, albeit challenging, future. For every story offered here there are many more that are not. It would behoove us all to seek those stories out — and listen carefully whenever we find them.

For now, it is our hope that after hearing the collective experience and wisdom contained in this book you will return to — or begin — your own anti-racist work more informed, more inspired, and more effective.

About the Contributors

The Alliance for Racial and Social Justice (ARSJ)

The Alliance for Racial and Social Justice (ARSJ) is a grassroots organization based in New Jersey whose mission is to promote safety in our communities, with expertise and focus as a watchdog for mental health, child protective and court-based services. We work for social justice and peace through unity, education and accountability regarding inequities arising from white privilege, and by initiating and sustaining social action aimed at eradicating racism, sexism, classism, homophobia, able-ism and other abuses of power. The ARSJ website is www.arsj.org.

Lisa V. Blitz

Lisa V. Blitz, PhD, LCSW-R is a social worker with more than twenty years experience working with people from a broad range of social and cultural experiences. Her commitment to social justice centers on incorporating antiracist and anti-oppression analyses and action into clinical, administrative, and academic aspects of social work practice. She is currently an assistant professor at Binghamton University College of Community and Public Affairs, Department of Social Work. Dr. Blitz is also the program coordinator for SHARE, a public school-based initiative under the auspices of the CCPA Center for Best Practices in Full Service Community Schools. Past positions include directing a network of domestic violence services in New York City that included shelter, community-based counseling and advocacy, and educational outreach; overseeing psychiatric rehabilitation services for adults with serious mental illness; and managing school- and community-based juvenile diversion and substance abuse prevention programs for youth. In addition, Dr. Blitz has a background in mental health, working in both agency and private practice settings, where she specialized in trauma recovery and life transition issues.

Gillian Burlingham

Gillian Burlingham was born in Thailand and raised in Thailand and Argentina until the age of four, at which time she became the 6th generation on her family's dairy farm in a predominantly white area in western New York State.

She's undertaken anti-racism work for 20+ years in a variety of settings. At Oberlin College, she received the Leah Freed Women's History award for her research paper, "'Triply Disadvantaged': The Effects of Race on the Life and Work of Mary Edmonia Lewis," about the first prominent African American and Native American sculptor and former Oberlin student. She holds a Master's degree from Antioch University in systems design, cross-cultural community-building, and mediation.

Gillian has worked as a community organizer, mediator, wilderness ranger, and anti-racism coordinator. She helped organize the first three Seattle Race Conferences (2003-2005), was secretary for the Commission on Racial Justice at the Church Council of Greater Seattle, established the Committee for Ministry on Racial Justice at University Friends Meeting, and was a co-organizer of the Washington State white anti-racist gathering in October 2005.

She is currently a union construction electrician apprentice and lives in Seattle with her partner, Sariya, and daughter, Amina.

Lila Cabbil

Lila Cabbil is a committed change agent with thirty-five years of experience in direct service, human potential development, and coaching, workshop design and facilitation, and organizational development. She is president and principal consultant of LMC Diversified Consulting, and President Emeritus, founding board member and current Director of Programs of the Rosa and Raymond Parks Institute for Self Development. Her work focuses on racial disparities in health, environment, economics, education, employment, and public/justice policy. Her mission is the empowerment of people, especially youth, through personal and systems transformation.

Ms. Cabbil was director of the Multicultural Experience in Leadership Development at Wayne State University for fourteen years. A few other examples of her vast local and national organizing include designing and leading Youth Peace Summits at the United Nations (2007 and 2009) and White Anti-racist Summits (held at the White Privilege Conference from 2004 – 2009), and serving as lead consultant for the Race Relations Initiative for the City of Detroit. She is currently active with the People's Water Board, the Urban Agriculture Food Justice Task Force, and the Rosa Parks Institute's Dialogue for Racial Reconciliation. Part of Ms. Cabbil's life/work commitment to the movement also includes maintaining accountability partnerships with white anti-racists on an annual basis.

Lila serves as a resource trainer with the People's Institute for Survival and Beyond and sits on the board of the Center for the Study of White American Culture. She earned a Bachelor of Science degree in Occupational Therapy and a Master of Science in Human Development and Resources at Wayne State University. Lila had the blessing of being mentored by Mrs. Rosa Parks for over forty years. Because of that close relationship, she had organized her community participation around promoting, protecting and preserving Mrs. Parks' legacy. Lila credits her professional competency to the gifts that God gave her to fulfill her life purpose.

Ronald Chisom

Ronald Chisom is the executive director and cofounder of the People's Institute for Survival and Beyond. He has organized tenants, fisherman, cane cutters and poor people throughout the South for over thirty-five years. He was cofounder and associate director of the Treme Community Improvement Association, which won several significant Louisiana victories in New Orleans in the 1970s. He also served as the main plaintiff of the *Ronald Chisom v. Charles E. Roemer, Governor of Louisiana Et Al.* case. This case challenged the Lousiana state supreme court to achieve equal representation for the predominately Black city of New Orleans. Ron has served as an organizer, advisor, lecturer and consultant to a wide variety of community, legal and church groups. Some of these organizations include the Fisherman and Concerned Citizens Association of Plaquemines Parish, New Orleans Legal Services, Southern Organizing Committee for Economic and Social Justice, Southern Partners Foundation and Philanthropic Initiative for Racial Equity. Ron has led numerous workshops around the country on Undoing Racism™, community organizing, and leadership and strategy development. His networking and community organizing extends throughout the United States and South Africa. He has received many prestigious awards, including the Bannerman Fellowship, the Petra Foundation Award, the Pax Christi Bread & Roses, and the Tenant Resource Center Achievement Award. Ron has been married for forty years to Jerolie Encalade Chisom. He has one daughter, Tiphanie Chisom-Eugene and is the proud grandfather of Jessica and C.J. (Cory Jr.).

Bonnie Berman Cushing

Bonnie is a social worker, a celebrant and an anti-racist organizer and educator. She has worked in the mental health field for over 22 years as a psychotherapist and group facilitator. She received her MSW from Adelphi University and trained as a family systems therapist at the Multicultural Family Institute of New Jersey. In 2004, Bonnie co-authored a chapter for the book *Human Development and Faith* by Chalice Press.

She was certified as a celebrant by the Celebrant Foundation of North America in 2003. Working as a "cleric without borders," Bonnie has collaborated on and officiated countless weddings, civil unions, baby namings, memorials, and other rites of passage.

She is a member of the People's Institute's Leadership Collective and is cofounder of the North Jersey chapter of the AntiRacist Alliance. She sits on the board of the Center for the Study of White American Culture and the Diversity and Cultural Competency Committee of the NJ chapter of the National Association for Social Workers. Bonnie co-facilitates workshops for clinicians on issues of white culture, white privilege, and white identity.

She lives in Montclair, NJ with her husband David. They have two children — Molly and Jerry — who are her greatest inspiration for working for social justice.

Mickey Ellinger

As a daughter of anti-racist Catholic labor organizers in Texas in the 1940s, Mickey says that she was born to activism. When she was a student at the University of Texas in Austin in 1960, she and other students began sitting in at the local Woolworth's, inspired by the sit-ins of Black students in Greensboro, North Carolina. As a graduate student at UC Berkeley in 1964, she participated in the Free Speech Movement, inspired by SNCC's organizing in Mississippi.

Mickey was an active member of the anti-racist, anti-imperialist Prairie Fire Organizing Committee, and the John Brown Anti-Klan Committee, two organizations that modeled anti-racist solidarity politics among white activists in the Bay Area from the mid 1970s until 2000.

Mickey and Sharon Martinas cofounded the Challenging White Supremacy Workshop (CWS) in 1993, after they participated in an Undoing Racism™ Workshop of the People's Institute Survival and Beyond. Mickey supported CWS throughout its organizational life. When CWS ended, Mickey began working with the Catalyst Project's transformative 'Anne Braden Program.'

Mickey is a free-lance journalist, poet, and fiction writer who thinks a lot about place, about the US as a country of the displaced, and about what happens to us, the displaced and the displacers. Ever an organizer, she is a member of the National Writers Union.

European Dissent

European Dissent (ED) is a collective of people of European descent who "dissent" from the ideology of white supremacy, and organize together with other whites and with people of color to undo racism. ED was created in 1986 at the urging of the People's Institute for Survival and Beyond cofounders Jim Dunn and Ron Chisom. Founding members included David Billings, Diana Dunn, Margery Freeman, LaVaun Ishee, Mary Lundy Semela, Meredith McElroy and Joey Napoliatano.

Many have contributed to European Dissent's organizing efforts over the years, including Doug Anderson, Orissa Arend, Suzie Bundy, Mary Capps, Randall Carpenter, Jyaphia Christos Rodgers, Gina Clausi, Becky and Jeff Conner, Renee Corrigan, Emily Drew, Lee Eaton, Kelly Frisch, Ben Gordon, Lance and Eileen Hill, Stacey Keane, Bridget Lehane, Laura Manning, Kendra Rodgers, Hamilton Simons-Jones, Audry Warren, Judy Watts, Jason Weill, to name a few. From our work in the 1980s with the Rainbow Coalition to our post-Katrina organizing efforts in support of the right of return of New Orleans and Gulf Coast residents, ED has taken direction from the People's Institute. Our accountability to one another and to the larger justice community has impacted antiracist white groups across the country.

Margery Freeman

Margery Freeman has been an educator and organizer for 37 years. Her experience includes public school teaching (middle and high school), early childhood education and child advocacy, and adult literacy education. She has directed programs with local and national organizations, including the National Council of Churches and ProLiteracy.

Margery roots her work in the principles and practices she has learned through her twenty-seven-year relationship with the People's Institute for Survival and Beyond, a multi-racial, anti-racist organization that promotes organizing for social change. She is a core trainer/organizer with the People's Institute, leading Undoing Racism™ workshops across the country, primarily with human service and educational institutions.

In New York, where she lives with her husband, David Billings, Margery is actively involved with the AntiRacist Alliance, promoting equitable and humane institutions throughout the Northeast region. Margery and David have three children and three grandchildren. In the fall of 2010 they will relocate to McComb, Mississippi (David's home town just 100 miles north of New Orleans), where Margery expects to continue her anti-racist organizing work. Her personal website is www.margeryfreeman.com

Jacqui "Adhi" Hermer

Jacqui Hermer wrote her essay as a reflection piece for college in 2006, where she received a BA in Health and Environmental Justice. She is currently organizing with Jewish Voice for Peace-Seattle, Resource Generation, and Education Transforming Community Health, a homeless health education program. She lives and studies nursing in Seattle. For questions or conversation, Jacqui can be reached at Jacquelyn.hermer@gmail.com.

Jeff Hitchcock

Jeff Hitchcock is executive director of the Center for the Study of White American Culture (Center), an organization he cofounded in 1995. Altogether, he has more than thirty years managerial experience in the nonprofit and private sectors, ranging from small organizations to Fortune 100 companies. He also heads up the Center's publishing operation, Crandall, Dostie & Douglass Books, Inc. Jeff received his MBA from New York University (Stern School) and his MA in social psychology from Rutgers University. He is author of the book *Lifting the White Veil: An Exploration of White American Culture in a Multiracial Context.* Jeff lives in Roselle, NJ. He is European-American and his partner is African-American. They have two sons, now young adults. He and his family are members of the Quaker meeting in Plainfield, NJ. Jeff is also a long time member of the Plainfield Chapter of the People's Organization for Progress.

Ben Kohl

Ben Kohl, PhD, LCSW is a social work practitioner, manager and educator whose career has focused on services to children, youth and families in congregate care, day treatment, hospital, outpatient and preventive service settings. He has directed the antiracism practice and research efforts of a large urban human service agency and has been an adjunct faculty member in the social work graduate programs of New York University and Salisbury University. He has a research interest in evaluating the association between experiential and didactic training models, and practitioners' cross-racial/ethnic self-efficacy. Ben is the author of several articles on cultural competency and child welfare services, a reviewer for the *Clinical Social Work Journal,* and a frequent presenter at professional conferences.

Cameron Levin

Cameron Levin has been a radical white community organizer for over twenty years. He has worked in Los Angeles and New York with youth and students, welfare recipients, homeless people, immigrant workers, and community members. For the past ten years he has consulted for social justice organizations in Los Angeles. He has been an anti-racist workshop facilitator and trainer for over twenty years. Seven years ago, he cofounded AWARE-LA (Alliance of White Anti-Racists Everywhere) in Los Angeles, CA. AWARE-LA is dedicated to organizing in white communities to build alliances with people of color in Los Angeles and working for racial, social, economic, and environmental justice. Cameron is the co-author of the paper "Towards a Radical White Identity," which offers an alternative white racial identity to the one created by the White Supremacist System. The anti-racist community organizing model he developed is being used in communities across the United States. Cameron is now a parent who has to learn a whole new world. More information is available at www.awarela.org.

Sharon Martinas

When Sharon Martinas heard SNCC call for white anti-racist activists to 'Go organize against racism in your own communities,' back in 1966, she decided that she was going to do that for the rest of her life.

Learning how to do that work, with accountability, solidarity and commitment to racial justice principles has been her life-long goal.

Her anti-racist political education came from the inspiration of SNCC, the Black Student Union and the Black Panther Party while she was a student at San Francisco State University in the late 60s. As an active supporter of the Third World Liberation Front strike at SF State in 1968–69, Sharon learned, by error and trial, what is might mean to be an anti-racist solidarity organizer.

Sharon has expressed her passion for anti-racist solidarity work primarily as an educator of grassroots social justice activists who want to become anti-racist organizers. Her vision of 'education for liberation and self-determination' was inspired by SNCC freedom schools and the student-initiated, community-based political education programs at SF State that led up to the TWLF strike.

Sharon's goal was to 'pass on' what she had learned from the Black Liberation movements of the 1960s to a new generation of (mostly white) Bay Area social justice activists in the 1990s.

In search of a principled and effective way of 'passing it on,' Sharon, with her colleague, Mickey, participated in a People's Institute Undoing Racism™ workshop in New Orleans in 1992. They grounded their creation of the Challenging White Supremacy Workshop (CWS) in many of the fundamental principles of the Undoing Racism™ workshop, while adapting its language and organizing strategies to the radical, mostly white, social justice constituency of the Bay Area that the workshop was created to reach.

Since CWS closed in 2005, Sharon has worked in solidarity with grassroots racial justice organizations in New Orleans working for the right of return for 'internally displaced persons'; and as an active supporter of the Catalyst Project's 'Anne Braden Program.' In 2009, Sharon and Cile Beatty began co-facilitating a new CWS study group called 'White Anti-Racist Organizing Since 1960.'

Matt Meyer

Matt Meyer is not only a founder of Resistance in Brooklyn (RnB), but is also founding chair of the Peace and Justice Studies Association and author, with Bill Sutherland, of *Guns and Gandhi in Africa: Pan African*

Insights on Nonviolence, Armed Struggle, and Liberation (Africa World Press, 2000). Still active with the War Resisters League, Meyer recently edited *Let Freedom Ring: Documents of the Movements to Free US Political Prisoners* (PM Press, 2008), and co-edited, with Elavie Ndura, *Seeds of New Hope: Pan African Peace Studies for the 21st Century* (Africa World Press, 2009). Meyer is educational director of a small, Manhattan-based alternative high school program, and his current political work centers around the raising of two wonderful, beautiful, and brilliant children.

Jeb Aram Middlebrook

Jeb Aram Middlebrook is an antiracist scholar, organizer, and rapper. He is a doctoral candidate in American studies and ethnicity at the University of Southern California, and past managing editor of *American Quarterly: The Journal of the American Studies Association*. His dissertation, *Challenging the White Supremacist System: Antiracist Organizing and Multiracial Alliance in the United States,* explores a historical lineage of white antiracist organizing from 1960 to 2010. Jeb directs the Solidarity Institute, lectures nationally through the Institute for Democratic Education and Culture, organizes with the Alliance of White Anti-Racists Everywhere - Los Angeles (AWARE-LA), and raps with AR-15. His work has been recognized by the Ford Foundation, the Harry S. Truman Foundation, the Council of Editors of Learned Journals, the Associated Press, MTV Networks, *Complex Magazine,* Def Jam Recordings, and Hot 97 radio in New York.

Kimberley Richards

Dr. Kimberley Richards' home is Mississippi and she was raised in Farrell, Pennsylvania. She is the daughter of Mrs. Martha Alfred Richards and the late Henry W. Richards and she has three sons and one granddaughter. Dr. Richards is an organizer in her community and is the co-director of Southwest Gardens Economic Development Corporation, founded by her mother and other residents of Farrell. The organization operates a home for men in recovery and a facility for women who are seeking permanent housing, as well as other housing and community-building programs. Dr. Richards is also an organizer and trainer with the People's Institute for Survival and Beyond. She holds an undergraduate degree from Clark-Atlanta University (formerly Clark College) in education and theatre. Her masters in Education Administration was earned at Westminster College in 1982 and her doctorate in Policy, Planning & Evaluation from the University of Pittsburgh in 1995.

Her graduate and post-graduate work has centered on internalizing an anti-racist analysis within the fields of community-based organizing/organizations and the process of program planning, development and evaluation. She is particularly interested in how and where internalized racial oppression and superiority impacts communities of color and efforts towards social justice and equity. She serves as a consultant internationally as well as on national boards including the Development Leadership Network, Crossroads ministries, Southern Grassroots Leadership Development Design Team, and the newly developed Institute of the Black World.

Christine Schmidt

Christine Schmidt, LCSW, is a social worker. Her forty-year commitment to anti-racism and social justice began as a youth organizer for Martin Luther King's Poor People's Campaign in 1968 and as a non-violent direction action trainer for the Quaker Project on Community Conflict during the Vietnam War. She led an organizing campaign with District 65 to bring union representation to NYC publishing houses in which the lowest-paid jobs were held by people of color and women. At Non-traditional Employment for Women, she advocated for women in blue-collar trades, and at the Jackie Robinson Foundation she organized tenants in city-owned buildings. She participated in an eight-year campaign to end the death penalty in New York State and has participated as a therapist in NYS prisons with the Osborne Association's Longtermers' Project.

Since 1983, Christine has worked for the New York City Department of Education as a school social worker, a clinical supervisor in special education, an educational administrator for alternative education programs on Rikers Island, and a principal for a GED program. In addition, she maintains a psychotherapy practice in Brooklyn, New York.

Her three sons attended New York City public schools. Christine earned degrees at Hampshire College, Hunter College School of Social Work, and the Post-Graduate Center for Mental Health.

Shelly Tochluk

Shelly Tochluk is the author of *Witnessing Whiteness: The Need to Talk About Race and How to Do It*, a book that helps people understand why race remains an essential issue, and how race affects people's daily lives and interactions. She recently completed writing a free companion curriculum for the book, available at www.witnessingwhiteness.com.

An educator with a background in psychology, Shelly Tochluk spent ten years as a researcher, counselor, and teacher in California public schools. She received her PhD in Depth Psychology at Pacifica Graduate Institute, where she investigated how white racial identity impacts friendship relationships. She now trains teachers to work with Los Angeles' diverse school population as the Chair of the Education Department at Mount St. Mary's College.

Shelly also serves on the leadership team of AWARE-LA (Alliance of White Anti-Racists Everywhere-Los Angeles), a community of white anti-racists that has reached hundreds of people in the Southern California area and draws approximately 30 people every month to Saturday dialogues. With AWARE-LA's workshop planning group, she co-created a workshop series that leads white people into a deeper understanding of their personal relationship to race, white privilege, and systemic racism. More information is available at www.awarela.org.

Larry Yates

Larry Yates' social justice and anti-racist commitment began in the mid-1960s working against housing segregation in Virginia's Washington suburbs. While at the National Low Income Housing Coalition, Larry was the first national organizer of tenants in at-risk privately-owned assisted housing, and an early user of e-mail for organizing. He also served as the grassroots organizing mentor at the Center for Health, Environment and Justice, as founding executive director of the Virginia Housing Coalition, and as Shenandoah Valley Organizer for the Virginia Organizing Project. At this writing, he is open to new projects.

Larry's other writing on race and related issues includes a chapter on the history of housing organizing in *A Right to Housing: Foundation for a New Social Agenda,* and his response to David Horowitz's attacks on reparations for slavery in *The Debtors,* published by Caucasians United for Emancipation and Reparations. He plans to self-publish his first novel *Bloodroot: First Flowering* in 2010. He and his wife Carol moved to Winchester, Virginia in 2009. Larry previously lived in Richmond, the Washington suburbs and the Shenandoah Valley in Virginia. Larry belongs to the National Writers Union, the NAACP, and the National Organizers Alliance. His personal website is www.user.shentel.net/llyates.